Quotes CH
CH

D0327255

Equ, ty

78 Contribution
Results

101
factor adj

→ p116 Nice Quote!!

128 -129 Expertise
131 monk's law

MANAGING COMPENSATION

MANAGING
COMPENSATION

J. Gary Berg

amacom

A Division of American Management Associations

Library of Congress Cataloging in Publication Data

Berg, J Gary.
    Managing compensation.

    Includes bibliographical references and index.
    1. Compensation management.   I. Title.
HF5549.5.C67B47   658.32   76-9809
ISBN 0-8144-5418-6

Second Printing

CONTENTS

PREFACE

"TO learn is far more important than to know" says J. Krishnamurti in *The Urgency of Change* (Harper & Row, 1970). This book *is* a learning process. The field of wage and salary is a constantly changing one. The forces that bear on salaries are many—economics, labor supply, management attitude, employee attitude, the union movement, the organization's ability to pay, and, of course, the pay program itself.

It's impossible to account for these many variables as they currently exist in the reader's organization. The hope is that the reader will benefit from the experiences that these words in the book reflect. They are the experiences shared during more than seven years of seminar teaching. These seminars on wage and salary are held approximately 12 times a month at various locations in the country. The ideas and solutions exchanged by their hundreds of participants have greatly contributed to the growth of the wage and salary field.

This book, then, is dedicated to those participants. My deep gratitude goes to them for permitting me—whether as chairman, speaker, or participant—to share a moment of closeness with them and to gain a real learning experience myself.

J. Gary Berg

·1·

Pay for Contribution

In the wilds of Afghanistan, the big car of an American tourist broke down and refused to start. No one could figure out what was the matter; even the factory representative who was flown in gave up. The tourist was ready to abandon the car and go home when someone remembered that an old blacksmith who lived beyond the mountains some fifty miles away had, in his youth, tinkered with engines.

In his despair, the tourist sent for him. Three days later, the old man appeared on a mule. He took one look at the car and asked for a hammer. He gently tapped one spot on the engine twice, and said, "Start her up," and the engine purred as smoothly as if it had just left the test stand.

"What do I owe you?" the grateful tourist asked.

"A hundred dollars."

"What, a hundred dollars for two taps with the hammer?"

"Well, I can itemize it for you," the old man said: "For two taps with the hammer—ten cents; for having known where—99 dollars and 90 cents."

PETER F. DRUCKER
Landmarks of Tomorrow

A part of the tragedy of our times is that we are willing to pay for action but not for contribution.

J. G. B.

THE many seminars in compensation, wage and salary, benefits administration, executive compensation, sales compensation, and personnel administration all suggest the tremendous emphasis that has come to be placed in

1

this important area. The number of administrators and analysts, too, has grown inordinately. Yet with this growth and interest there have not been many books that address themselves to the field. There *are* books, yes, but few of them are anything but revised editions of older texts.

Wage and salary has not been considered a glamour area. Recruitment, labor relations, and development and training have been the areas of heavy concentration, in which books abound.

However, the large number of seminars and meetings already alluded to not only suggests the overwhelming interest in compensation but supports the contention that there are but a limited number of books on the subject. Without up-to-date books, analysts must rely more heavily on meetings and seminars for exposure to the latest views and techniques.

In a sense, the very lack of books suggests that compensation is neither static nor sterile, but a very dynamic force in our society. The contemporary techniques used to pay people may not be found in books, but they are around us every day. They are in the periodicals, newspapers, and bulletins. Compensation truly *is* a glamour area and can be an exciting one if the pay problem is approached with a sense of contemporary dynamics.

Probably the most significant change occurring in the field of compensation is the shift from programs based on job content to those based on contribution. Too long have wage and salary programs been given a job content orientation, on the colossal assumption that the activities of a job suggest the value of the job. It ain't necessarily so!

Certainly George Odiorne's work and that of others have fostered the new awareness of the value of contribution in the higher echelons of the organizational hierarchy. And Peter Drucker has said that "the focus on contribution is the key to effectiveness" in one's work and in one's relations with superiors, associates, and subordinates.*

That companies pay for input, not output is still all too true. Such companies fail to recognize that pay should be used as a motivator for higher achievements in quality and/or quantity or in the results of the job activity, and that programs based on results or contribution will be more successful than those based on job content. This does not mean that these organizations will go out of business. "Institutions exist," as Robert Townsend says, "not because of what they're doing but in spite of it." †

All this is not meant to imply that the issues in compensation are clearcut and simple. On the contrary. Students in my classes frequently come up to me asking for a reference book which may provide insight into some of

---

* *The Effective Executive* (New York: Harper & Row, 1967).
† *Up the Organization* (New York: Alfred A. Knopf, 1970).

the contemporary ideas on wage and salary. They are usually looking for a given text which will categorically cite techniques for them to follow. Many of those students are disbelieving and discontent when I refer them to this periodical or that one which *suggests* what to do. What they seek is a ready answer, a "how to do it" solution. They fail to appreciate the complexity and diversity of business organizations, characteristics which make panaceas impossible.

Most persons who have had any exposure at all to the compensation field are aware that the practice of pay distribution appropriate for their organization is seldom to be found in another organization; a practice of its own must be developed for each organization in order to be compatible with the organization's style, size, product line or service, locale, employee numbers and skill levels, and other similar characteristics. Because of the great variety of elements among organizations, there is also a great diversity of approaches to compensation.

The failure of the Nixon administration's dismal approach to wage control program was an example not only of a lack of understanding of that diversity but, more alarming, of the lack of awareness of persons in the field who should have been able to guide the administration on a successful course.

Even when the American Compensation Association, the largest professional group in the field, approached the administration, there was little evidence of its influence in the activities of the control program. ACA seemed to function merely as a reporting agency for its members. Whether this was because the administration refused to listen or because the Association proposed no new ideas is hard to say. The fact remains that the series of governmental phases failed to arrest inflation.

The field of compensation has not spawned many who can think creatively about the pay problem. Most of its practitioners do nothing more than rehash what has always been done. Their approach to resolving the problems of the present and anticipating those of the future is to draw on the tired techniques of the past. It doesn't work! New approaches must be sought. The successful practitioners in compensation today are, and those in the future will be, people who are mindful of the past practices but who trained in areas other than the traditional personnel-oriented courses.

Compensation administration has been done so badly for so many years that the novice is better off with his limited experience in the field. I once had a newly appointed boss in wage and salary. It galled my colleagues and me to have a newcomer lead us. He had little knowledge of the technical side of wage and salary. One day he told us, "Look, I know I don't know all that's gone before in developing what we currently have, but wage and salary is simply a process of *logic*. If we look at everything we do from that stand-point, it should work." We did, and *it did*.

Wage and salary seems to have attracted many who are very pragmatic, set in their ways, and generally afraid of new ideas. Consequently they've made few innovations. Anyone who does make innovations is suspect and seen as a maverick and not to be trusted with the "company jewels." Most of the wage and salary programs in force today were developed in the five-year period between 1945 and 1950. Just think of the changes that the United States has undergone since World War II, yet most companies use pay sys-tems created prior to the onset of many of those changes. Even the most popular point system in the country today, the Hay system, was developed in the thirties in Philadelphia. I wonder what W. C. Fields would say about that considering the way he felt about Philadelphia.

As an analyst in years gone by, I realized that the task of wage and salary was largely one of classifying and codifying people and jobs. We were thought of as postal mail sorters. This meant putting everybody in mail cubicles which were not only prearranged but very inflexible and put in to stay.

This "conforming process," putting everything and everybody in a nice neat box, made me realize that I was actually promoting mediocrity. There was no room for variation from the norm. Any deviations were looked upon with disdain and incredulity, and every effort was made to make everything fit into the existing setup.

This, of course, created many problems, which, if resolved at all, were resolved through political pressures and harangues. Those that were not resolved created lots of confusion and set all kinds of precedents which, of course, produced more harangues, jangled nerves, and bad stomachs. There had to be a better way, I thought, and there was.

The successful compensation administrator is one who will develop pro-grams based on contribution rather than job content. The word "success" is being used here to refer not only to how compensation administrators are received by their peers, subordinates, and superiors but—even more impor-tant—to how they perceive their own performance. People are the most crit-ical judges of themselves and their achievements.

To prepare for their role, compensation administrators must equip them-selves with a proper understanding of the forces acting upon compensation and of the basics underlying successful compensation administration. These basics are certain principles of economics and the behavioral sciences. An-other essential ingredient in the success of compensation administrators is their frame of mind. The self-awareness and attitude set promoted by the recent transactional analysis movement have no greater application than in compensation.

It's by now a fairly old and well-known tale that personnel people were given that job when they failed in others—and there's been a lot of truth in it in the past. But in recent years, at least, many people have been preparing themselves exclusively for personnel work. They took the "right" personnel courses, pursued personnel job openings, and got ready for the life of a personnel administrator.

There was another oft-told tale about people in personnel. This one claimed that they went into personnel because they "like people." This implied that one was automatically soft in the heart, or the head, or both, for being in personnel. Many with the scars of personnel work will attest to the fact that liking people is not necessarily a good mental set or qualifying asset for pursuing personnel work. Nevertheless, the field did attract many persons with a humble-pie attitude.

Concomitant with that popular misconception of personnel people was another humbling situation: the prima donnas in the company who had to be treated *right*. These included not only the engineers but also those purchasing the material that went into the product. This situation prevailed when American industry was primarily product-oriented rather than service-oriented and a huge part of the product cost was the material cost.

As a result, those procuring the material were to be treated with kid gloves. So special were they that material had to be spelled m-a-t-e-r-i-e-l. The change in spelling alone was worth some money! At any rate, the personnel person was certainly playing second chair to the materiel specialist because labor costs were not as significant as material costs. This humbling effect still prevails among many personnel people in product-oriented companies where labor costs are equal to or greater than material costs. However, even in service-oriented companies where material costs are minimal and labor costs are substantial, personnel people are still frequently playing the role of Mr. or Ms. Humble Pie.

All this is not meant to launch personnel people on a crusade, but to try to make them more aware of their responsibility and consequent influence on the success of the company. The high labor costs incurred today by organizations can thrust those who handle compensation into very responsible roles—*if* they are ready to accept them. It can't be simply a matter of luck that enables a personnel person to assume a responsible role; it must be the result of preparation. "Luck," it has been said, "is the result of meeting opportunity with preparation."

Of course, in order to prepare for a more responsible role, many personnel people and, more specifically, compensation administrators must first divest themselves of their too humble, and, for some, their definitely negative, mental attitude. Transactional analysis is showing how we can come out of this shell and assume a more positive and contributing posture in our organization.

In terms of transactional analysis, T. A. Harris would say that humble or negative attitude can be summed up as I'm Not OK—You're OK.* This humbling approach is not only ineffective but it shirks the responsibility of compensation administration. This is basically a 1,9 approach (people-oriented, no production concern) using Blake-Mouton Managerial Grid® terminology.† It is a Theory X posture as well, since it is wrought with negative feelings about people and certainly self. Persons with this posture usually depend on the organizational hierarchy to make decisions which they can follow instead of contributing to those decisions.

I'm Not OK—You're OK best typifies this posture; however. I remember an engineering manager frequently touting me with, "Aren't you tired of being overhead and not contributing to anything?" That's a pretty negative position in which to be placed. Try to belly up to a line person in a negotiation with that attitude set!

Gamesmanship abounds in this humble role, too. There's a feeling of "Oh, me, what can I do?" Sometimes there's a little bit of the "Let's you and him fight" attitude, not to mention the ever popular "If it weren't for you . . ." game.** Basically, a person in this negative position is fighting for the lower needs satisfaction (according to Abraham Maslow). He is merely trying to survive in a world that is too much for him. His actions are motivated by *"What will be my best chances to stay alive* in the organization?"

The person in this role is often merely "coming from" his Child, usually the Adaptive Child, doing whatever he is told, responding to Parent types and tapes.††

This posture is not what we would look to and revere or seek, yet it is one that many compensation administrators assume. Unfortunately, they

---

* *I'm OK, You're OK: A Practical Guide to Transactional Analysis* (New York: Harper & Row, 1969).

† I remember taking an intensive management grid course at Texas Instruments, and it was a very worthwhile experience. When I was first assigned to my group and they learned I was from the personnel section, they immediately assumed and wrote down that I was 1,9. They made this snap judgment apparently from other personnel people they had known or from the stereotype!

** Eric Berne, *Games People Play* (New York: Grove Press, 1964).

†† The concepts developed in transactional analysis by Berne, Harris, Jungeward, and others, enable us to categorize people's behavior in ordinary language, which everyone can understand. The reader is referred to the several books in this area, especially Harris, *I'm OK, You're OK* and Jungeward, *Born to Win*.

think it is a posture from which they will emerge unscathed, but this is not true. In this position people compromise themselves so much and find themselves so difficult to live with that they become quite nervous. Many compensation administrators have developed ulcers or become alcoholics because of the disappointment in their daily work. This is not a happy end.

The other negative life structure that is frequently seen among the more aggressive compensation administrators is I'm OK—You're Not OK. Whereas the first life structure is demoralizing, this one can be destructive. It thrives in a Theory X atmosphere in which negative thoughts abound anyway.

Playing politics is the order of the day and is seen as a sport and perhaps the only way to survive in the organizational jungle. In this role Parent tapes are played in "quadraphonic" sound, and the dictates supporting the statutory position draw the line of battle. Compensation administrators feel compelled to match wits with their opponents on every count. The signing of a pay change, for instance, is a win-lose proposition, a triumph or a defeat.

This approach does seem to allude to a higher need, ego satisfaction—which by no means makes it right, however. In this role there is a tendency to be nonproductive by working in either a pragmatic or reactionary manner to most ideas. Needless to say, this attitude is not very satisfying and will cost the possessors ulcers *if* they last that long. They are like the proverbial used-car salesman with his name written in pencil on his business cards. Administrators of this type are seen to be constantly updating their resumes and moving from company to company. As soon as management can dump them, it will, and they leave with scars unhealed.

If I seem to be leading to a particular conclusion of the proper life structure to assume, then my deliberate attempts in this direction have not been in vain. Even before I was fired "successfully" and joined the ranks of the unemployed, I became convinced that to do compensation administration from the "inside," that is, as an employee of the company, is nearly impossible. My address book seemed to be testimony to this. It was filled with the names of associates that I admired. Although their names were in my book in ink, their companies were in pencil, since they had a habit of relocating frequently. I am convinced, however, that the job of compensation administration can be done successfully once compensation administrators assume a healthy mental attitude. The one that I would recommend is I'm OK—You're OK. This is a positive attitude in which compensation administrators and everyone they deal with may meet on an entirely different plane from those described above.

I can think of no other job which requires this life structure more. Compensation administrators assist management and employees alike in a very important trust, directing the payroll dollar to those jobs and persons contributing to the success of the organization. They are accepting responsibility for what is in many organizations an ever-increasing cost and often, as our economy becomes more and more service-oriented, the most significant cost of doing business. All compensation administrators have to do is prepare themselves and they will have great opportunities to do well for their enterprise and for themselves.

The assumption of the Adult role is the epitome of the compensation administrator. The Adult is that role in which we draw from our *total* frame of reference: all of the experiences we have had, the Parent tapes we've stored, all the learning we have amassed and, also, the empathic feeling from our Child. Using this mass of data, we can react to each situation, new or old, and determine its merits. This position is Theory Y at its best. It suggests strong positive feelings for all within our midst. It suggests that we want to encourage input from others, as we are not blinded by our own insight. We are concerned with people, but we also have assumed the more fiscal role of concern for production and the organization's success. Our authority rests on our personal attributes, and we use logic and reason to back up our moves and recommendations. We can explore new heights in the pursuit of our job which will be gratifying and self-actualizing. Our job assumes the posture of professionalism, and we enjoy the fruits of success and good health.

The mental set of the compensation administrator is crucial to the success of the compensation program. With an unhealthy mental set, the administrator may create just another program dealing with a sensitive item, handling it in a mediocre way, with mixed results of bad "press" and a general lack of enthusiasm and motivation on the part of the employees. The compensation administrator's first step in establishing a valid compensation program is to assume a healthy mental set.

· 2 ·

Economics —

A Basis for Job Evaluation

In Canada there is a small radical group that refuses to speak English and no one can understand them. They are called Separatists. In this country we have the same kind of group. They are called Economists.
                                                                    Nation's Business
                                                                    (March 1975)

THE romanticists won't agree, but it's really economics that makes the world go 'round, not love. The sooner compensation administrators become aware of this, the better they will be at their job.

I've already mentioned that the mental set the compensation administrator should assume is I'm OK—You're OK, the Adult posture. Once done, the compensation administrator is ready to take the next step in the development of a viable compensation program. This is to assume the role of internal consultant. I said earlier that at one time I thought the compensation job was just too difficult to do as a member of the political organization. I've already revised that stance and said that it can be done—with the proper mental set. In addition, let me suggest that the compensation administrator use this new mental set in the role of internal consultant. The term "consultant" suggests several things. It suggests objectivity, professionalism, and expertise in the field. It suggests independence, if not mobility. Putting all these thoughts together, it suggests that as internal consultant, the compensation administrator can approach the compensation problem equipped with characteristics from the best of two worlds: the intimacy of the organization as its member with a personal interest in its success and the success of its members, plus the objectivity of the consultant. To prepare for this role, the compensation administrator has to view the problem of compensation administration through new eyes, the eyes of the head of the organization. Since most organizations call their chiefs by different titles, let us merely refer to this person as the chief executive officer, hereafter referred to as the CEO.

Let's look at some of the similarities and dissimilarities the CEO has with the employees.

People are sometimes surprised to learn that CEOs are *not* the omnipotent, independent, and fearless despots devoid of feelings that they are made out to be in some stereotypes. They feel pressure from several groups—the stockholders and board for whom they work, the employees with whom they work, the customers, the public, the unions, and more and more, "Big Brother" government. CEOs must focus their attention on each of these pressures, usually one at a time, in order to keep from getting the screaming meemies. In general, the measure of their work is usually first, last, and always the dollar. How they use it, how much they were given to work with, and the return on the buck in both the short and long term. The compensation administrator must be cognizant of the economics, both macro and micro, in order to develop a program that will satisfy the needs of the CEO.

The organization is only a small part of several interrelated economic systems—the organization, industry, domestic economy, international economy. Presumably, the need is for a program which will mesh with economics of the present and the future. The past is prologue, and one must be aware of what has occurred. Santayana has said that he who cannot remember the past is doomed to repeat it. Economics is not an easy subject to grasp. The constant train of economic consultants in and out of the White House gates is proof that few know the magic of its workings. Nevertheless, compensation administrators should equip themselves with the basics of economic theory and the several interacting forces which cause certain trends to occur. Thus prepared, they can anticipate these trends and apply them to their own organization or industry. Compensation administrators need not go heavily into the science of economics, since they may come out with an inordinate awareness of statistical data but without the awareness that it is people and people's attitudes which often develop economic phenomena.

The future and its secrets are important to the success of the compensation program. Anyone can look at what is occurring during this or any year and anticipate certain trends. If the economy is currently going up, going down, or holding steady, what is the anticipated trend two or four years from now? What changes in Washington or other world capitals will cause changes in the economy? Does your organization's economy mirror any national economic trend? Does it seem to rise and fall with private sector spending, or is its state a function of public sector spending? How long before the multiplier principal acting on public money impacts on your organization's growth? What political power is in Washington, liberal or conservative, Republican or Democrat, and how do their spending habits differ? When is the next election, how may its results affect the general economy and consequently your organization?

If your organization tends to be in an industry which is capital-intensified or labor-intensified, will it remain this way? What would be affected if your company decentralized or centralized? What role does labor cost play in your organization? Is it on par with your industry as an element of cost or sales? What is the output per employee? Is it higher or lower than it once was? What is its trend compared to sales or costs or profits?

What setting will your organization be in during the next several years? You must understand as many of the variables as possible. The rate of inflation, the sales volume trend, the cash flow concern, the capitalization plans of the organization, the budget growth and control, merger and acquisition expectations, and people growth. All of these are matters that compensation administrators must take into consideration if they are to perform successfully.

The organizational dilemma of the mid-seventies regarding pay practices was caused by a lack of understanding of economics by compensation administrators in particular and personnel people in general. They were apparently not trained in it, nor did they believe it was important. The problem was worsened by the lack of Depression babies coming into their own who could assume the compensation administrator's role. Furthermore, the younger persons who did come to these positions were reared in an era of affluence.

The tragedy was that those personnel programs which were born and nurtured in the boom era of the sixties were not only inappropriate in the seventies, but the people responsible for reacting to the changes of the seventies could draw upon nothing but the economics learned in the boom period. These techniques were 180 degrees out of step. In the boom period of the sixties there was a high demand for labor because of a rapidly growing gross national product and a lack of supply of labor. Personnel programs reacted well to that need; it's a pleasant problem to have growth and boom and to do things to entice people to come and work for your organization. There is ample money to play with, and management is inclined to use it.

The seventies, however, present a different story. A lagging GNP and a reduced demand for labor, coupled with a tremendous supply of labor created by the war-baby boom, have completely changed personnel economics. Compensation administrators must react to this change and alter their own approaches to the pay program. They cannot simply look at the "way it used to be done" and apply those tenets. The ball game has changed, the momentum has altered, and compensation administrators must change too, or they are doomed. Dramatic, yes, but economics can be exciting, glamorous, or devastating.

Many economists are predicting a modest real growth in the GNP through the seventies and into the eighties. A fact which is irrevocable is the growth of the labor force. International economics has already shown the United States that it does not enjoy an open market. American industry has found that it must keep its labor costs down and increase productivity if it is to compete in the world market. Pay, influenced by a constantly rising rate of inflation, must be directed where it will do the most good. Compensation administrators can play a large role in reinvesting the payroll dollar properly so that the return for that investment is enhanced as much as possible. By assuming a more fiscal role in the administration of the compensation dollar, compensation administrators can contribute much to the success of their organizations. Pay programs based on contribution, rather than job content, and in which the payroll dollar is used to optimal advantage, must be instituted. Compensation administrators must assist in controlling labor costs. This doesn't mean that they should depress or hold them down. It means that they must control them by assuring management that pay is being properly directed to the jobs and persons that are contributing to the success of the organization.

The maturation of an organization is a worthy subject to consider regarding the kind of program that would be suitable for the organization. The maturation cycle is usually tied to the economic growth of the organization, that is, as an organization prospers, it grows. There are several plateaus in the development of a company which are important to identify because the compensation administrator can have a significant influence on the organizational health of the enterprise.

It has already been suggested that the economy experienced in one decade may be different from that of the past decade, and the training, techniques, and knowledge gained from one decade will not be advantageous for another decade. Change is imperative in the approach that business people must take to their businesses. I know of no better source for understanding change and its implications than Alvin Toffler's book *Future Shock*.

Perhaps before exploring the "change" issue, it would be a good idea to look at the maturation cycle of organizations. Northcote Parkinson, in Parkinson's third law,* traced the growth of bureaucracy using the British admiralty as the subject. Taking our cue from that entertaining and informative book, let's expand the idea and apply it more broadly.

Organizations are formed by people who want to do something a little different. Though some fail, some succeed. The only difference between nonconformists and leaders is that the latter have followers. As the ideas grow and gain acceptance, the pioneers gather about them associates with whom they can relate. They seek associates who can contribute to their particular idea; they are "buying" conformity. The pioneers may be unorthodox in their manner, perhaps unsophisticated and naive, even rude and crude, but they and their ideas grow, nevertheless. The interesting thing about this development syndrome is that it can be used to describe the growth pattern of *any* organization, whether it be a company, a religion, a country, a society, a neighborhood, a club, or even a political movement.

As the idea gains success, the enterprise gathers more persons about the nucleus who contribute to the main idea, but the "dues" for joining are to surrender some creativity and conform to the organization. As the organization grows, new employees are hired primarily for their conformity to the main idea. Some companies even hire industrial psychologists to help prevent the nonconformists from joining the organization. Before long, the organization's growth pattern is "organized" and smoothed out. No longer is there that excited scurry to get things done. Things have settled down to an orderly pace. Policies and procedures are written which further refine the activities of the organization.

The organization has by now reached the acme of its success and feels compelled to erect a monument to itself. This may be in the form of a new facility, a plant, statues, an office; a tome of published rules, regulations, dogma, policies, procedures; or an inflexible compensation program. At this point conformity *is* the rule. Nonconformists are screened out, no wave makers are welcome. This is an advanced state of bureaucracy and the beginning of the end. Because of its bureaucracy, the organization is certain to gradually fail and collapse. Smaller companies are created which compete, and because of the élan which prevails in those younger maverick companies, the "established" institution cannot cope with the younger, more aggressive ones. The newer companies "eat the lunch" of the larger one, enjoy success, and establish their own brand of growth and, unfortunately, bureaucracy.

Creativity is the result of the identification of need and the opportunity to fill that need. Compensation should be paid for the creative work done.

---

* *Parkinson's Law* (Boston: Houghton Mifflin, 1957).

The compensation program should be flexible enough not only to accommodate growth of the company but to actually reward, if not inspire, it. As I've said before, the successful compensation program is one in which *contribution* is the basis of pay, not job content.

It should be noted that the use of Theory X or Theory Y management techniques in the extreme is ultimately nonproductive. In the mid-sixties a certain company with which I was familiar was very Theory Y in its management philosophy. It was so Theory Y that one could spend much time creating, but to implement was near impossible. To implement meant to coordinate with all kinds of people—superiors, peers, and subordinates. Most people would simply throw their hands up in the air and utter, "What's the use?" It was an example of too much of a good thing.

The status of the organization in its growth cycle is critical to the design of the pay program. Compensation administrators should analyze the status and try to abet the growth, not the bureaucracy, of their organizations. A good rule to follow is one I learned at the knee of a close associate a number of years ago. That rule is simply the KISS principle. It stands for "Keep It Simple, Stupid." The simplicity of a system will go a long way toward the success of the system. The key to success is flexibility. The compensation program should be one which can not only accommodate the growth of the company in its current product mix but also external possibilities, such as horizontal growth, merging and acquiring companies with products or services complementary to one's own; and vertical growth, merging or acquiring companies which contribute to the making of one's product or service or to which one's product or service contributes.

Readers who think that the growth pattern drawn from Parkinson's idea is wrong should review any company with which they are familiar, or a church, an association, a club, the United States, or any other country which can be viewed.

This organizational pattern does not necessarily end in collapse. However, the bureaucracy must be arrested to avert the decline. New ideas must be encouraged. Turnover of employees at a nominal rate is advantageous, not detrimental, to a growing organization. The strength of an organization in both the short and long term is the ideas of its members. Good ideas will prompt continued growth; the lack of ideas will accelerate decline.

• 3 •

Behavioral Science —
A Basis for Job Evaluation

There is always an easy solution to every human problem . . . neat, plausible, and wrong.

IT was mentioned that compensation administrators have two major foundation considerations, economic and behavioral. Having explored the economic foundation, we now move on to the behavioral foundation. Some may consider this to be the more important of the two, but we mustn't forget that that is exactly the bias compensation administrators must overcome. To be successful in the role of the internal consultant in compensation administration, it is necessary to remain as objective as possible about the several forces which bear upon the problem. Nonetheless, the behavioral side may still be the more interesting since it deals with people and their reactions to certain stimuli, and we find it easier to relate to that situation than to the abstraction of economics.

Much work has been done by behavioral scientists, most of which has been ignored by compensation administrators. Perhaps the "typical" wage and salary administrator has always been too much of a "numbers" person or "systems" person, and too insensitive to people. This attitude was certainly not encouraged by the behaviorists, who have stated repeatedly that money doesn't motivate. I was once told that the behaviorists were much in demand to speak on the subject "Money Doesn't Motivate." Asked to speak, the first response of many of these behaviorists was, "How much does it pay?" Nevertheless, the theory was loudly proclaimed and gained much attention—especially from many executives who, with a glint in their eyes, said, "Good, that relieves the pressure, let's cut back on the salary increases."

Perhaps the fallacy of the postulate was that its application was too general. "Money doesn't motivate" is a pretty sweeping statement. What exactly was meant by "money"? Pay, incentives, the program, the total compensation program. To whom was it meant to apply? Everyone? Blue-collar workers? White-collar workers? All ages? All walks of life? All classifications? Generalizations are tricky and all of them, of course, are false, including this one. We have a way of emphasizing our theorem by pronouncing it as all-inclusive in application, when in effect we really don't mean "all." People *are* motivated by money at some time in their lives, depending on the conditions in which they find themselves.

Since money and motivation are key to the compensation program, we will spend considerable time in developing some thoughts about the role the compensation program can play in motivating the employee. To this end, it is appropriate to look at the makeup of the employees, the people we are trying to motivate.

Figure 1 shows the birthrate in the United States for the years 1920–1960. This simple graph reveals much to us now in the latter half of the seventies. It can be seen that the birthrate was increasing rapidly until the Great Depression. At that time the birthrate dropped abruptly and remained low for several years. As the economy recovered, the birthrate increased. During World War II, the birthrate waned. After the war, it increased at a rapid pace. Although these data are affected somewhat by the death rate during these years, the curve is basically accurate in showing the population distribution in the country today.

Figure 2 shows that the population groupings in 1975 fit into three distinct age groups. In 1975, the Senior Employee, between the ages of 45 and 54, represents the largest number of persons in this age range the country has ever had. This is the group that is usually found at the helm of the many organizations, private and public sectors combined. These are the persons who will approve or disapprove of the programs that are installed.

Much has been written about the Depression Baby. Not many of them were born. These persons, who in 1975 are between the ages of 35 and 44, are in short supply and presumably in high demand, since this is the age group normally sought for higher levels of managerial responsibility.

The person in the 20 to 34 year old range, the Challenger, is in huge supply. These are the "war babies," so called because they were born during and after World War II. The number of persons between the ages of 20 and 34 increased by 40 percent from 1965 to 1975. This is by far the largest age

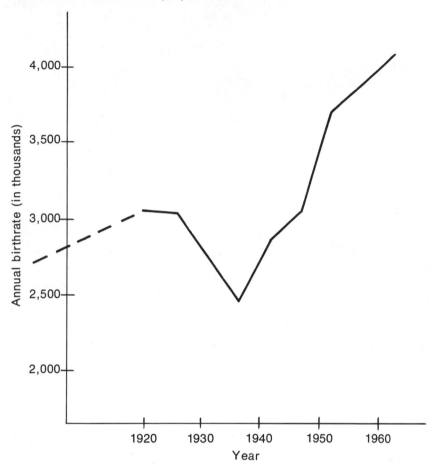

Figure 1. Birthrate in the United States for selected years.

group in the United States. One need only go to restaurants, department stores, offices, and other places where groups of people can be found to see the degree to which these people abound.

By 1980 the Senior Employee will be from 50 to 60 years old, the Depression Baby from 40 to 50, and the Challenger from 25 to 40. Due to the normal retirement and mortality rates, the Senior Employee's numbers will be even smaller and the Depression Baby will be even less evident, but the Challenger will be in his prime. He will be the controlling force not only in the labor market but in industry. His attitudes will prevail, he will assume the reins of management and politics, his ideas will be those fol-

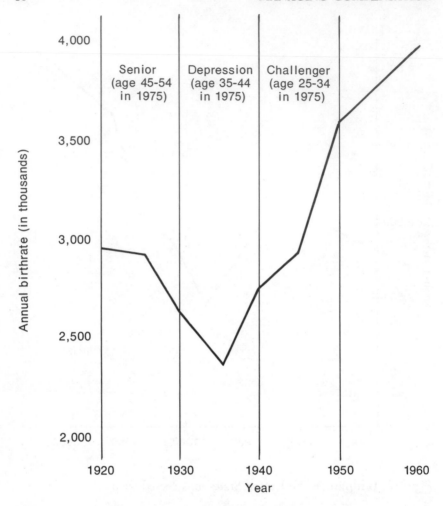

Figure 2. Labor force in the United States by age groupings.

lowed. Each organization must make sure that it has the best of these Challengers on board. Organizations had better take advantage of the time between 1975 and 1980 to attract, retain, motivate, and develop their own leaders. Compensating them properly is a key to effectiveness in this manpower planning. The compensation administrator has a great opportunity to provide a valuable service to the organization by meeting the challenge of the Challenger and his needs.

These three groups, then, are the persons we are trying to motivate in our companies, institutions, and organizations today. The Depression Baby forms the valley between the Senior Employee and the Challenger. The differences and similarities between these groups are very interesting. They suggest the type of programs we need to implement in order to optimize the return on the payroll dollar investment.

Chances are the populations in all organizations are distributed as suggested in Figure 2. If anything, there are even more Challengers in organization populations because of the many new organizations in our midst. Which type of organization is yours? You must take a careful look at your organization, its current makeup, its dynamics, its position with regard to Parkinson's third law, and, most important, what its needs are going to be.

First, let's look at the differences in the Senior Employee, the Depression Baby, and the Challenger.

These differences seem to be more basic than merely what one would expect from age versus youth. They emerge as definite patterns or life styles. One is not to be criticized and the other honored; each style has drawbacks from being too naive or too cynical. It remains that there are differences, and it is this fact that concerns us in compensation.

Psychologists tell us that our basic characteristics and traits are the result of influences and impacts we encountered at very early, impressionable years. The differences in these groups, then, can probably be traced to the differences experienced in those youthful years. What is it that makes the Senior Employee seem overconscious of frugality and spartanism? Depending on which psychologist one reads, the impressionable years are from 4 or 5 to 10 or 12. What economic influences were being exerted on the Senior Employee when he was in his impressionable years? A stable economy or fluctuating economic cycles? The latter, of course. Nothing as traumatic as the Great Depression perhaps, but nevertheless an apparently unpredictable, uncontrollable, incomprehensible economy. Since 1900 and before the Great Depression, there were dire cycles of downturn every three or four years, with the post–World War I depression being particularly severe. When living is from "hand to mouth," certain attitudes and adages emerge. The wealth of sayings from Ben Franklin, which dwelt on the virtues of spartan life styles and *saving*, attest to the fact that these cycles plagued the country since its early times. "Save a penny for a rainy day," "Waste not, want not," "Take only what you need," and other similar sayings were the vestiges of prior generations. Saving was synonymous with virtue. It is no wonder that the Senior Employee has a high regard for the accumulation of material wealth.

Depression Babies, born between 1930 and 1940, obviously were affected by the Great Depression. Things were very rough in those growing-up years. "Drink every drop of milk in your glass." "You're lucky to have it in the first place." "There are people starving all over the world." "Clean up everything on your plate." "What you don't eat today you'll see tomorrow in a stew of leftovers or potato pancakes." My mother was master of "leftover conversions." They may not have been tasty, but they did have food value and bulk. "Those crumbs you're leaving on your plate would feed a family of five for a week in Europe." An exaggeration, perhaps, but the point was made. Depression Babies, few in number, are not unlike their predecessors in attitude toward security. Depression Babies were further influenced by the law of scarcity when in the early war years they were part of the rationing scene. Food, sugar, butter, meat—all essentials were hard to come by. If normal frugality didn't make its point in the thirties to the Depression Baby and the Senior Employee, the War Ration Board made believers of them.

By the time Challengers came along and were "aware," things had changed. They were reared in an age of affluence (they were later to criticize their elders for the effluence of this age of affluence). They were borne in a golden chariot, they drew from the horn of plenty, and suffered no lack of indulgence from Dr. Spock's teachings. This "good times" attitude was even encouraged by their elders who had suffered greatly themselves but wanted their offspring to have what they had not had while growing up. Abundance was everywhere. If you didn't finish everything on your plate, so what, there was plenty more where that came from. Survival needs were satiated. Indulgence, free spirit, and little discipline reigned supreme. The Natural Child and the Little Professor were encouraged and abetted at every turn. A whole generation was enjoying what previous generations had not had. Furthermore, the older generations were proud to provide it.

Individual freedom, nonconformity, and a rebellious attitude were considered at first to be cute and later the "in thing." To "do one's own thing," became the catch phrase of the time. This attitude prompted these young persons to challenge everything that the establishment put before them.

The result was the emergence of a new breed, physically giants, mentally superior, and spiritually free. They shunned the accumulation of material goods. Their attitude was "Why amass wealth? It takes too much time from the pleasurable pursuits, it takes too much out of a person. Look how worn out my dad is, and besides there's always more where that came from." Unshackled by the air of prosperity, Challengers could aspire to more noble pursuits.

Abraham Maslow's hierarchy of needs theory can be used to understand the needs of our employees. Understanding this hierarchy and improvising upon it in applying it to our employees can be helpful in developing a compensation program that best suits both the employees and the organization.

According to Maslow's needs hierarchy, we have very basic physiological needs. We need to fortify our body with food and water. We also need to protect ourselves from the elements. When our basic needs—that is, for food and shelter—are satisfied, we try to satisfy still greater needs. We seek acceptance, love, and affection—social needs.

The significance of Maslow's needs hierarchy is that each need must be satisfied before we can begin to fulfill a higher need. If our basic needs are challenged or even displaced or dislodged, all that we had built on top of them falters and falls about us, and we are compelled to rebuild and restack the needs hierarchy.

Once we have satisfied our social needs, we seek further gratification by satisfying our ego needs. It seems somewhat paradoxical that in the very group in which we sought acceptance as peers we now seek a measure of detachment. We want to be recognized as being different or better, of a higher status. "Going through the chairs" in clubs or associations is the "approved" process for the older institutions. We seek ego gratification or esteem fulfillment by achieving some position of authority and power. Appreciation for this position is usually generated from outside ourselves, or so it seems.

Again, if basic needs are not satisfied or are threatened, we will give up the manifestations of higher needs satisfaction in order to recover and fulfill the lower needs. Persons who have achieved places of authority in their groups will give them up if they can no longer fulfill their own and their family's survival needs.

According to Maslow, our highest need is for self-actualization or self-fulfillment—a feeling from within that what we have done is truly worthwhile for a group with which we can relate. Note that the difference between self-actualization and ego satisfaction is the source of the appreciation. In ego satisfaction the appreciation is generated or perceived to be generated from without. In self-actualization the appreciation comes from within. External appreciation may *not* be forthcoming at all from a self-actualizing act. Self-actualization is a personally rich fulfillment. It is the satisfying of our most severe critic, ourselves, in the accomplishment of a meaningful task.

Acts performed by people who are primarily motivated by the fact that as a result of them they will receive recognition from others are probably acts of esteem satisfaction. Acts performed with the realization that few people, if any, will know of their accomplishment are probably acts of self-actualization.

The theory states that we are motivated to satisfy these needs, one at a time, building the blocks, as it were, toward the highest need, self-fulfillment. The tendency to strive constantly to satisfy these needs is natural and affects everyone. If one has a low threshold of satisfaction for a particular need, that need will be satisfied more quickly than if one has a high threshold of satisfaction for that need. Persons with a strong need to amass material wealth to ward off the fear of impoverishment will be preoccupied with gathering about them all things which protect them from that fear. Persons who don't fear impoverishment will spend very little time gathering material wealth about them. Whereas some of us relate to the former and laud them for their industry, others will deride them for their narrow existence and point up the things that they are missing. Others will applaud the latter, relating to their ability to put something away for the future but not to forsake the present in doing so.

Most of us probably feel that neither is entirely correct and that a position somewhere in the middle should be assumed. "Live today as if you were going to die tomorrow, plan as though you were going to live forever," is an adage worth considering. Nevertheless, there are persons who reach certain levels of the Maslow hierarchy but never are able to go higher. The type of compensation program installed should be tuned to the level aspired to by your employees. What is that level? Do the levels vary by income? background? age group? sex? What are some guidelines on this?

Most of us would like to aspire to the higher needs, but are so caught up in surviving that we cannot. This can be seen in terms of transactional analysis: Senior Employees and Depression Babies had to grow up quickly. Frequently they were unable to permit the development of their Natural Child or Little Professor. These tendencies were restrained, and they were encouraged in their role of Adaptive Child. Now as adults, they may be unable to bring their Child into their attitudes and therefore from their executive suites manifest only their Parent. The younger persons, however, having been given license through their upbringing to give full vent to their Child, Natural Child, and Little Professor, with a minimum of Parent tapes, will find it easier to face problems in a more realistic state coming from their Adult.

Differences seem to be correlated with the age groupings of the employees. Senior Employees, influenced during their formative years to be frugal and to save to ward off poverty, seem to be inordinately concerned with survival needs—so much so, that few have been able to pursue the satisfaction of higher-level needs.

The next need is the social need. For many Senior Employees, this is the highest-level need satisfied. Fraternal and social organizations, the Elks, Moose Lodge, American Legion, VFW, all abound with persons of the Senior Employee age group. Is this a coincidence, or is it a manifestation of the highest need these persons have been able to aspire to and satisfy?

Senior Employees who have progressed to higher needs satisfactions such as ego needs are not in the majority. Status symbols, executive perquisites, and organizational placement charts are the manifestations of these achievements. This is in no way a condemnation of these accomplishments; it is merely a recognition of the differences between Senior Employees and how they covet these things as opposed to other employees. As we have seen, few of this generation have been permitted to seek the self-actualization level.

Depression Babies are not unlike their predecessors. They, too, were brought up in a period of want. They amass material goods, are "joiners," and frequently emulate their superiors in their quest for ego gratifiers in organizations. With few exceptions, they, too, have not been permitted to achieve self-actualization.

Challengers, however, are different. They were born and raised in a land of plenty. Plenty to eat, plenty to wear, comfortable surroundings, and the promise of more. They have been conditioned to believe they would be cared for "from cradle to grave." Their threshold of want is very low, permitting them to aspire to higher-level needs. Even when times are bad, Challengers have an enviable resilience. They seem unaffected by what appear to be dire circumstances to older employees.

Maslow wrote,

> People who have been satisfied in their basic needs throughout their lives, particularly in their earlier years, seem to develop exceptional power to withstand present or future thwarting of these needs simply because they have strong healthy character structure as a result of basic satisfaction.*

In his book *The Greening of America*, Charles Reich further states the derivation of the Challenger's life style, calling it Consciousness III. Reich says,

> The new consciousness is the product of two interacting forces: The promise of life that is made to young Americans by all of our affluence, technology, liberation, and ideals, and the threat to that promise posed by everything from neon ugliness and boring jobs to the Vietnam War and the shadow of nuclear holocaust. Neither the promise nor the threat is the cause by itself, but the two together have done it.†

---

* Abraham H. Maslow, Ed., *Motivation and Personality*, 2nd ed. (New York: Harper & Row, 1970), p. 53.
† *The Greening of America* (New York: Bantam Books, 1971).

This set of conditions, coupled with rearing by parents who wanted "something better for their children than they had had," created Challengers. Their attitude toward life, with their Natural Child showing, and educational systems which fostered their Little Professor and repressed their Adaptive Child instincts created energetic individuals bound and determined to do something different, if not great. If America ever wanted to create a super race, this was it—healthier, both psychologically and physically, intellectually superior, with a zest for life and a reverence for everything natural and vital, if not ethereal. In Reich's words, "The most basic limitations of life—the job, the working day, the part one can play in life, the limits of sex, love and relationships, the limits of knowledge and experience—all vanish, leaving open a life that can be lived without the guideposts of the past."

The combination of experiences Challengers have had, which made them the kind of people they are, are incomprehensible to the older employees, who run the organizations that hire these people and who are trying to motivate them. The attitudes Challengers display are just not understood: "In the world that now exists," Reich says, "a life of surfing is possible, not as an escape from work, a recreation or a phase, but as a life—if one chooses. The fact that this choice is actually available is the truth that the younger generation knows and the older generation cannot know."

"I just don't understand these young people" is a phrase heard over and over. It usually refers to their lack of initiative and go-getter spirit, which is frequently the result of a Theory X management using Theory X rationale to motivate Theory Y people. It just doesn't work, nor do the people; hence the 1970s' productivity rate. Young people refuse to be part of a machine which cannot satisfy their needs.

In the past, the differences between the manager and the managed were very great. They date back to the Industrial Revolution, when immigrants came to the United States without even the ability to work for their living in the huge industrial scene. In response to that situation, management created simple jobs that could be performed with a minimum of training and know-how. Theory X assumptions flourished then and still live today in the heads of many; Theory Y assumptions are as close to Reich's descriptions of Consciousness III as they can be (see the table). Is it any wonder that young persons do not commit their energies to the decadence found in most organizations today?

Challengers' social need, next on Maslow's hierarchy, has little attraction to them because this need has long been satisfied. Generations before theirs were "vertically aligned," that is, people related to institutions such as family, church, neighborhood, school, city, state, nationality, race, and country. Challengers, however, relate "horizontally" to persons in their generation. As Reich put it:

> As the new consciousness made youth more distinct, the younger generation began discovering itself as a generation. Always before, young people felt themselves tied more to their families, to their schools, and to their immediate situations than to a generation. But now, an entire culture, including music, clothes, and drugs, began to distinguish youth. As it did the message of consciousness went with it. And the more the older generation rejected the culture, the more a fraternity of the young grew up, so that they recognized each other as brothers and sisters from coast to coast.

THEORY X ASSUMPTIONS	THEORY Y ASSUMPTIONS
People by nature:	People by nature:
Lack integrity.	Have integrity.
Are fundamentally lazy and desire to work as little as possible.	Work hard toward objectives to which they are committed.
Avoid responsibility.	Assume responsibility within these commitments.
Are not interested in achievement.	Desire to achieve.
Are incapable of directing their own behavior.	Are capable of directing their own behavior.
Are indifferent to organizational needs.	Want their organization to succeed.
Prefer to be directed by others.	Are not passive and submissive.
Avoid making decisions whenever possible.	Will make decisions within their commitments.
Are not very bright.	Are not stupid.

If the institution cannot motivate or encourage camaraderie through social needs, what about ego needs?

At Texas Instruments, it was necessary to motivate the scientists and engineers who were working in the corporate laboratory, or "Sleepy Hollow," as it was sometimes referred to, because of its location and apparent level of activity. These scientists were chagrined if you referred to their work as *applied* research. They were doing *basic* research, and to tie their efforts to some commercial result was unthinkable. They were discovering things by serendipity, and serendipity is hard to schedule—and never was an attempt made to do so. Nevertheless, the scientists were well paid, and a means was needed to motivate them. Recognition, ego gratification, was perceived as the highest need they had not achieved. A whole program was generated, therefore, to give recognition to their efforts. New titles abounded, attesting to their scientific supremacy. Much attention was given to their presentations, papers, and lectures. "Ego trips" were the order of the day. This was T.I.'s way of trying to motivate them. It worked, but there was an even more challenging method—an attempt of self-actualizing.

Esteem and ego gratification are important, and if this is the need of the employees, it can work. It seems, however, that given the size of the Challenger generation, and all commercial items being marketed to cater to its whims, their ego needs are already satiated.

According to the Challenger, ego and status symbols seem to go together, and status symbols are material goods and, therefore, held in disdain. Child psychologists, from Dr. Spock on, remonstrated for "Letting the little one have his head, let him do whatever he wants to do, get him those toys and clothes that build his ego." He was smart enough to see through titles, office trappings, and other such ego trips. All of these have been tried without success.

Reich says,

> The foundation of Consciousness III is liberation. It comes into being the moment the individual frees himself from automatic acceptance of the imperatives of society and the false consciousness which society imposes—the individual no longer accepts unthinkingly the personal goals proposed by society; a change of personal goals is one of the first and most basic elements of Consciousness III. The meaning of liberation is that the individual is free to build his own philosophy and values, his own life-style, and his own culture from a new beginning.

The organization seeking to attract, retain, and motivate the Challenger has a choice. It can either continue to play the same games that have been used in the past, based on the lower-level needs of the hierarchy—survival, social, and ego needs—thereby permitting the Challenger to seek self-actualization in nonorganizational satisfaction in pursuit of higher productivity and consequently higher profitability. It makes good Theory X "cents" to do things in a Theory Y sense.

Most will recall the mid-sixties campus scene of wild demonstrations against the establishment. The revolt or challenge was thrust at much of society. It touched the lives of everyone because of its dynamics, enthusiasm, and impact. As Elton Reeves summarized it:

The greatest effect of a subculture on the rest of the population is a forced re-examination of fundamental values by society. Starting with their original protest against the Vietnam War, the hippies made the American public crystallize its thinking about this war, the validity of the universal draft, the position of the home in our society, marriage as an institution and the ethical and moral values in the use of psychedelic drugs. . . . The hippies have made the American public take a good, long look at the underlying ethics of our society.*

These young people aged, then gradually became integrated in the labor force. Their hair is less unruly if no shorter, their clothing conforms to the published or tacit dress code, their mannerisms and conduct are toned down so as not to disturb those who are "working." The scene that greeted this youthful clan was best described by J. D. Batten: "The halls and offices were filled with well groomed, polite, proper people. Emotion was rarely in evidence and neither was vigor. Meetings were characterized by pleasantness, blandness, large vocabularies, and little accomplishment. At 5:00 P.M. the vast building emptied miraculously within a couple of minutes." †

Wide-eyed zealous youth had joined the establishment. This is where they were to spend the next 40 or 50 years carving out "their thing." They must have looked about themselves, carefully noting which people got ahead and what their styles were, realizing that if they, too, were to progress, they must emulate those who got ahead. Seeing the pattern emerging, they must have wanted to bolt the scene. Some did, only to wander back with their disdain matching their need for income. So join the establishment they did. And once in a while elements of their old selves would surface, and they would try to change the bureaucracy that they were trapped in. But the older employees were usually successful in sabotaging the new ideas, using games and techniques that amazed the young-timers and, in fact, teased their creative powers.

Surely these youngsters can think of even more confounding games to play. The challenge intrigues them, reminding them of their college days. Thus they begin to play the politics game, and their creative energies are tapped. What suffers? Productivity? Profit? If Challengers aren't allowed to contribute to the organization's growth, they'll devote their energies to the game of getting ahead through the bureaucratic maze. It's just as challenging and tricky and requires ingenuity as well. Besides, now that the young-

* *The Dynamics of Group Behavior* (New York: AMACOM, 1970), p. 155.

† *Beyond Management by Objectives* (New York: American Management Associations, 1966), p. 18.

timers are providing for spouses and perhaps children, why take risks—at least until they make ends meet?

This sad tale explains the dilemma of Challengers as they enter the business world. No wonder that their old creative flair has disappeared. The institution discourages creativity, and they seldom see risk-taking being rewarded. They are no longer part of a cohesive, organized group, as they were on campus. They are, instead, in a new environment, as they were in their freshman year at college. They are amazed and awed by all they see, a situation which is further complicated by the seriousness of it all and the consequences of making a mistake.

There is another force modifying the behavior of Challengers. This is seen in the game of "marital bliss." Whether legalized by the state or not, two cannot live as cheaply as one. As a bumper sticker put it, even "Free love costs too much."

In spite of the many single people in our midst, society encourages mating, and Maslow considers it as a need. As the couple begins their life together, they are in a "cash-now" position. They need many items for the nest—a refrigerator, laundry appliances, pots, pans. At this time outgo is often greater than income. In such a situation, no matter what one's background is, money motivates. Disposable income, income left after all the takeouts, such as taxes, seldom matches expenditures. As income increases, through salary raises and career progress, one could move toward a breakeven point with the expenditure level *if* that level remained constant. However, at the same time there is a tendency to raise one's standard of living, and things that used to be luxury items become staples. Thus, a breakeven point is not reached, for the expenditure level keeps rising. Additions to the family introduce new expenses, and the chase for the buck goes on. Because consumer goods take such a large percentage of the disposable income at lower income levels, persons at these levels of income frequently are highly motivated by money. Many families whose income remains low are always motivated by money. Other families who raise their living standards without discipline and never quite make ends meet are also highly motivated by money.

The staple needs of persons in highly technical occupations and other positions commanding high wages and salaries are met easily, and because a breakeven point is reached, the motivating power of money is increasingly diminished.

By combining Maslow's needs hierarchy and the individual's inclination toward money, the role of money as a motivator can be traced. Figure 3 shows this relationship. The Y-axis represents pay. The X-axis represents energy output for pay, measured in ergs. One's indifference to money as

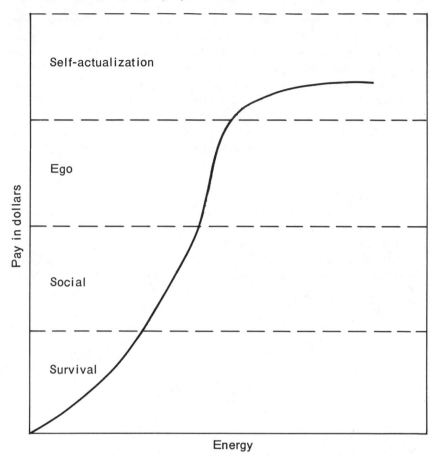

Figure 3. Personal indifference curve: needs hierarchy.

represented by the heavy black line was traditionally believed to begin in an elastic plane, become inelastic, and finally bend backward as one's pay became higher, and one became indifferent to pay. However, the graph suggests that this is not so. In the graph all of the needs are in equiwidth bands even though it is believed that this is not so, since, as discussed before, strength of needs is affected by one's age and upbringing. For simplification however, the bands of needs are displayed as being equal for all.

The graph suggests that people who have not reached the breakeven point, where income equals outgo, will put out a reasonable amount of energy for a reasonable amount of pay. To be more accurate, it is likely that more energy is put out in the beginning of the curve since the need for money is so great. As people reach the breakeven point, assuming for simplicity a constant expenditure level, they ease off and need more money in order to be motivated for greater energy output: once our survival needs are met, and the breakeven point reached, it takes more money to motivate energy output when we perceive we are trying to satisfy our social needs. It may be noted that an increase in income is perceived as an ego satisfier, as executive income; since much of it is syphoned off into taxes, it takes more money to induce more energy. It has been observed that when people perceive that they are performing tasks of self-actualization, they will expend much energy for no more pay received. Because Challengers' thresholds of survival needs are low, they are able to aspire to self-actualization earlier than others. This is made possible by the ever-increasing wages and salaries paid new entrants to the labor market and by the Challenger's natural inclination toward satisfying the higher-level needs.

The organization has several options. One important primary option is in manpower planning. The organization needs to look at itself, to see its current population makeup by age, performance level, sex, skill level, and so on. It should look at its expected future needs with regard to dynamics in competition, technical obsolescence, profitability, product mix, and so forth. Having done so, the organization needs to look at the manpower supply available to it. There are three relatively distinct groups: Senior Employees, Depression Babies, and Challengers.

The Senior Employee's greatest advantage is experience. This overwhelming consideration is what prompts many organizations to do no college recruitment. They seek only experienced persons at the exempt and nonexempt level. They want persons who can "hit the ground running." There is no time for training. Competition demands a pace only an experienced person can maintain. Often, Senior Employees bring with them a great deal of loyalty. They are vertical-institution oriented, that is, they have strong ties to "family, God, and country." This suggests stability and solidarity. It suggests maturity, though maturity is not necessarily linked with chronological age.

Senior Employees also may bring obsolescence and unchangeable methods of doing things. Their motivation may have waned due to physical impairment, family situation, or simply lack of enthusiasm. There are both disadvantages and advantages in seeking the Senior Employee.

Challengers offer the zeal of youth, new ideas, and current technology. The creativity and élan that can come from such a source are invaluable to an organization no matter what its age or stage of maturation. In a new organization Challengers are not bound by tradition and can make rapid progress. Mistakes will occur but ingenuity and dynamics will ensure speedy recovery and success in the long run.

Depression Babies seem to offer a reasonable compromise between the two extremes. They appear to have the good traits of their predecessors and yet identify and understand the Challengers. The greatest disadvantage for the company in seeking Depression Babies is that there are so few of them.

The organization must decide which age group will ensure greater success for the organization. If an organization seeks to attract and retain Senior Employees, the type of program needed will differ from that of the organization that seeks Challengers. It would be based primarily on helping employees satisfy the lower levels of the hierarchy—survival, social, and, perhaps, ego needs. Basically, this is the traditional approach. The limited effect this has on Challengers is in evidence today in most organizations and has already been alluded to here.

A program designed to attract and retain Challengers will be based on higher-level needs, primarily the satisfaction of self-actualization. It is interesting that while the program designed to attract and retain Senior Employees will have a pronounced negative effect on Challengers, the reverse is not necessarily the case. A program designed to attract and retain Challengers will attract and retain the better Senior Employee. This suggests that the latter approach has advantages over the former.

You may have noticed that Depression Babies have not been considered with regard to their being the target of a program. There are reasons for this. Not only do Depression Babies have inclinations that resemble both Senior Employees and Challengers, but there are so few of them that it is not practical to design a program to fit their particular characteristics. However, the law of supply and demand is in favor of Depression Babies. The need for their talents will always be high because there are so few of them.

One last comment regarding these three groups. It has already been mentioned that Senior Employees have tendencies resembling past managerial attitudes, traceable to the Industrial Revolution. These tendencies have been labeled by MacGregor as basically Theory X attitudes toward people. If there had been a normal birth pattern in the thirties, producing a normal number of babies who in the mid-seventies would be from 35 to 45 years old, rather than a reduced number of babies who have been dubbed Depression Babies, chances are there would not be the tremendous gap in attitudes toward people. It is likely that there would have been a normal evolution of thought, resulting in Theory Y attitudes. Instead, as we have seen, there has been a revolution in thought. The lack of Depression Babies created a chasm which has been euphemistically called the Generation Gap. The lack of Depression Babies merely dramatized the differences in management styles between the two polarized groups, the Senior Employee and the Challenger. The techniques of Theory X management must be understood. No one is entirely Theory X or entirely Theory Y; everyone has tendencies in both directions. However, when things get rough in business, such as a cutback in personnel, a sales drop, or a recession or depression, there seems to be an inclination to take on more Theory X attitudes. It behooves the compensation administrator to understand Theory X techniques in order to deal effectively with them.

· 4 ·

Motivation
Through Involvement

There is the story about the wealthy retired businessman nearing a ripe old age who invited his six married sons to Sunday dinner. As they sat down to the table he announced that he had not made any arrangements in his will, owing to his disappointment that he was not yet a grandfather. So as a bonus, he announced he would give the first grandchild $50,000. After asking the blessing, he looked up to find he was the only one at the table.

THE substantial difference between motivating the Senior Employee and motivating the Challenger is in the needs each has. For the Senior Employee the aim is to satisfy the lower-level needs, the hygiene factors or the maintenance factors, and for the Challenger the aim is to satisfy the higher-level needs, or the motivational factors. One is relatively negative and threatening and based on fear. The other is optimistic and promising.

Management by fear is a short-term stimulus, one that has to be repeated often in order to get any results. Power based on fear is relatively short-lived. "When the cat's away, the mouse will play," is apt here. Anyone who has reared teenagers knows that fear no longer helps when that teenager is either bigger and more powerful or out on his or her own. The Parent tape of fear is not long-lived and is frequently the root of spiteful actions on the part of the teenager. As the saying goes, "He who uses power to sustain authority ultimately loses it . . . often before he knows it."

John J. Fendrock puts it this way:

While fear can be used occasionally to stimulate individuals to better performance, prolonged periods of fear create ennui and indifference. Instead
of intensifying a man's effort, the threat of losing his job frequently has the
opposite effect. After seeing heads roll on all sides, managers develop a fa-
talistic belief that nothing matters, that all is in the laps of the gods. Organizations begin to drift. What might have started as healthy competition
among employees is suddenly viewed as a contest in which only a few will
survive.*

The apparent level of sophistication to which the Challenger has evolved
is dramatically different from his predecessor generations primarily because
of the gap created by the lack of Depression Babies. The techniques and
programs that used to work no longer will work. The movie *The Immigrants*
was excellent for its portrayal of Scandinavians migrating to the New Land
with high hopes. They were intelligent but naive and found it very difficult
in the new environment. Communication was the primary problem. The
lack of skills was certainly key also. This, coupled with the giants of industry
around the turn of the century and their zeal for greatness (or rape if you
would follow Reich's logic in *The Greening of America*, Consciousness I)
created simple jobs based on fear, reward, and punishment.

Peter Drucker points out the rapid changes that have occurred. "Everybody is employed by an organization. . . . Seventy-five years ago this was a
tiny minority. . . . There were more domestic workers than there were blue
collar workers. . . . Fifty per cent of the population worked on the farm." †
Drucker calls it a "society of institutions." The level of sophistication of
leadership and motivation has not caught up with this technological change.
The employee has changed dramatically; the organization must react to that
change and change also. Most systems in use today are based on the theory
of reward and punishment. Through the offer of rewards, the proverbial carrot, and the threat of punishment, or lack of gainful employment, the employee is pushed, not led, to a desired end. According to Don Fabun,

Historically, these institutions were forged in a tough furnace; they were
created in a world economy of scarcity—a largely agrarian society where
rewards were meager and hard to come by, and, therefore, treasured, and
where punishment was apt to be sudden and severe, and for that reason, all
the more feared. In an increasingly affluent society, the power of money
rewards as a motivator decreases, because beyond a certain point the difference in living styles becomes marginal and for this reason less motivat-

* *Managing in Times of Radical Change* (New York: American Management Associations,
1971), p. 89.
† *Management: Tasks, Responsibilities, Practices* (New York: Harper & Row, 1974).

ing. In an increasingly socialized society, punishment is less of a motivation because the loss of a job is not as disastrous as it used to be.*

In fact, the various programs to assist the unemployed have in many instances encouraged persons to be unemployed. Fabun's summation is:

> Primitive man was *driven* by cold and hunger and thirst to perform certain
> acts. Modern, technological man is *led* through the manipulation of sym-
> bols to choose the direction in which he will expend his energy. The study
> of human motivation thus becomes an examination of the stimuli a tech-
> nological environment can provide.

In July 1972 *Nation's Business* cited not only the need'for increasing
productivity but also the results of a survey done on filling that need. The
article reported that 260 firms were surveyed regarding whether or not they
had tried any programs to increase clerical productivity. Ninety had tried but
60 were disappointed with the results of those attempts. Thirty were glad
they had tried because output was measurably higher in the first year and
subsequent years. Firms that had been successful stated that their programs
were based on goal setting and job enrichment, both of which allude to the
higher-level needs. This is opposed to the approach of using work measurement techniques, the traditional reward-punishment method. This article
cited the need for increasing clerical productivity since "in the last seventy
years, for each seventy-five cents spent in wages, productivity rose only by
twenty-three per cent." The Bureau of Labor Statistics predicts that by 1980,
there will be 25 million more clerical workers as our economy turns more
and more to a service economy. The question is no longer *should* we do
something to increase productivity, but, rather, *what* can we do? The traditional methods don't work with Challengers. In order to be successful in
motivating them, an organization must seek to challenge them "where they
live." They must be given the opportunity to satisfy their self-actualization
needs.

In a most refreshing book dealing with leadership and organizational
motivation, Louis C. Schroeter wrote, "The continuity of purpose, the
commitment to honorable action, and the sense of duty all reside in the *will*
of the individual, not the intellect. Organizational elan will thrive only
when there is a feeling of mutual trust and confidence when information
leads to action and the achievement of goals." †

From Don Fabun again:

---

* *On Motivation* (Beverly Hills: Glencoe Press, 1969).
† *Organizational Elan* (New York: American Management Associations, 1970).

The basic concepts of the "new" motivational theory are to make the job itself so challenging that it becomes its own reward, and to create an institu-
tional environment in which the employee finds opportunity for personal
growth and the development of his own personality and self-fulfillment.

The employment contract between the employee and the organization,
which David Belcher has so aptly characterized, is the relationship in which
the employee brings to the organization a certain degree of ability and a
level of motivation. The degree to which he will perform is directly related
to *his* perception of how well the organization uses and enhances his ability
and motivates him. In terms of performance, there can be no more sensitive
area of dynamics than the system which determines the employee's compensation. Compensation administrators have tremendous opportunities to
"turn on" or "turn off" the employees through the programs they administer. Remember that in the compensation program as in all policies, we are
dealing with *how the employee perceives* these programs. The best-designed
program will be useless if the employee's attitude toward it is bad. Furthermore, an employee's perception is not necessarily the result of cool, well-
thought-out logic. It is frequently the result of hastily drawn conclusions and
casual but repeated observations.

This is not to suggest that we need to play games with employees and
present them with a slick façade. This also has been attempted, with terrible
results. Instead, it is suggested that employees be recognized as whole individuals with their own "right to work" laws. They must be convinced that
the program is well conceived, based on logic, carefully developed, and,
above all else, equitable. The compensation administrator should recognize
quickly that every employee is a wage and salary expert; each employee has a
perception of equity. The program must measure up to this perception of
equity in order for it to be successful. The compensation administrator must
not follow the path taken by the missionary who was determined to make
many converts because of his superiority in his field. Upon reaching the
desert isle he met a native and, convinced of his own expertise and the
strength of his will, he began to convert the native by first teaching him the
language. He pointed to himself and said, "Man." The native replied,
"Man." Thus encouraged, the missionary pointed to a tree and said,
"Tree." The native dutifully said, "Tree." Just then a huge plane flew
overhead, catching the attention of both. Looking up, the missionary mused
aloud, "I wonder what kind of plane that is?" To which the native replied,
"I think it is a DC-10."

In *Every Employee a Manager*, Scott Myer suggests that almost every
problem facing an organization could be better resolved by a group of dedi-

cated employees on a task force charged with the problem's resolution.*
This technique is an extension of the method Texas Instruments used with
employee attitude surveys. The attitude surveys, which were dubbed improvement surveys for subtle, super-smooth, employee edification, were
conducted at TI with considerable success. The questions were well chosen,
well written, and TI knew enough to take action on the results. That action
amounted to collating the results, categorizing them, and assigning the
problem of resolutions to employee task forces. The recommendations of the
task forces were usually well conceived and well received. The acceptance of
the recommendations by the employees was much higher than if the problem had been shoved underground or the results worked on by an ivory-
tower group.

Taking a cue from this method and from Scott, it seems that of the several possibilities open to an organization as to who should design a program,
the employee task force approach has many advantages. In fact, from my experience in leading several employee task forces toward the design of evaluation programs during the last several years, I have come to the conclusion
that there are *no* disadvantages, only advantages. The advantages are many
and varied and in some ways surprising. The only qualification for designing
a program would be that although such an approach works admirably in a
nonunion group, it would probably not succeed in a union group, which
has someone to bargain for it. The outcome of such an approach is directly
opposed to the objectives of the union movement. In a bargained-for group,
the name of the game is to intervene between the "represented" employees
and the management. In involving employees in such an endeavor, one of
the great byproducts is a new level of understanding and communication. A
union steward would not tolerate that.

Improved communications, then, are a major advantage in involving
employees in the design of their own program. Another advantage of such
involvement is that it negates much of the attraction of the union movement. Employees seek union representation for several reasons, foremost of
which is the lack of communication. When employees see that they have no
communication link, all else is lost, seniority, wages, security; every element
of their working environment is in jeopardy. In this situation, they are
inclined to seek a third party to represent them.

The best place for the union from the standpoint of both management
and employees is right outside the gate. In such a position it exerts pressure
on management to treat the employees reasonably and with respect. From
the employees' standpoint, management's anxiety about a union permits

* *Every Employee a Manager* (New York: McGraw-Hill, 1970).

them to get what they want through pressure and without paying dues. The loser in this situation is the union—it expends time and money trying to get inside the gate but is *not* rewarded with increased membership or dues.

Trade unionism is a worthwhile movement—in someone else's shop. Without the presence of the union movement many employers would not treat their employees fairly. The majority of management is Theory X, and in the absence of unionism, the American worker would not be where he is today. It is regrettable that the union cause has been marred by many abuses. Unions, like many other institutions, have followed Parkinson's law and become bureaucracies perpetuating themselves rather than following their pristine objective of helping the worker.

Most employers and many employees would rather function without a union in their organization, because it greatly reduces the flexibility of the organization, and the individual. The Theory Y employee does not perceive his goals in the context of the union movement—he wants freedom of thought. It is regrettable that once a union movement gets going, the momentum is hard to stop, and the NLRB actually abets the union cause in that it prevents management from correcting the ills that initially caused union interest among the employees. It is usually a minority of people that swings a union vote. And within that minority there are only a few personally motivated individuals who initiate and maintain the necessary momentum. If these few can be reached before they seek outside help, a union can be avoided. They can be reached by involving them in important decision-making processes, the very essence of participative management.

From working with family-owned companies, I've come to recognize the time when conditions are ripe for union organization. It is when the employee no longer relates to management. In family-owned or single-proprietorship companies, the critical time is very clear. In these organizations, management is personified; it is characterized by the head of the company who is cited by name as having done one thing or another in exercising his executive prerogative. The reference is usually done with respect, as in "Mr. Johnson changed the way we do it," or "The Old Man decided we'd do it this way." There is a time in every company when the top management has newcomers who don't carry the family name. These strangers start influencing the decision-making process, and before long, reference is made this way: "They decided to do it this way." Who are "they"? It's that new group—with whom the employee no longer relates. This is when the organization is ripe for unionizing. If I were a union organizer, I'd go around the country and listen to employees speak of their management. If I found an organization in which the employees were saying *"They* did this" or

"They did that," I'd know I'd found myself a "live one" and begin the campaign.

Probably the most significant advantage of involving employees in designing their own plan is the resultant plan itself. A more basic plan is likely to result using employee input, ideas, and skills. Employees' most frequent complaint about a compensation program is that they had very little to say about it. Therefore they reserve opinions about it or are downright critical of it. Employees want to give input about the sensitive area of their pay and if they are not permitted to do so, they can be very critical about the program.

One advantage that might have been expected but was not was the appreciation employees had for the managerial problem in pay distribution. In the role of being involved, employees are suddenly thrust into a sensitive position. Whereas before they could simply criticize their management for the program, now they *are* management and they can't go under cover. Whereas once there may have been a big difference between manager and managed, I've learned through the involvement of employees that the difference today is slight and often due to circumstances such as birth, education, and position. Employees are frequently equally logical if not more so than their managers. Management people are often so involved in game-playing that they go along with the façades seen in business. Not so with employees; they are the last to be fooled. Their approach to a problem can be direct and to the point. The employees involved in the company's activities and programs will be dedicated productive contributors. It's a wonder why management doesn't share the involvement with them more often.

Another advantage in employee involvement is that it permits the evaluation of the participant's abilities and potential. Assessment centers are useful tools in this process. Assessment centers in training programs provide activities in which the participants have opportunities to work out business problems to display their business acumen and to show their fitness for positions of authority. The issue of compensation is one of the most significant problems that can be tackled. The involvement process is an excellent arena for the employees to engage in real problems, develop usable solutions, and be observed. This byproduct is a meaningful outcome for the growing organization.

Perhaps the most important advantage of the involvement exercise is the motivational aspect. Theory Y attitudes are closely linked to commitment. Employees will work hard toward the achievement of realistic goals when they can relate to the organization of which they are a part. Too often, Senior Employees criticize Challengers for their lack of commitment, despite the fact that, according to Senior Employees, Challengers have been given all the "advantages." In psychology, this is called "projection." Senior Employees project their own needs and desires on Challengers, and seeing that Challengers have satisfied those needs, Senior Employees are disappointed by their (Challengers') lack of appreciation. Challengers are not turned on by the same things that turn Senior Employees on. That is why Challengers appear to be noncommittal. They can be motivated, however, by being permitted to satisfy their self-actualization needs. Involvement is definitely a means of satisfying that need. Challengers and other employees will be motivated if they perceive that they may pursue the satisfaction of a need through involvement.

When employees are involved in the development of a program, the acceptance of that program is very high. The organization can be scattered over the whole country or can be a tight unit in one building. Its population can be heterogeneous or homogeneous. It can have several products or services, or just one. The larger the organization, the greater the need for employee acceptance of programs. The program must run on its own. When employees know and understand that their peers are involved in the development of a program, their level of satisfaction is increased. This can be communicated to them by a variety of methods. Face-to-face meetings are the best. Supervisor notifications, memos, bulletins, newsletters are also good. Company newspapers and notices can also spread the word. When the employees themselves contribute thoughts or ideas to members of the task force, their satisfaction is again heightened. According to Elton Reeves,

> Involvement of group members insures a continuity of action hard to come by from any other source. Ego and self-actualization needs are on the highest level of the pyramid, and their satisfaction is more rewarding than the satisfaction of lower-level needs. When a man takes an objective for his own, there is less need to monitor his activity in the group. It only seems to be a paradox that man's best individual efforts are often his contribution to the group.*

Warning! The technique of involvement can be habit-forming! I'm being a little dramatic, perhaps, but employee involvement is very exciting. One client who developed an exempt and nonexempt program using employee task forces found the technique so rewarding that he was besieged by the company president every time a problem came up. The president was so elated over the success of employee involvement in the development of compensation programs that he used task forces to resolve other business problems—with great success. Employee involvement works in most organi-

---

* *Dynamics of Group Behavior* (New York: American Management Associations, 1970).

zations. The rapport that develops reduces the distinction between the employees and management, and remaining differences have a way of working themselves out when the chasm between these two mythical opponents is bridged.

Because the program resulting from employee involvement is simpler, it is easier to implement, less costly, and less time-consuming. What's more, the simplicity permits a more facile administration of the program, thus reducing gamesmanship. Unless the compensation administrator is looking for a gobbledygook way of administering the program (there are those who, in attempting to ensure their own security, actually do seek a mystical system that only *they* can understand), the involvement approach will result in a plan which in the long run will be a better administrative program.

The participative approach has long been cited for MBO, job enrichment, work simplification, and other similar programs. Using the technique in the development of a compensation program will lead to other opportunities in personnel program development.

If the technique is so good, why hasn't it been used more often? This is a typical question asked about the technique. A reason for the use of this "new" approach that immediately comes to mind is one already touched upon, that is, today employees themselves are vastly different from any that we've seen in the labor force before. They are intelligent, well educated, and have a tremendous desire to fulfill the higher-level needs. Yet, involvement is not new. "Over 2000 years ago, Aristotle said, 'Men love that which they have made.' . . . Acceptance of change is directly related to the knowledge that affected members have of it and the degree of influence they have been able to exercise in controlling its extent and direction." *

The best way to introduce change into an organization is to involve some or all of those who will be affected by that change. Specifically, if a compensation program for a nonexempt group is needed, a task force should be composed of members of the nonexempt employee force. This means that the membership on such a task force should consist of secretaries, accounting clerks, draftsmen, technicians, machinists, assemblers, inspectors, and other nonexempt employees. With guidance from the compensation administrator, the task force develops the program.

A task force for an exempt program should be composed of representatives from the exempt population. As many departments as possible should be represented. And the members should be peers to prevent any conscious or unconscious intimidation. For example, a task force of managers should not have a director or a vice president on it, since this person's rank may be

---

* *Organizational Elan* (New York: American Management Associations, 1970).

intimidating to the nonofficers. Persons of a higher level can work in a subgroup without intimidating members of the main group, but it takes special people to do this.

In addition to developing a compensation program, a task force, particularly at the exempt level, has many opportunities to solve other problems as well. In one company the CEO wanted to eliminate the barriers between the several departments that had built up over the years. It was a mature company and each department had its own compensation plan, since the company had none. There were allegations that one department paid well, that another didn't, and so on. The task force was made up of principals from each department. They developed a compensation program common to the whole company. A side benefit of this program was the elimination of the barriers that had built up. In another instance, the organization was the result of several merged companies who were still fighting each other. The CEO appointed principals from each of the merged factions to serve on the task force. The result was catalytic. Not only was a compensation program developed, but the merged companies came closer together as a result of working together and resolving their differences.

Still another company was convinced that it was so diversified and so highly technical that no one program could properly compensate its several disciplines. There were marketing people, administrators, accountants, employees with doctoral degrees, medical doctors, electrical engineers, mechanical engineers, and members of associated technical disciplines. The answer was to compose the task force of representatives from each discipline. A common program resulted.

The selection of the task force members is critical to the success of the program. It is interesting to watch a management team make these selections. Once the management team embraces the concept of task force and involvement, it zealously selects members for the force. Realizing the significance of the task force's work, the team exercises great care in selecting members who will properly represent their departments. In some instances, the most vocal persons are selected; in others the troublemakers; in others the sensitive, thoughtful ones. I've not seen yet a group chosen that couldn't work together. Each management projects its personality into the selection of the task force members and thereby a good representative group is formed.

A task force is vastly different from a committee. It's been said that a committee is a group of the unprepared appointed by the unwilling to do the unnecessary. Not so with the task force. There are several characteristics that set it apart from the committee.

First and most important, the task force moves by synergism. All individuals are encouraged to participate in the proceedings. No "holdbacks" are permitted. The weak voices are given as much attention as the loud ones. No one is permitted to take over the group's action. The matter of compensation is too vital to allow factions to develop and bias the resultant program. Progress in developing the program is made only when *all* members concur with the action proposed. The importance of synergistic action cannot be overstated.

As already mentioned, and repeated here for emphasis, the members of the task force are peers in the company. They are appointed by management. The work of this task force is vital to the organization. If the employees elected the members, these "popularity" votes might not produce the best task force. Moreover, people who are elected may feel bound to the group that elected them and take a partisan approach to the problem. Task force members must assume a more broad-minded and unbiased role in their work. The election of employees to serve on a program, personnel-oriented or otherwise, smacks of union procedures. In unions the biggest event of the year is the election of officials, officers, stewards, and others. It seems inappropriate to follow a procedure reminiscent of union activities in the selection of task force members.

Further, make no mistake about it: we may live in a democracy, but within the universe of a given organization, the regime is authoritarian. The organizational hierarchy is not to be denied. Involvement of employees does not displace the management team or the hierarchy, it complements it and is an adjunct to it. Finally, the management team should select the task force members because it is responsible for running the organization and for the policies that are developed and administered. It is also the management team that will approve the work done by the task force. Chances are, the members management chooses for the task force are the same ones the employees would elect anyway. However, actual selection of the task force members rests with management.

The size of the task force is important. If there are too few members, there will be little discussion and few inputs. The actions decided upon may be expeditious but perhaps not as well thought out or deliberate as if there were more members on the force. If there are too many members, the task force has a tendency to bog down. Cliques could develop and it would be difficult for the members to reach any agreement. As a rule of thumb, there should be no fewer than three members and no more than seven. The group should have one or more members of the personnel department who will lead the task force. Remember that the role of compensation administrators or personnel persons is as a mostly silent guide. This is a difficult role to play since, as the experts, they will constantly be looked to for direction, at least until the task force carries the ball.

Task force meetings are like seminars. They are not a series of lectures or presentations by authorities. The first few task force meetings may be presentations on setting goals, reviewing the background of the problem, and establishing the frame of reference. But beginning very early in the meetings, the leader must gradually assume less and less control. The leader's value is as a *resource* person.

The selection of the task force members should be guided by some simple but important principles. The members should be communicative and reasonably intelligent. One task force was composed of four whites and one black. In the beginning of the series of meetings, the black person had difficulty communicating with the rest of the group, primarily because of his manner of speech. His ideas were excellent, however, and when he spoke, others listened attentively. Thus encouraged, he spoke more deliberately and more clearly, and the whites "caught on" to some of his colloquialisms, and there was good communication. The inclusion of minorities and women on the task force strengthens the composition of the group. The ideas are more universally applicable, and the results have wider acceptance. The members of the task force should represent the various departments, skills, disciplines, plants, offices, divisions, companies. The members should reflect the variations in tenure, age, sex, and other characteristics of the population they represent. They should be in positions to observe the company's methods, the products and services, and the people producing them. The most important consideration for the selection of task force members is that they must be worthy of employee trust. This point cannot be emphasized too much. The sensitivity of the issue of pay, the integrity of the company, the perception of employees as they review the results of this program are dependent on this last principle.

In a company in which there were some union rumblings, the CEO decided to develop a compensation program using the involvement technique. Having been informed of the characteristics needed by members of the task force, the CEO thought it would be a good idea to name to the task force a particularly outspoken character who was suspected of being the union organizer. The individual was in his mid-thirties, held a leadman's job, and was nonexempt and very enthusiastic. He was intelligent and strong-willed, had a big ego, and was interested in self-actualization. The first few meetings of the task force were difficult ones. He was convinced it was merely a ploy; that management wasn't really going to let *them*, the employees, play such an important role. He fussed and challenged and purposely threw in some monkey wrenches and rushed down blind alleys to see the reaction of the leaders. With time, a great deal of patience, a little persuasion, and good but subtle guidance, the group became cohesive and developed a sound program. To the end, he was devil's advocate in the group.

When the work was finished, however, he became the program's most ardent supporter. He was convincing and dedicated, and he "sold" the employees on *his* program. The company never was petitioned by the union and remains nonunion today. This individual had a need to be heard. He needed to satisfy his ego and to be recognized by his peers. The union offered him the opportunity to do this as an organizer, with the possibility of being made shop steward. The company also offered him an opportunity, and he took the company's offer instead.

A person may be chosen for the task force because of his belligerence. At times this is done to allow that person to vent himself, as in the case described above. More often though, the choice is made because both management and the employees feel that no one is going to pull the wool over that person's eyes. If that person can be convinced, then the rest of the employees will be convinced. With such a person as a member, the task force will experience trying times, times when serious consideration will be given to ejecting that person from the task force. With patience and an I'm OK— You're OK position, the problem will resolve itself and, in fact, this member will become one of the task force's strongest supporters.

Occasionally some members, though qualified, will be reticent to participate in the group. This may be due to natural shyness, skepticism, or age. For example, Senior Employees were reared in a Theory X environment in which the social need is the highest one aspired to. These persons have never been asked their opinion before, and now when asked they don't know how to respond. Patience and encouragement will usually induce these people to participate and the result, obtaining their wisdom, fully justifies the effort made with them. Keep in mind that a mixture of age and youth is important to the balance of the task force.

The responsibilities assigned to the task force will vary with the organization. How much the group may handle corresponds with the style and personality of the company and its executives. Conservative management's first inclination is to permit the task force to have some meetings to discuss the compensation problem and to formulate the plan. As management gains confidence in the technique, the responsibilities of the force will be increased, and as discussed earlier, management may want to greatly expand the concept to include the resolution of many of its other problems.

To get an idea of the typical responsibilities of a task force, let's enumerate some of the jobs the force could do and the order in which they could be done. Each company can decide how much it wants the task force to do. Decisions as to the scope of the responsibilities do not have to be made at the outset. In fact, it may be difficult to anticipate the many things the task force will get into as the meetings progress. In the beginning of the program, the task force deals with the basics and moves gradually into specific problem areas. Note that members of the task force never get into the actual distribution of pay to individuals. The task force doesn't work on individual salary determination and will never know what individuals are being paid. Thus, it is possible to maintain strict confidentiality of the payroll yet deal with the sensitive problem of pay. The task force discusses the issues of *how* to determine pay, not *what* to pay. The purposes of the task force are to:

Establish economic and behavioral considerations.

Discuss fundamentals of job evaluation.

Explore different approaches.

Establish objectives of program.

Develop compensable factors.

Encourage broad employee participation.

Develop job collation means and techniques.

Test evaluation system on key jobs.

Recommend survey techniques and surveyees.

Develop structure policies.

Develop salary administration recommendation.

Assist in communication of the program.

The first issue to be discussed deals with economics. The members should be apprised of the significance of the payroll dollar in the company and of the company's position in the economy. It is in the early stages of the task force that each member becomes fiscally responsible. To this end, each member is asked to view the pay problem through the eyes of the organization's CEO. (Just as the compensation administrator must become sensitized to the status of the economy, discussed in Chapter 2, so should each task force member become economically aware.) The company's place in its product market, the elements of its cost, the impact of labor costs should be brought to bear upon the problem. The purpose of presenting this information is not to show why the company *can't* pay, but rather to acquaint the members with the facts of the economic life in the company.

Since one desirable outcome of development of the compensation program is motivation of the employees, the behavioral aspects of the pay issue must be explored. (Behavioral elements were discussed in Chapter 3.) The purpose is to identify the needs of the employees and to show that those needs are *not* dissimilar from those of the CEO. For economic reasons the CEO wants to pay for *contribution*. Self-actualization is linked to doing something worthwhile, or put another way, to making a contribution. Thus the objective of both the CEO and the employee is to pay for contribution— to direct the payroll dollar to those jobs and persons who are contributing to the success of the organization. The goal of the task force is to design a means for doing this.

There are several approaches to job evaluation, some of which are better than others. Each should be explored and a determination made as to the right one for the organization. These approaches will be discussed in later chapters. Similarly, all items proposed for the task force program from this point on will be discussed in later chapters. Our purpose here is to mention the items and to put the work of the task force into perspective. The items include:

⋄ the establishment of the objectives of the compensation program,
⋄ the formulation of a list of compensable factors,
⋄ the encouragement of wide employee participation,
⋄ the use of job descriptions or other job specification techniques,
⋄ the testing of the program and ways of implementing it.

Some management persons may feel that certain issues are too sensitive for an employee task force to discuss. However, credibility of the pay program will be enhanced if the task force has discussed them. These issues include:

⋄ survey jobs and companies to be surveyed,
⋄ structure design and policy,
⋄ salary administration policies,
⋄ the evaluation process itself.

It is during the evaluation process that the pay grade to be assigned to each job is determined. This usually is a very sensitive, and sometimes traumatic, part of the entire program. It is where "memory scars" are made that never quite heal. The potential for trauma exists in plans which are ill conceived or which are written up in language that is artificial and unconvincing. The flexibility of the task force technique suggests that the task force meetings are the ideal place for the tools of the evaluation process to be designed. The management team receives these tools and does the evaluation. This transfer of power is desirable, and the check and balance adds to the program's credibility. If the task force has kept it simple (following the KISS principle mentioned earlier), and the whole exercise has been done in a primarily Theory Y atmosphere, the evaluation process will be neither sensitive nor traumatic. Furthermore, the evaluation of the jobs need not be done by the management team. It can be done by the existing task force, by another task force set up to do the evaluation, or by the employees themselves. More will be said about this later in the chapter.

The issue of communication of the program to the rest of the employees is a difficult one. How much can be disclosed and to whom are the subject of Chapter 19. Realize, however, that no matter how extensive the communication is, it can be done more successfully by the members of the task force. These people were chosen because they were communicative and intelligent and worthy of employee trust. They are representative of the group for whom the program was designed. What better persons are there for communicating the program? Employees standing before peers with *their* program will achieve far greater acceptance than the smoothest of higher-level presenters. It must be remembered that we are dealing with the employee's perception. Chances are, that perception is a mixture of fact and fancy, emotion, logic, past and present impressions, and lingering doubts. A pay program is better received when it is presented by its designers, and when presenters and presentees are peers, the acceptance of the program is even greater.

When the program is presented to the employees, its acceptance will be enhanced if elements of the program are recognized by employees not only because they have already been discussed in informal gatherings but because they have been contributed by the employees themselves. The wider the employee participation in the development of the program the greater its acceptance. There is a direct correlation between the degree of participation and the level of acceptance. The task force members should be apprised of this early in the task force meetings. This will encourage them to actively seek employee input. The confidence of those who present the program is increased if they know they are presenting data with high employee input. It therefore behooves task force members who will be active in the presentation of the final program to actively solicit employee input.

The involvement technique process by which the compensation program is developed is simple. It usually starts with the compensation administrator presenting the concept to the executive management group. This allows management to see the purpose of the concept and to determine which employees will serve on the task force. Management's approval of the process is all-important. It would be a disaster to develop a program with an employee task force, present it to management, and have it disapproved. Approval starts and ends with executive management. To preclude disaster, the compensation administrator must always remember that executives, like the rest of us, hate surprises. They are charged with the management of the company and must know what is going on at all times. Management does not lose control by using the task force technique; just the opposite, it retains control that way.

Even though management does not serve on the task force, it should be kept informed of the force's progress, employee inputs, and the status of the developing program. If management is displeased with the program as it is developing, the compensation administrator has the opportunity to share the reasoning and thoughts with the task force and appropriate modifications can be made. I know of no situation where an impasse was reached using the involvement technique when discretion was used in guiding the task force and keeping the management informed. The task force is acting in a staff capacity, and like a staff group, it makes recommendations. If the staff has done its work well and has had guidance from management, the recommendations will be well received and implemented. The task force concept does not imply a carte blanche arrangement. Diligence and reason and a feeling of working together for the good of everyone must prevail at all times.

The next step in the process is to communicate the intention of the involvement technique to the employees. Although a face-to-face group meeting is the preferred method, other means of communication can be effective, such as through closed circuit TV or the company newspaper. The purpose of this initial communication is to inform the employees that some of them will be asked to serve on a task force, and that those chosen will not represent any special group or interest, and to encourage them to contribute to those selected any thoughts or ideas or questions they may have regarding the pay program.

The importance of selection of the task force has already been discussed. Because of the sensitivity of the pay issue, managers will be inclined to appoint their best people to the force. Nevertheless, the compensation administrator would do well to assist the managers in their selection of task force members in order to ensure a good working group of competent people.

The meetings of the task force follow the lines discussed when the responsibilities of the force were explained. The first few meetings consist of selected persons making presentations about economics, behavioral science, and traditional wage and salary programs. Subsequent meetings are low-key seminar-like discussions in which the personnel representative or the compensation administrator assumes the role of resource leader. Ideal frequency and length of task force meetings have been found to be one or two half-day sessions a week. The number of sessions required to design the program depends on the ability of the group to interact and ideate. The design process is likely to take about six to eight weeks.

Once the program is designed, the compensable factors must be tested on a representative number of jobs. All jobs will be evaluated eventually, so data about the jobs will be needed. This brings up the issue of Job Descriptions, the topic of Chapter 14. Management may then elect to evaluate the jobs, have the task force do it, or appoint a totally new group to handle the evaluation. More will be said about the process of evaluation later, in Chapter 6.

Like any program, this one needs to be "priced" in the market. Surveys and structure building are discussed in Chapter 15 through 18. Next, the program is communicated and implemented (Chapter 19). With the involvement technique, this communication to the employees is a pleasurable and casual happening. The reason for this is that most of the program will already be known by the employees through the most effective communication device in the organization, the grapevine. The employees will recognize elements of the program that they feel personally responsible for, and the tone of the communication will be one of information-giving rather than acceptance-seeking. The agony of the speakers in communications to employees when they have not been involved is in not knowing whether to duck or smile after delivering the essence of the program. In such programs speakers do not know whether to expect bricks or flowers to be thrown at them. This is not the case with the involvement technique. The employees have participated in this program. They know its contents. To criticize it would be criticizing their own efforts—and such criticisms were ironed out at the meetings before the program was completed. The acceptance of the program is, therefore, high.

In addition to involving employees in the development of a program directly affecting them in order to increase their acceptance of that program, two other goals are accomplished by the involvement of the employees.

The first is that employees are enabled to strive to satisfy their need for self-actualization. Involvement engages their intellect, their will, and allows them to contribute in a meaningful way to an organization that acknowledges their existence, importance, and individuality. With so many institutions being challenged and destroyed today, the business organization may be one that deserves and commands the commitment of the individual.

The other goal is to ensure that employees understand the program and that it relates their efforts at their jobs to their feelings of self-actualization, namely, through paying for *contribution*.

The involvement technique is a means and an end. It is a means for self-actualization and it results in a product which can be used to measure contribution and thereby motivate the employee to higher levels of productivity.

· 5 ·

Fair Labor Standards Act— A Basis for Job Evaluation

Government is not a substitute for people, but simply the instrument through which they act. In the last analysis, our only freedom is the freedom to discipline ourselves.

BERNARD M. BARUCH

THE basic foundations of the wage and salary program have been discussed. The economic foundation seems to be obvious since compensation is an economic unit. The behavioral foundation may be equally obvious since we are investing that economic unit, pay, in our human resources. There is another basis for pay also. It is the legal basis as stated in the Fair Labor Standards Act (FLSA), also called the Wage and Hour Law. Although the FLSA may be not as personally compelling a basis as economics and behavioral science, it is nonetheless important, and the compensation administrator must have a good working knowledge of it in order to build a solid program.

While governmental influence is not always welcome, it seems to be always present. There is often a tendency to resist the influence and "get around" the law. A company once was so antigovernment that it purposely devised a program paying no heed to the FLSA. The method of dividing employee groups was contrived and illogical. The management team fought what turned out to be a gradual realignment of natural work groups which very nearly resembled the FLSA approach. The point is the FLSA is not an unreasonable law nor an illogical one. In retrospect and in the perspective of

51

the many legislative influences business now has in the form of EEOC, OSHA, the Walsh Healy Act and others, it seems like the only old friend of the lot. The FLSA can actually help the organization to better manage the people, control costs, and develop more meaningful compensation programs. Wise compensation administrators will read the law, understand it, and put it to work for them.

A background of the law and its intent are important to the compensation administrator in the utilization and administration of its mechanics. The law was prompted by the failure of businesses to regulate themselves, an old story in the United States. It is a result of Consciousness I, referred to in Reich's *Greening of America*, wherein unscrupulous employers take advantage of their employees.

The law was paternally oriented in the beginning. It was intended to protect women and children from exploitation. This need was recognized as early as 1912 in Massachusetts, and 17 states had minimum wage laws by 1923. The FLSA appeared in 1938, a landmark year.

The aim of the FLSA is to "eliminate labor conditions detrimental to the maintenance of the minimum standard of living necessary for health, efficiency and general well-being of workers" in the United States.* Simply put, it was an effort to raise the standard of living for the American worker. It has succeeded in doing that. It sought to provide a base of pay which would ensure decent living standards. The law was designed to protect the employee.

Some employees bring constant pressure to bear on the compensation administrator to exclude them from the coverage of FLSA. The reasons for this pressure are usually based on status and ego needs. For example, the employee may want to identify with executives, who don't have to "punch in." The employee may also feel he can, in the long run, receive more pay and better fringe benefits and experience greater career advancement by being exempt from the law. However, it seems ludicrous that employees should want to be excluded from coverage, whether they do so individually or collectively, for status reasons or whatever. The compensation administrator should remember this when discussing the law with employees. It is *their* law. It was enacted for *their* protection. To be excluded from its coverage may jeopardize *their* well-being.

The enactment probably followed the typical game plan of legislation. Politicians and business executives got together and said, "We need a uniform approach to this common need." It was an early attempt at national

---

* M. E. Haynes, "Minimum Wage: Where Are We Headed?" *Personnel Journal*, June 1972.

evaluation or classification of jobs and employees. It made gross generalizations as to the logical groupings of employees. It excluded many industries in order to preserve the homogeneity of the act. Many of those previously excluded have since been included primarily because of the fairly universal way of approaching employee relations problems in the private and public sectors of the economy.

The initial thrust of the law was to provide a common "livable" base for the setting of wages for work done in a specific time span. All work done in excess of the time span would be paid a premium rate. Business executives probably balked at that, saying that there were certain jobs in their organizations that just didn't lend themselves to a set number of hours to be worked and further that the type of work involved in these jobs could not be monitored since it involved mental not physical work. The government finally conceded and the term "exempt" emerged. The government agreed that certain employees would not be covered by the law and would therefore be called "exempt from the provisions of the Law." Persons categorized as "exempt" would not be subject to the minimum wage or the overtime payment consideration.

Next the problem of further categorization and classification had to be tackled. Someone had to define what jobs would be specifically exempt. They certainly couldn't go to each organization and name each job that would be exempt. Similarly, they couldn't permit business to decide, so guidelines were established.

Those guidelines, essentially unchanged since the beginning, established four basic classifications which would be exempt from the provisions of the FLSA. They are, in the order of the ease with which they can be identified, outside sales, executive, professional, and administrative.

The source for the latest provisions of the FLSA is basically the Federal Labor Department office in the area of the compensation administration. Other sources also provide understanding of the law. Notable among these are various clearinghouse publications. These publications not only detail and restate the law but also interpret it and cite court cases which add further understanding of the law and its provisions. It is highly recommended that compensation administrators equip themselves with a thorough understanding of the FLSA in order to establish the legal basis for their compensation programs. The decision as to whether a position or employee is exempt or nonexempt is not an arbitrary one made by the compensation administrator. The decision of exempt versus nonexempt is made on the basis of the law. The judicious use of the logic found in that law will go a long way to establish and maintain the credibility of the compensation administrator.

Becoming acquainted with FLSA administrators should also be considered. Enforcement of the law is becoming more and more the province of local administrators. These officials have been given more authority in the selection of cases, audits, and follow-up programs. It behooves compensation administrators, therefore, to get to know the persons who could affect their companies' wage and hour status. Compensation administrators should know and understand how their particular FLSA administrator interprets the law. With or without disclosing the names of their organizations, compensation administrators can get preliminary information on the law from the FLSA administrator. The FLSA administrator is a source of information and help to the compensation administrator in this relatively difficult and sensitive area.

The categories of exemptions listed earlier were given in order of the ease with which they can be used and justified. Each exemption status is defined in terms of the characteristics a position must have in order to be considered exempt. The several guides available for determining exempt or nonexempt status are called the "long test."

There is also a "short test," which is used to make cursory reviews of the several jobs to make preliminary judgments as to their status. Remember the purpose of the law—it is designed not only to protect the employee, but to establish an ever-increasing standard of living. Therefore, essentially the short test asks, "Is the employee making a good salary in this economy?" If the answer is yes, the basic principle of the law has been met. It might be added that if an employer is willing to pay an employee a high salary to do minimal work, this is the employer's concern, not the government's. How much is enough? As the minimum wage goes up, so does the amount required as one of the tests of exemption status. Two compensation programs are necessary for each organization—one for exempt jobs and the other for nonexempt jobs. One program will not accommodate both groups. The scope and outcomes of exempt and nonexempt jobs differ, and so must the rationales used to pay for them.

For this reason, wise compensation administrators have a good understanding of the law and categorize their employees as exempt or nonexempt *before* developing the wage and salary program. For those who believe that this can't be done before the program is developed, the discussion that follows will help them see the importance of categorizing employees prior to developing the program.

The Fair Labor Standards Act can be seen by employers as an assist if they use it properly. The law identifies those jobs which are to be paid on an hourly basis and actually tends to reduce the number of high-paying jobs and in so doing reduces payroll. It also assists in recognizing bona fide "salaried" jobs and enables a rational base for the separation of lower-level jobs from higher-paid jobs. It is actually the foundation of the wage and salary program.

Violations of the law bring penalties. An infraction brings with it a fine against the employer for each instance of willful violation. The aggrieved employee and the FLSA office establish the number of hours worked overtime by the employee for the past two years for which he was not compensated. The settlement is based on premium pay, and the employer is *not* a party to these negotiations or calculations, but is liable for the money to be paid the employee. Perhaps the most costly penalty, however, is the unfavorable publicity resulting from such an investigation. If the company serves the public directly or makes a product for the consumer, the unfavorable publicity from such an investigation can cause significant loss in consumer support and purchases. If the employer enjoys a solid public image, that image can be severely tainted by such an investigation. If an employer was vulnerable to unionization or was in contractual relations with a union, its position is greatly weakened by an investigation of this kind.

Not all employees in the industries covered by the law are subject to the law. Employees or jobs not covered by the law are said to be *exempt* from the law. The FLSA specifies which jobs are exempt from the law. The four categories of exemption are executive, professional, administrative, and outside sales. Although much is to be found in the act defining jobs falling into these categories, there is much to be desired with regard to clarification. The easiest exemption to be "pushed into" is the administrative one. It also is the most difficult to defend because of the wording of the exemption. It behooves the company to strictly control and adhere to the Wage and Hour Law not only because it is legally and morally correct to do so, or because it makes good economic sense to control salaried jobs, but because when found in violation of the law, the company must show reason why a particular job is exempt. The company is on the defensive. It is therefore to the advantage of the company to maintain a strong moral position within the limits of the law, rather than to be subject to such an inquisition.

Employers may incorrectly exempt a job from the FLSA because they believe they are doing the employee a service or an honor. It must be remembered, however, that the law was enacted for the benefit of the employee; to remove an employee from coverage from a protective law may be a disservice to the employee. It is frequently such an employee, exempted from the law by a patronizing employer, who later "turns on" the employer and calls for an investigation claiming that he has been wronged.

An FLSA investigation by the Labor Department can be instituted in several ways. The employee may ask for an audit by the Wage and Hour office. The FLSA administrator may come in, unannounced and uninvited, for an audit. The employer is obligated under law to permit such an entry and is further required to disclose all records, files, and other data bearing on the subject.

The reason for most audits, however, is that of the disgruntled employee. Any employee, exempt or nonexempt, may "blow the whistle" on his employer and request an FLSA investigation. Once an investigation is requested on one job, all jobs within the company are investigated, subject to audit and action. Over the years, every company, young or old, large or small, product-oriented or service-rendering, usually has an ample number of suspect jobs.

An FLSA audit and investigation by the FLSA administrator is costly, not only from the standpoint of the fine, back pay for overtime, and public embarrassment, but from the time and energy spent on the audit itself by the several employees involved in the investigation. This includes top executives, middle management, all personnel functions, payroll personnel, and selected employees as well.

Rather than permit the company to be subjected to such an audit, the company is able to perform a *self-audit*. Such an audit has many advantages. Not only is it a controlled exercise, that is, the number of persons involved is limited to only those immediately concerned with the problem, but the audit is performed with utmost discretion, creating a minimum of unsettling situations.

The self-audit also permits the company to retain the initiative, in action resulting from the audit, and the options available can be deliberated discreetly, which would not be the case with a government audit.

The self-audit also permits the company to take a look at its jobs, positions, organizations, and people. This rare exercise in introspection can help to stem the growing bureaucracy in the organization. The FLSA actually can be a *positive assist* to the company for the reason that the law says that only truly *responsible* jobs should be exempt from the law and therefore be the higher-paid jobs. Used in a positive and therapeutic environment and atmosphere, the law can help management to "keep lean."

The self-audit is not without drawbacks. When "exempt" positions are found to be nonexempt, or covered by the law, the company is placed in the position of taking some direct action. If it does not, it is subject to the charge of willful violation, since it has become aware of the violation. As with any other business decision, the company must assess the degree of risk involved and decide to act or not to act in any given situation. Often, when violations are pointed out to executives, and the decision is for inaction, the reason they give is that they don't want to dishonor, embarrass, or demote the person holding the job in question. This decision may be based on a paternal feeling for the employee, on the employee's physical condition, or on some other personal reason. It must be repeated here, however, that it is often this employee who later turns "sour" and complains to the FLSA administrator.

Should the company elect to correct the exemption status, that is, reduce the status of the job to its correct level, nonexempt, it must determine the amount of back pay due to the employee for the unpaid overtime the employee performed during the last two years in that job. Although such action may seem harsh and demotivating to the employee, with regard to instituting a self-audit, this still permits the company to retain the initiative, and in this case the company *is* a party to the determination of back pay for overtime due the employee. What's more, such action precludes FLSA action by the government, in which the company's position would be considerably less favorable.

Another important consideration when reducing a job to nonexempt status is the determination of benefits lost or, possibly, gained by the employee(s) affected by the change. It is entirely possible that the employees affected by the change can retain the salary, though now calculated on an hourly basis. Obviously, the employees are now eligible for overtime pay and their annual earnings may actually be enhanced as a result. Other benefits also must be scrutinized to allow the company and the employee to come to an understanding. This is another reason for a company to encourage a "classless society" among its ranks by having benefit plans accrue to both exempt and nonexempt employees. The more perquisites or status symbols a company has, the more difficult it becomes to "sell" an employee on nonexempt status and its advantages.

Of all the options available to the company performing a self-audit and perhaps one of the most significant advantages, outside of economic-realignment considerations, is the opportunity to correct a situation in a very positive manner. If a job is found not to qualify for exempt status, the company can enrich that job in such a way so that it truly is an exempt job. Everyone benefits from such an action. The employee is doing a more rewarding job with greater responsibility and opportunity for advancement, the company has fulfilled its legal obligations to the FLSA, and gains by getting its value out of the money being paid for the position by having it be more responsible.

The execution of the self-audit is, at best, a political bombshell. It affects many people in various parts of the organization. It gets into operational activities and makes organizational analyses and draws judgmental conclusions frequently involving the personalities of the employees. So politically tinged is such an audit that although it can be done by a person within the company, it is best to have it done by an outside person. Although it can be argued that only an inside person knows the organization well enough to explain the positions and their responsibilities in detail, this can also be a most significant disadvantage. The inside person may know too much about the internal workings and lose his objectivity and ability to apply the law's provisions properly.

By far the most serious disadvantage, however, is the political sensitivity of such an audit. Very few organizations and very few persons within those organizations would be able to perform a self-audit in an objective manner and not feel sensitive to that political organization. It would, in fact, be unfair to put anyone in the position of performing a self-audit in an organization of which he is a member and thus subject to the influences, pressures, and personalities of that organization. If he receives his pay from the organization, he is hard pressed to be free of political influence.

A self-audit can be best accomplished by a trusted, knowledgeable outside party. This person need not be an attorney. In fact, it may be tremendously costly to use an attorney, and the intimate knowledge of the FLSA and its implications for the company and for the company's wage and salary programs seems *not* to be found among those practicing law. The ideal situation seems to be a combination of an outside party familiar with the FLSA and wage and salary programs, the personnel or wage and salary executive, and the company's attorney. The outside party brings to the company expertise, objectivity, experience, and patience. The outside party permits freedom from political interference, influence, and pressure. Working in conjunction with the company personnel executive, the consultant can develop the audit and refer the analysis to the company's legal counsel for confirmation of the findings. This then develops the basis for understanding, legality, and action.

The combined efforts of the company's personnel executive, the outside party, and the company's legal counsel can make a significant impact on and contribution to the company's success in not only identifying exempt positions but in auditing and analyzing the company's operations. The resultant jobs are more responsible, the employees more satisfied, and management has the assurance that not only is the organization fulfilling its moral and legal obligations but the payroll dollar is being more wisely invested.

The question of what job is exempt and what job is not often winds up as a personal duel between the compensation administrator, who is familiar with the law, and the supervisor of the job in question, who is unfamiliar with the law, and who suspects the compensation administrator of being arbitrary in making decisions. This need not be the case. Any of several mature approaches to determining exemption status can be used.

Because the legal observance has been within the charter of the financial department, the determination has often had its roots there. The observation has been made that decisions about exemptions arising in the controller's department are proclaimed as if sacred, and because many decisions emanate from that department on a variety of legal matters, the decisions have rarely been challenged even though they have not been well received. This is truer in smaller or younger companies in which the personnel organization is not fully developed. Even after personnel departments are operating, the decisions frequently remain in the controller's department. These decisions can be good or bad, depending on the expertise and style of the person making them.

Organizationally, it doesn't seem logical for the controller to continue to make these decisions; the controller's time could be better used in financial activities, especially when there is a fully operative personnel department. Financial departments have frequently been accused of being huge sprawling organizations both deep with supervisors reporting to supervisors reporting to supervisors, and broad with many small groups each with its own supervisor. This is the result of the controllers' acute sensitivity to the FLSA. The controllers, aware of the four exemptions—sales, executive, professional, and administrative—needed to have a means of promotion for their people. Accountants have frequently been low in demand, not college graduates, and not overly ambitious, and the controllers realized that for promotion's sake the accounting personnel didn't really qualify for the sales, professional, or administrative exemption. Therefore, the best route open to controllers in promoting their people to higher income levels was to create oftentimes redundant organizational places to which these people could be moved. This led to accountants being exempt by virtue of the executive exemption, which resulted in the creation of huge, sprawling financial departments. Although this practice still exists, accountants have become professional in their approach to the financial problem. They are highly sought graduates and command good salaries in positions that make use of their training. These accountants usually qualify for the professional exemption, making it unnecessary for the financial department to build huge, costly organizations to justify exempt status.

The language of the FLSA has remained unchanged since its inception. The jobs in industry have changed dramatically. Yet the applications of the law made in 1938 and since are still in use. The result is confusion, chaos, and misunderstanding of the FLSA. The FLSA is not to be kept at a distance and viewed with awe. It is to be used by industry for the good of both employee and employer.

It is an obvious alternative to appoint compensation administrators as guardians of the FLSA. In this capacity, they can equip themselves with the knowledge of the law, use it as the basis for the wage and salary program, and use it to help define the work assignments of both the exempt and nonexempt jobs. When the exemption status of a job is in question, they can exercise authority and expertise in reaching a just decision. They are also a source of advice to management on the FLSA.

Frequently, compensation administrators do not want this kind of authority. Sometimes they find the law difficult to understand and don't feel qualified to administer it. Often they feel it is not advantageous to them politically to make such controversial decisions. Others feel that line management should make these decisions.

Whatever the reason, a common practice is to have line management complete a form generated by personnel which lets line management administer the FLSA. In such a form, the several exemptions are enumerated and FLSA descriptions are paraphrased. The supervisor, knowing the job in question, can then compare that job to the exemption test and determine the exemption status. While this seems like a reasonable exchange of power between line and staff, it really is a degeneration of staff responsibilities. Line managers may be highly motivated to "take care of their own" and usually will be so occupied with that notion that they will elect to exempt positions which really ought not to be exempted. The responsibility for the action is "assumed" by the supervisor at the time, but if an audit were done by the Wage and Hour Division, there is no doubt as to who would have responsibility, the personnel department. It will always fall to the compensation administrator to show why certain positions are exempt in the company when they really are nonexempt under the law. In view of this, it is clear that the compensation administrator must take and maintain the initiative in making decisions about exemption status and in ensuring that the company complies with the law.

Compensation administrators who want to encourage participative management within their organization without divesting themselves of the charge of FLSA administration can do so. With participative management, compensation administrators assume the role of internal consultant rather than that of watchdog.

The way to do this is to have review board action. This works in the following way. A review board composed of line management is established. For best results the members of the board should all be at the same level in the organization. They should represent several of the major groups of the company. As with task forces, selection of the members of the board must be made very carefully. The board will have considerable influence and, therefore, many departments will want their own representatives. In the interests of good group dynamics, the board should be large enough to be representative yet small enough to be manageable. This means three to seven members. The members should obviously command respect and be reasonable in their approach to problems. They should be appointed by management and perceived by employees to be fair-minded persons. They should be permanent members who can devote their time and energies to the problem at hand. The problem in this instance is the FLSA. The board should be a "standing" board. That is, it is not a board which will perform an act and then disband. It will be asked to meet regularly. This will be anywhere from monthly in a dynamic, growing, or large company, or to semiannually in a relatively static environment. The purpose is to act as the conscience of the organization with regard to the FLSA and its ramifications. Test cases found in the various clearinghouse publications should be used as precedents for the actions of the board.

The compensation administrator serves as the board's *guiding* secretary. In this capacity, the compensation administrator receives the request or initiates the action regarding a promotion or consideration of a position for exempt status. The compensation administrator does all the research in the case and prepares a brief, much as an attorney would do for a client. He should remain as objective as possible and explore all details and possible effects of the action proposed. What effect will it have on the current employees? Other classifications? Other employees? Does it meet the standards of the FLSA? What status is most applicable? The compensation administrator's presentation of the case to the board should be accompanied by a recommendation that the job in question be accepted as exempt or rejected for that status. Obviously, if he has done his work properly, this recommendation will be supported and the board will act on it as recommended. The significance of the board's action is that it acts as an objective check and balance on the work of the personnel department. The board actually is in a position to screen applications and deem whether or not a position should be accepted into the "fraternity" of exemption status. Many examples of this screening may be found, notably in engineering. Often a "mustang," a person with limited academic training, becomes a technical specialist in a narrow field. As a nonexempt technician, he has become ultravaluable, knowing everything there is to know about a certain subject in which the organization is greatly interested. There is often a tendency to "give away the plant" to him to ensure his continuance in the organization. Everything must be done to make the person stay. There is an overwhelming push to give him exempt status, pay him more, and increase his standing in the company. The compensation administrator finds it difficult to deny him exempt status. He may not know all the elements of the job, may not even want to; it may be so unpolitic to deny the action that he inevitably succumbs to the pressure. Whether the action should be taken or not is not the point. The point is that the action is not the result of rational behavior.

When there is a review board, the compensation administrator prepares the brief, submits it to the board, and the board can take the action. In some instances, the change is warranted. More often, however, the board will deny the action on the grounds that the job is not exempt since the professional clause is not truly satisfied. There are two other reasons that the board will deny the action. One, they realize that the employee's training and expertise are not broad enough for true professional application and the employee will be at a disadvantage when and if that particular need diminishes. This is the situation regarding obsolescence. For example, the expert on propellor blades may be indispensable while propellor blades are essential, but when they are no longer used, that technician is hard pressed to do a job worthy of exempt status because he does not have the ability or training to expand into other areas. The other reason for denying the action can be laid to a kind of snobbery. Any profession has pride, and the members have a tendency to want to keep their fraternity close-knit. For this reason a group will look askance at someone trying to gain membership who is not extremely well qualified. The motive may be questioned; the phenomenon may not, it does exist.

There are other ways of expressing appreciation to respected employees. In fact, employees may actually be done a disservice if they are made exempt. The FLSA was enacted to *protect* employees and give them certain rights and privileges, overtime pay being the primary one. Take those rights and privileges away, and employees are actually hurt. The other consideration is the position in which employees have been put. They now have to contend and compete with persons who may be better equipped to do the job than they. This puts them at a distinct disadvantage, and should their expertise no longer be needed, they may really find themselves lost and out the door.

The board approach has many advantages. It permits the organization to honor the FLSA more objectively and with greater adherence. It also views each application for exempt status more rationally, with more participation for decision making. Employees, too, are ensured a fair shake, for the action taken will be the result of a reasonable body, working with facts and counseled by an expert. One can feel certain that the final decision will be in the best interest of all concerned. The board approach certainly is an Adult—Adult transaction which utilizes the expertise of the internal consultant, the compensation administrator.

The Extension of the FLSA—stating that persons doing the same-level work, with the same standards of performance, should receive equal pay—was the result of a mistake, and before I'm branded a male chauvinist pig or a sexist, let it be known that this "rider" was attached to a piece of legislation in an attempt to bog down the passage of the whole piece. It didn't. It was enacted into law, and it states what should not have to be said at all.

However, abuses by industry spark legislative action. It's regrettable that EEOC dictates and age and sex legislation even exist. Compensation administrators are obligated and dedicated to achieve equity in pay. It is old, traditional systems in wage and salary that have permitted inequity to exist. Programs based on job content permit inequity in pay. Programs based on contribution do not. The laws are the means by which industry is forced to do what it should have been doing all along, paying for work done without bias of any sort. Resistance to those laws is to be expected. Laws can change actions right away, but attitudes do not change so quickly. To some people, the laws represent a catastrophic change. The shock is difficult for them to handle, and making the change depends on a variety of conditions, the most significant of which is not attitudinal but economic.

Note that with all of the influence exerted by EEOC and age and sex legislation in the first half of the seventies, the last half of the seventies will see a gradual erosion of the influence because of the change in the relationship of labor supply and economic demand. This erosion is manifest in a very glaring way: unemployment statistics. The first reports on unemployment figures in the mid-seventies revealed that most of the unemployed were blacks and women. Their departures from the workforce were both voluntary and involuntary. The change is what is noteworthy. As an observer of and commentator on these data, I may be characterized as a sexist with a KKK sheet over my head, but I am not. The point is that economics dictate the action taken by people. When the lower needs of the hierarchy are threatened, the higher needs are sacrificed. In this case, all the good intentions of legislated equity are displaced by the will to survive.

Nature abhors imbalance, and things have a way of seesawing back and forth until balance is achieved. Equity as a principle remains unchanged, and compensation administrators are remiss if they don't always aim for equity in the payment of the organization dollar. It is within the purview of compensation administrators to establish systems which prevent inequity from occurring in pay systems. The addition and removal of persons from the payroll is a manpower function presumably based on micro economics. But even if the pressure for equity wanes, the compensation administrators should continue to ensure it. It makes good *economic* sense to achieve equity in payment. The need is to direct the payroll dollar where it will do the most good, to reinvest that payroll dollar into those jobs and persons that are contributing to the success of the organization. This is done on the basis of contribution, not some Parent-tape bias or egoism. It makes good *behavioral* sense to ensure equity. When employees perceive that the contributors are rewarded and get ahead, they, too, will strive for higher performance levels. Motivation is improved when equity is achieved. The perception of equity by itself may not be motivating, but equity must be achieved before any motivation can occur. The bases for the importance of the achievement of equity are seen in economics, behavioral science, and law.

• 6 •

Job Evaluation—
The Keystone of Compensation

A proposal to raise faculty salaries at a small state agricultural college was brought before the legislature. The farm bloc was solidly against the measure—they couldn't see why the state should pay those college professors $5000 a year just for talking 12 or 15 hours a week. Faculty representatives made no headway with their arguments until one of them, who had done some farming, had an inspiration.

"Gentlemen," he said to the lawmakers, "a college professor is a little like a bull. It's not the amount of time he spends. It's the importance of what he does!"

THERE is an old saying, "Philosophy bakes no bread—but if it weren't for philosophy, there wouldn't be any bread baked." The philosophy of a sound compensation program has economic, behavioral, and legal bases. They've been discussed; now let's "bake bread."

The method of evaluating jobs is the most important basis for the organization's compensation system. Without a sound method of evaluation, there is little order. Thus, the choice of a method must be made with great care.

The judgment technique exercised in evaluating jobs can range from informal "gut" feeling for the values of jobs to the overly precise quantitative methods sometimes used. There is no one technique that is ideal for all settings. Each organization must choose the one that best suits it.

The formality or informality of the technique must be compatible with the aims and style of the organization. Methods which seem too informal are often referred to as the "cigar box" type. This is where compensation decisions are reached by the "old man" who has all the data in a cigar box in his middle desk drawer. At the other extreme are the overly zealous technicians who have created inflexible systems which tend to advance the complexity of systems design but little else. Here, as in many pursuits, moderation is the key.

An engineering manager visiting a client company found that his task was to convince those he was speaking with of the need for an evaluation plan of greater substance than the BG^2 ("By Guess and By Golly") method they were using. The meeting had gone on and the participants were getting restless. Many felt there was no need for a real evaluation plan and that what they were doing was crude but adequate. Suddenly the engineering manager had an idea. He said, "We've been sitting in this room for five hours today. You've all been in this room before, several times. Tell me, what's the volume of this room?" They all sat back, pleased at the diversion, and each responded with a calculated guess. One geologist said, "It's 15,000 cubic feet." "Naw," said the petroleum engineer, "it's about 25,000." "You're wrong," said a production engineer, "it must be over 35,000 cubic feet." This went on until all present had submitted estimates. Finally they all looked at the originator of the question for direction. They were surprised that there could be so many "wrong" answers that varied from their own "correct" one. The engineering manager asked, "How wide is the room?" They answered almost in chorus with fairly close estimates. "How long is it?" Again a quick but accurate response from all present. "How high is it?" Once again they responded. "Now," the manager said, "what's the volume of this room?" The point was made. They all saw the parallel with the need for a job evaluation system. Once they quantified the parts, the "whole" took on proper dimensions. All were agreed that a job evaluation program was needed.

An informal evaluation system, in which we guess how much each job is worth, is as good as the results that this group of technically qualified people got when they each first responded to the question about the volume of the room. There are two points to be made. One, when given the dimensions of the item, several persons arrive at similar conclusions. Two, the more quantified the dimensions of the problem, the more accurate the conclusion will be.

The need for a substantial evaluation plan is best seen when we examine the needs of the two alleged poles of an enterprise, employees and management. Management needs control of the organization's costs, wants to be sure the money in the payroll is not being wasted on nonproducers. Management wants desperately to pay for contribution, and needs some way to measure that contribution—first, which jobs are contributing, and then which persons are contributing. Employees want an income to satisfy their survival needs, a place to work where they can find satisfaction, and an opportunity to make a contribution to something. If the workplace is not that place, then they'll find some outlet, some institution or group, that will permit them to make their contribution. Both employees and management want the same thing. They are not so different after all. Their needs can be satisfied by a meaningful evaluation plan which permits and encourages management to recognize contribution and employees to be rewarded for it.

Industrial economics tells us that money, machines, and people produce the income. Money, measured in such things as cash flow and costs, is carefully controlled. Machines, likewise, are all tagged, inventory counted, desks marked, and other assets carefully and methodically controlled. How about people? The numbers are counted, the payroll counted, but what control exists? Usually people, what most companies claim in their annual reports to be their most important asset, are carelessly left to their own devices. An evaluation plan can not only make it possible to quantify the numbers but also to qualify the numbers and ensure that that precious investment, the payroll dollar, goes where it will do the most good. In spite of these compelling needs to develop an evaluation plan, management still is reluctant to go ahead.

There are two possible reasons for this. First, although management knows the need exists and appreciates the logic of measuring jobs and employees, it has seen so many unsuccessful attempts at job evaluation that it hesitates to do anything. Second, the authority to issue pay dollars to employees is the only prerogative left to management in this world of control. It represents management's last vestiges of power and, therefore, any attempt to take it away is resisted. In other instances, it is the old story of entrepreneurs who refuse to believe that they cannot continue to personally dole out pay just as they did when they started their company. The companies may be huge now, but they still regard them very personally and paternally and feel that it is their duty to maintain this last vestige of personalization. These persons are, perhaps, the hardest to convince because they are coming from such a sincere position. Unfortunately, it usually takes hard, sometimes ugly, data on turnover, productivity, or the like to convince them that conditions no longer permit them to continue in that manner.

Job evaluation is the keystone of an integrated personnel program. A job evaluation program will define the parameters of a job, exempt or nonexempt. With this done, any approach to management by objectives or similar programs is facilitated. Job evaluation can help greatly to reduce job duplication and overlap, resulting in tremendous cost savings. This kind of definition can assist in the formulation and streamlining of the functional organization. Job evaluation can also identify the staffing needs of the company, thus reducing cost in superfluous hiring practices. With the jobs identified, the qualifications for those jobs may become evident and lead to selective hiring practices—hiring the right persons for the right jobs, not overhiring, not underhiring, which in turn help in modifying and creating enlightened job design, eliminating "dumb" jobs, enriching jobs, and promoting motivation. Job evaluation can also provide the basis for a successful performance appraisal program. It is difficult if not impossible for a performance appraisal program to work if there is no job evaluation program. The job evaluation program establishes the parameters of the job, and a performance appraisal program measures how well that job is done. Without the former, how can you have the latter?

The need for an evaluation program is clearer than the need to modify or replace one that exists but is no longer valid and working. However, there are detectable symptoms of the need for change. They are discussed in some detail in the rest of this chapter.

Abundance of job descriptions. The sheer number of job descriptions in a file may indicate the need for a change. The number may indicate that the current program is too exacting, requiring detailed job descriptions for each job in the organization. Such a program is costly, though highly personalized. Such a program can exist in a static environment, but in a dynamic one there will be an accumulation of job descriptions, since jobs sometimes change imperceptibly, leaving an old one unchanged but creating a new one requiring a new description. Often the analyst becomes disenchanted with the program and ignores the accumulation of job descriptions, knowing that to dive into them means much fruitless toil, with the possibility of a great deal of pressure from various people and departments. To avoid this, the analyst allows job descriptions to pile up and become hopelessly out of date.

Job descriptions out of proportion to number of employees. In a working system in which the program permits more than one person in the same job, there should be fewer job descriptions than there are employees. This seems obvious, of course, but in many instances this is not the case. New job titles are entered, the old ones not discarded, and before long there are many jobs that are not held by anyone. Again, the system may be so specific that the slightest change in job prompts a new title, job description, and possibly a new grade. Such a system is costly. The proponents of such a system claim that it permits more exact pricing of the job. Many disagree, saying that the change in a job's scope rarely causes a decrease in pricing. There could be no saving at all, just a costly maintenance process.

How many jobs should there be? A company which permitted more than one person in the same job once had 4,000 employees and 4,000 job titles. A painstaking effort of screening, auditing, and analyzing revealed that the number of job descriptions needed was 1,000. This seemed to be a great many but was a workable number. The ratio of 4:1 in a working, mature system in a relatively large company is a fairly good rule of thumb. In a smaller company, there will be proportionately more jobs, in a larger company fewer. The technology, number of products, product mix, and the evaluation plan itself will suggest the ratio appropriate to the particular organization. Too many job descriptions in relation to the number of employees may suggest the need for a change.

Job descriptions out of date. A collector of antiques could have a heyday in the files of job descriptions around the country. The collector may find value in relics of the past, but for the compensation administrator, old job descriptions probably suggest the need for change. The dynamics experienced in the country during the last ten years in virtually all organizations preclude the possibility that old job descriptions are useful. Strictly speaking, job descriptions are outdated as soon as they're printed. The older they are, the less useful they tend to be. There is often an unwillingness to update them because of the work involved in revising a job description. The cause for simplicity is made again in terms of this issue. Every effort should be made to develop a simple job description in the first place. Next, a simple procedure for its revision will make it easier to keep job descriptions up to date. The need for change is in direct proportion to the age of the job descriptions.

Meaningless compensable factors. Perhaps the best reason to change the compensation program is the realization that the compensable factors no longer measure the value of the job, if, in fact, they ever did. A survey revealed that most of the plans in existence today were designed and implemented in the five-year period right after World War II. The answer to the question Have there been changes in this country since 1950 in technology, methodology, skill, laws, and the like which would influence the compensable factors? is a resounding yes. Yet, many of these plans are still "prospering" in languishing organizations. One notable plan in the country even antedates World War II, and yet its popularity is very high because of very effective marketing and the lack of sophistication which also abound in compensation technology.

There is a good way to tell if the compensation factors are no longer valid. There is a time when we find jobs no longer priced "right." We find that the market has advanced and is paying much more for the job than the system says it's worth. This is a most disturbing situation for the compensation administrator. There are several options open to him. He can redefine the job, in hopes of obtaining a higher evaluation and consequently a higher grade, which will permit competition in the labor market. He can simply go back to the evaluation, change it, compromise the integrity of the system, and get a higher evaluation and a higher grade. Or, taking the really easy way out, he can call the job an "anomaly" and pull it out of the system. The use of this word, which is worth at least $53.50, offers several advantages. It often causes the listener to wince, nod, and scurry back whence he came. It permits the compensation administrator to retain the old system and reduce his own effort. It also permits the company to hire successfully in the market whenever an anomaly can be "found." Once, an administrator who was obviously titillated by the word became quite adroit in its use. He found several anomalies in his system, pulled them out, and proudly grouped them together in what he called his "anomaly structure."

Getting serious again, this phenomenon usually occurs when the dynamics of technology or methodology produce a new job, such as when the key-punch operators first happened on the scene. The simple economics of the matter were that there was a high demand for them and a low supply. The result was that wages for them rose dramatically. Yet, when the duties of key-punch operators were compared with traditional compensable factors, the job didn't evaluate high enough to command a grade sufficient to facilitate hiring. The key-punch job when thus reviewed was similar to the clerk-typist position. The operator typed at a keyboard resembling a typewriter, from copy like that used by a clerk-typist, produced copy that was used elsewhere that was again similar to that produced by the clerk-typist. Right? Wrong! The analyst should ask himself, "Why do other organizations want the services of key-punch operators? Why is the demand for that job so high?" It's because the supply of key-punch operators is low and the demand is high that the price is so high. But why? It should have become obvious that key-punch operators were so much in demand because of the impact of that job.

To place value on a job by comparing the *activities* done in a job rather than the *contribution* made by the job is where the error lies. Traditional programs based on activities or job content rather than on contribution miss the whole intent of job evaluation. This system was unresponsive to the real world. It measured things which were nonessential. There would be no anomalies in a system in which the compensable factors are timely and properly oriented to contribution. Anomaly jobs are a manifestation of out-of-date compensable factors. A system of evaluation that rewards those jobs which are contributing to the success of the organization will not have anomaly jobs.

Turnover too high or two low. The coming and going of employees has often been seen as an indication that something is wrong with the organization. This is unfortunate. Times have changed so much that employees *not* coming and going should be viewed with alarm. This would suggest that while some turnover is good, too much or too little turnover is not so good. Frequently a company is aware of high turnover but seldom is sensitive to the problems causing low turnover.

Further, the concepts of high and low are perceptions of those viewing turnover. Those perceptions are the result of their frames of reference. In the West, turnover and tenure are viewed very differently from the way they are viewed elsewhere. On the West Coast an engineer who stays with a company more than five years is viewed with no little suspicion, as one without much ambition. In the Midwest however, an engineer who stays with a comapny for less than five years is viewed as a transient and a "job hopper." The quality of those persons leaving the company's employ also tends to influence whether the turnover is high or low. There may be few employees departing, but if they are quality employees, the perception of those remaining is that turnover is high.

Nevertheless, turnover is calculable. It should be used to measure the success of the compensation plan in general and the actual evaluation plan specifically. Although there are some occupations that seem to be more mobile than others, certain numbers can be generated to use as criteria for high or low turnover. Any such norms, however, must be viewed with respect to the economy. If the economy is recessed, employees detecting the insecurity of the times will have a tendency not to move and this will result in lower turnover. In a dynamic, fast-growing economy, employees will tend to be more opportunistic and turnover will be high. The mobility of Challengers is much higher than of their predecessors and, consequently, turnover will be increasing through the years in which they are dominant figures in the labor force.

With turnover data thus qualified, it can now be stated that the typical turnover among exempt employees is 10 to 12 percent annually. Typical turnover among nonexempt employees is 25 to 30 percent annually. If the organization's turnover varies considerably from these typical figures, it can be pronounced high or low. Turnover which is considerably lower in either category is seldom noticed, yet it can be worse than high turnover. High turnover often reflects undercompensation. Employees are seeking "greener pastures" where their services will be more appreciated and better rewarded. Low turnover often reflects overcompensation. Employees remain because they have found a safe, secure nesting place. Low turnover and the better employees leaving in small numbers may seem to suggest no problem, but in fact the organization may be dying. Better employees leave because they are seeking an organization which will reward their services over and above the others. Low turnover and overcompensation are usually found in maturing organizations in which everyone or nearly everyone receives an annual increase. In such an organization, bureaucracy has set in and the Parkinson's third law syndrome is in evidence.

Product or labor difficulty in marketplace. In a downturn economy or any instance in which the success of the product or service is waning in the marketplace, organizations often look to their compensation plan as being faulty. Labor costs in a competitive product market can make the difference between success or failure. Compensation administrators have an excellent opportunity to contribute to the success of their organizations by more carefully controlling compensation. Control does not necessarily mean keeping compensation levels down; it means directing the compensation dollar to those jobs and persons that are contributing. Labor costs will be kept down since productivity will thus be increased. The labor market is usually the most obvious place where the need for change in a compensation plan manifests itself. When employees leave for higher pay, when it's difficult to extend offers of pay in the labor market for fear of upsetting internal equity, and when the recruiter is constantly in battle with the compensation analyst—all these are very loud signals that the compensation plan needs to be improved.

Aging of labor force; youth in labor force. A problem which is somewhat tied to turnover and somewhat tied to labor market woes is the manpower staffing analysis on the demographic problem at the company level. The organization's manpower should result from purposeful action. It seldom does. The employees are usually the result of haphazard acquisition. Chances are that most organizations mirror the bimodal age distribution, that is, quite a few Senior Employees and a large number of Challenger employees. Some companies, because of their compensation plan, or in spite of it, have an inordinate number of one or the other age group. The organization may have too many Senior Employees because its policies do not attract or retain Challengers. Such a situation will be detrimental to the organization since "new blood" will keep the organization growing and dynamic. Too many Challengers can also be detrimental. The zeal of youth is wonderful, but it is mistake-prone. The youthful zeal must be tempered by the experienced Senior Employee to create stable long-term growth. The compensation plan, identifying and rewarding contributors of all ages, will ensure the proper distribution of age groups and, more important, will ensure the attraction and retention of contributors.

A *bureaucratic environment.* This is one in which the key to success or at least longevity is to assume a PYD attitude. PYD, standing for "Protect

Your Derriere," means that the systems dare employees to risk anything because if they err in their risk taking, they are subject to harsh treatment. The compensation program, too, can add to bureaucracy by requiring an inordinate amount of paperwork when any action is taken. In such a case, the system has become an institution unto itself rather than being a system contributing to the good of the organization. Such a program should be replaced by a simple system that will clearly and effectively encourage risk taking and reward for accomplishment.

Huge and growing middle management. Probably the most obvious manifestation of bureaucracy is the size of the organization's middle management. These employees are the caretakers of bureaucracy, the GPD, the "Grand Protectors of Derriere." They are a costly bunch, yet often taken advantage of with regard to compensation. Executives have several options open to them with regard to their pay. The union takes care of the nonexempt worker. The ofttimes neglected one is the middle manager. It is ironic that the employee hurt the most during the abortive wage freezes of the Nixon administration was the very person who had elected him to office. Some may say that this was justice. Nevertheless middle management is a difficult group to deal with. It should be kept to a minimum in any organization. That in itself would reduce the problem of neglect. Simplified systems which eliminate the need for "backup" PYD systems would greatly advance the state of management and increase productivity in business exchanges.

Compensable factors unrelated to contribution. Much has already been said about this. There is little choice open to compensation plan developers. Either they want systems that will reward for contribution, or they want systems that will value activities or job content, for job content's sake. Either they want a viable, direct, and simple system that will guarantee them a place in management circles, or they want a confusingly worded gamesmanship vehicle which will give them secure mediocrity. Either they want a personally satisfying position, or they want a politically bent position which holds its authority through statutory policies and organization charts.

Employee attitude surveys. The best reasons for changing the present system are to increase employee acceptance, encourage motivation, and enhance productivity. What better measure is there for the present state of content than a well-constructed employee attitude survey? Much money is spent on installing various personnel systems because somebody thought they would have beneficial effects. Those guesses may be right, but why guess? Instead of putting in this or that program, an employee attitude study may show that something else is really needed. In increasing numbers, the employee wants to be heard and can greatly help in the company policies if permitted to do so. An employee attitude study will show whether a revision of the present compensation plan is needed.

Financial ratios. Of all the reasons for changing a system the ratios found in an organization are the most commanding. There may be several intangible manifestations of a need for a change, but until compensation administrators begin to identify real changes in the financial picture of their organizations, they have only "feelings" to work with. The ratios are many, with the most notable ones being those measured against payroll.

◆ *Payroll growth: sales growth.* Many companies as they grow find that the payroll is growing at a rate faster than sales. Although there may be an explanation for it, it nevertheless suggests that greater control is needed. Perhaps there is a little too much exuberance displayed in salary increases, new hires, or lack of productivity since it's taking more and more people to produce the same number of sales dollars.

◆ *Payroll growth: profit growth.* Often maturing organizations sacrifice profit for bureaucracy. This happens in a PYD situation where an organization has found that it has become more important to document the institution's activities than to advance them. This is the result of making little distinction between good employees and not so good employees. When general increases are given (a situation in which all or nearly all employees are given some kind of financial increase during the year for adjustment, promotion, or merit), the good employees leave, and all that is left is the sediment. To further secure its position, the sediment develops a bureaucracy which will hurt no one and benefit very few. The result is greater numbers of persons to perform the bureaucratic games and a waning profit.

◆ *Payroll growth: cost of sales growth.* The cost of putting out the product or service is called many things by the accountant: cost of sales, cost of goods produced, value added, and so forth. If it takes more people or payroll to produce the same kind of goods dollars, there may be a need to change who is getting the payroll dollar. Productivity has waned.

◆ *Payroll growth: productivity.* There are several ways to measure productivity. Recently the various governmental units have taken great pains to devise formulas to measure productivity. The easiest way is to merely measure output per employee. If it takes more employees to put out the goods than it used to, the organization may have a problem. The product may have changed. The technology may have changed. This simple measurement of output in dollars, volume, pounds, or whatever divided by the number of employees is an easy way to get a significant insight into what may be a serious problem.

Compensable factors mired in confusing language. The most common cause of the collapse of compensation programs is the weight of the program itself. This is often a literal weight—the weight of the job description. The more complex and confusing the program, the more job description information is needed. Employees fail to understand the program, analysts institutionalize the program by writing lengthy descriptions that few read and fewer agree upon. Before long, no one pays heed to the verbose program except those who enjoy splitting hairs in determining the meaning of the descriptions in the program, and sooner or later the program is compromised and aborted, weighted down by its own language—time for a change.

• 7 •

Job Content
versus Contribution

Seated in a hotel lobby was a party of businessmen attending a convention. Among them was a man who introduced himself as a mind reader and offered this challenge:

"I will bet any man in this group $10 that I can tell him what he is thinking about."

"I'll take that bet," said one of the businessmen.

The mind reader gazed intently into the other man's eyes for a few seconds, and then announced: "You are thinking of going to the city, buying $10,000 worth of goods, then going home, declaring yourself bankrupt, and settling with your creditors at 10 cents on the dollar."

The merchant did not answer, but reached into his pocket and handed over the $10.

"Ah," said the mind reader, "then I read your mind correctly."

"Not at all," said the businessman. "But the idea is easily worth the $10."

THERE are numerous reasons for developing a job evaluation plan, many of which have already been discussed. Each organization's reasons will be different. Even within an organization, those involved will have varying reasons for wanting to develop a plan. I've spoken with persons in an organization who have decided they need a job evaluation plan but who look at each other in bewilderment when they hear the reasons that each one has. In organizations that have had little or no control over compensation, the need usually manifests itself in a lack of control over salaries and a growing inability to control costs, which leads to problems in the product market. Employees are very sensitive to perceived inequity within their ranks. They, sometimes more than their managers, recognize productivity and the lack of it among their numbers. They also have a tendency to compare the amount of money they are receiving with the often exaggerated amount of money they think is going to a peer, which, though their guess is incorrect, is demotivating. Internal equity is a paramount goal of a job evaluation plan.

Other companies have different goals. One of the more frequent is to enjoy more success in the labor market. This is often the case with technical companies that are continually pursuing talent in the labor market. The aim of such an organization is to develop a system which will enable it to attract new employees. Often this concern is so overemphasized that all else is forgotten. External equity is achieved but at the high cost of internal equity. Soon the company recognizes the failing of the market-sensitive approach and the need for recapturing internal balance.

An example of this occurred in a large midwestern chemical company. The company was encountering difficulty in attracting chemical engineers. It had no evaluation system and its policy was simply a matter of "reaction to needs," even though it employed several thousand people. The CEO became upset with the company's inability to recruit. In an impulsive mood, he turned to the personnel director and directed him to "clean up the mess in such a way that we can hire anyone, any time, anywhere." The intimidated personnel director grabbed the compensation administrator and said, "Get a system, quick." A consultant was brought in who produced a plan which was "market-sensitive." In effect, it was a carte blanche—whatever the market paid, that's what the system paid.

After investing a considerable sum of money in the system, the company was able to bring in talent at market-competitive prices. The company found, however, that although it increased the traffic coming in the front door, traffic out the back door was similarly increased. As fast as the company could hire the people, they were going elsewhere. Upon investigation, it was found that the system had created gross internal inequities which prompted the employees to leave in droves. The satisfaction of external equity is an important goal for a job evaluation system to meet, but not at the expense of internal equity. Internal equity may not be as visible, but whereas external equity is more demanding, it is a short-run gain, while internal equity is the long-run gain. Both are worthy goals that should be met by the evaluation system.

The third goal of the evaluation system is *contribution*. When compensation administrators are asked the goals of an evaluation plan, external equity and internal equity are always offered. They seldom mention contribution as a goal. The reason for this is unknown. The fact that compensation administrators don't shout it from the rooftops is disturbing. When brought to their attention, compensation administrators generally say, "Oh, yeah, and, of course, contribution." But then they go right ahead and forget it as a goal of the evaluation system. Instead of developing systems that pay for contribution, they dredge up traditional systems that were designed by technicians 20 or so years ago which reward on the basis of job content. Traditionalists seem willing to pay for activity but not results. It's a tragedy that compensation administrators are willing to pay for activity but not for contribution.

Peter Drucker has said, "The focus on contribution is the key to effectiveness in a man's work . . . its content, its level, its standards, and its impacts, in his relations with others." * Yet most systems in use in today's highly competitive times are based upon job content, the activities of the job rather than the results of those activities. There is little wonder why productivity has headed downward. If the reward system is based on activity, the employee is inclined to merely increase that activity to receive greater reward. This is done regardless of the effect of that activity upon results, contribution or productivity. Needless to say, activity for activity's sake is usually unproductive and leads to a bureaucratic atmosphere. Programs based on job content or activity therefore are not feasible and do not contribute to the success of the organization. The measurement of contribution is and must be one of the goals to be achieved by the evaluation plan. Ironically, if the measurement of contribution is achieved, the goal of internal equity is also achieved.

There are three general types of evaluation systems. The first is any system which is exclusively geared to the labor market. It establishes relationships based strictly on the labor market, with no regard for the contribution made by the jobs. The second includes well-intended internally oriented systems which measure activity and base pay on job content. The third kind of system is established on the tenets of measuring the results of jobs and the contributions those jobs make to the success of the enterprise. This type is the only one that should exist in business today, but it rarely can be found.

The differences between a program based on job content and one based on contribution are many. The job content program is limited by definition and is strictly job oriented. Its very approach is to narrow the scope of the job and to indicate its every particular, which results in the creation of a lot of what Charles Hughes used to call "dumb jobs." On the other hand pro-

---

* The Effective Executive (New York: Harper & Row, 1967), p. 52.

grams based on contribution are broad in scope and oriented toward business objectives. Business objectives need not be limited to those commonly thought of such as profit, sales, budget, and so forth. Instead, they can be objectives to which nonexempt jobs can relate, such as tooling tolerances, letter outputs, claims processed, and the like.

Whereas job content programs tend to be detail-oriented, contribution programs tend to be goal-oriented. Content descriptions include every detail of activity to cover all the nuances of the job. Contribution descriptions deal with the results and goals to be achieved by the job and are simpler and more to the point. Content oriented programs are subjective. The several questions answered—why, how, what, and by whom—are good for making presentations for rewarding these jobs but deal subjectively with the activities of the jobs. Contribution can be measured objectively in numbers, and the more objectivity in measurement the better the program.

The fact that job content programs are traditional and contribution measurement programs are new is a distinction which may not impress anyone. New for new's sake is unimportant. The significance is really in the fact that job evaluation should assist executive management in fulfilling its responsibilities. That charter can be to turn a profit or render top service or minimize costs. In any event the "new" economy of frugality, bear market, lean GNP makes it imperative that a new approach be used. It probably is equally obvious that even in a boom economy the job evaluation plan should help management to fulfill its responsibilities charter and achieve the organization's goals. The traditional programs simply haven't worked. A new approach is needed. The measurement of contribution is that new approach.

As lengthy and verbose as job content programs are, they still tend to be insufficient in capturing everything about the job. What's worse is that even with the verbosity, they tend to be limiting. Employees are permitted to say that a particular duty is not included in their job, and they are "home free." Even in the TV series *Chico and the Man*, Chico disclaims having to do a particular task because, as he puts it, "Ee's no my yob!" Faced with that dilemma, personnel technicians completely negate the entire body of information found on the job description by "cleverly" putting as the final line: ". . . and all other duties assigned by the supervisor." If the purpose of the system is to recount the many duties performed and to itemize them for appraisal, what is to be done with "and all other duties assigned"? A result-oriented program needs no open-ended phrase. It identifies the contributions made by the job and does not confuse the issue by mentioning how that end is met or any of the peripheral activities leading to it. It simply states the reason for the existence of the job and what is expected of it. It directs the holder of the job toward the desired end. This person must perform any duty necessary to the fulfillment of those expectations; any task not included in those expectations does not need to be performed.

Programs based on job content permit the employer to unfairly discriminate against employees. If a major goal of the program is to ensure equity, such discrimination won't happen or won't be accepted. It is legally and morally proper to develop a program in which there is equity in payment. Job content programs do not encourage equity. Effort spent describing the activities of a job can be misdirected, consciously or unconsciously. The duties are not important; the results are. While it may be an important training need to describe what has to be done in the execution of a job, this is not essential to a contribution-based system. The main thing is to describe what the results are expected to be. A program based on results cannot be discriminatory since it does not assume that anyone cannot accomplish the tasks. Old problems such as the lifting of heavy objects, climbing, or other formerly sex-related activities are no longer relevant. The gamesmanship is over in contribution-oriented systems.

Programs based on lengthy descriptions can be discriminatory in other ways. It's long been suspected that the same job described in different ways will garner different evaluations—just like the professor grading papers. The professor throws all the papers up a flight of stairs. Some land on the higher steps while others flutter to his feet. Regardless of the content those on the higher steps receive an A, those at his feet receive a failing mark. Similarly, the job written in terse style in a job content program will often receive a lower rating than the job described verbosely. If this is true, the program is dependent on the employees' ability to communicate either directly or indirectly about the elements of their jobs. People who have not had the advantage of a good education may be unable to communicate properly or fully. They will suffer in such a system regardless of the impact of their job. Such discrimination is legally and morally wrong, and is economically foolish. People whose jobs make a large impact should be rewarded no matter how well they communicate. A result-oriented program reduces the need for employees to communicate in a particular fashion and is therefore superior.

Dealing with words in the job content system simply intrigues some people and taps the gamesmanship in most. There are certain "in" words, and the name of the game is to interject them in the description in order to "snow" the evaluator. Such "gamesmanship" drags the system down, and once more we are saturated with long-winded documentations and PYD bureaucracy. Contribution systems instead encourage professionalism and pride. This orientation reduces bureaucracy and enhances profit or budget efficiency.

Executives appreciate the utility of the contribution approach. They are delighted that compensation administrators are finally doing something grand and noble rather than getting wrapped up in language intrigue. Job content systems encourage nonutilitarian duties to be accounted for and recompensed. Job content systems itemize elements of a job which don't contribute to the success of an enterprise but instead are debasing to the individual. Such systems enumerate these items, structure pay programs accordingly, and pile money high on the table to overcome the employees' reticence about doing their jobs.

This last difference between job-oriented systems and contribution-oriented systems may, in fact, be the most important. It must be realized that Challengers are seeking to fulfill higher-level needs at every job. Contribution measurement satisfies both high-level needs of esteem and self-actualization. Job content systems dwell on survival needs. The former is Theory Y; the latter Theory X.

As stated earlier, the three goals that the wage and salary program and specifically the job evaluation program should meet are internal equity, external equity, and contribution. These three goals are succinct, yet all-encompassing. Put another way, the compensation administrator is charged with the responsibility of assisting the organization's management in "reinvesting" the payroll dollar, and to assure both employee and employer of equity in payment.

The questions of who should be included in the plan and how many plans are necessary frequently come up. As already mentioned, there is a distinct difference between exempt and nonexempt employees. The reasons for which they should be paid are also different, and a separate program is needed for each group. Furthermore, the labor markets in which they compete are different, making it desirable to have a different program for each. Upon closer inspection, it can be seen that while the exempt group is rather homogeneous, the nonexempt group is not. The nonexempt group, even in small organizations, service- or product-oriented, is divided into at least two major categories: those whose assigned tasks are physically oriented and those whose tasks are mentally oriented. An example of an employee with a physically oriented job is a turret lathe operator. Although there are calculations requiring mental skill, the contribution of the job is seen in the physical aspects of the work. An example of an employee with a mentally oriented nonexempt job might be an employment interviewer. The employee's task is to analyze the qualifications of candidates.

The labor markets in which nonexempt jobs are found vary also. Those who contribute to the success of their organization as a result of their mentally oriented tasks compete in a wider geographical market than those whose work is basically physical. (More will be said about this later in the discussion of the development of wage structures.) There are two major categories, one of which is often referred to as the office and technical (O&T) group, the other as production and maintenance (P&M). In larger organizations certain conditions warrant further separation of these groups. Office and technical may become two groups, and production and maintenance may become two groups. The major advantage in this further separation is seen in the labor market movement. Each of these groups (office, technical, production, and maintenance) may move at different paces through the years. Large populations would prompt separate wage structures or rate schedules to enable different movements of each group. For example if the technical group is largely technicians and draftsmen, their market may move considerably faster than the market of the office group. In order to remain competitive, it may be desirable to raise the pay ranges of the technical group and not those of the office group, since to raise both, if they were in one wage structure, would be throwing money away. (More will be said about this in the discussion of structure development.)

It was mentioned earlier that the exempt population is homogeneous and needs only one program. This opinion is based on the fact that even though there are four categories of exempt positions—executive, outside sales, professional, and administrative—none of the conditions mentioned in the discussion of the nonexempt differences exists in the exempt categories. They all participate in a wide market, if not national, then at least regional or sectional. The contribution each makes is largely the result of the "discretion" exercised in the fulfilling of their jobs. These two reasons suggest that they can all be accommodated in one program and one structure.

During the technology boom in the late fifties the professional employee was in high demand, and the labor market was national in scope. The administrative employee was largely a local market item at that time. It was desirable to move their pay structures at different rates. The boom waned, governmental bureaucracy increased, and the need for the administrative employee increased dramatically. The difference between the two diminished. The only reason to retain different structures was for prestige. Furthermore, the complexity of the administrative jobs and the growing numbers of quasi-technical jobs further reduced the difference between professional and administrative jobs. It was difficult to determine which job was exempt because it was administrative and which was exempt because it was professional. Moreover, what reason could there be for identifying for the whole world to see, especially the Wage and Hour administrator, how the organization was exempting the job? These conditions prompted most to combine the several programs and have one system for all exempt positions.

The outside sales job prompts considerations, too. Because of the several means of compensating the sales job, it could be the one exception to all exempt jobs being in one program. Even though the sales job is paid by commission, the job could be evaluated and priced with relation to other exempt jobs. Sales compensation is the result of working backward; it is known what the salesperson should earn under a certain set of conditions. The makeup of that compensation, or the relationship between salary and incentive, provides the magic of sales compensation development. The compensation level deemed optimal for the sales job is the market value; thus the sales job lends itself to placement in the salary structure. Likewise, the sales job is definitely a national market item, and the results of salespeople's work are due to their ability to "influence" customers, a discretionary act, again making it clear that the sales job should be part of the same pay program as all other exempt positions.

Now, for the sacred cow. The executive positions in an organization have long been among the missing in exempt plans. The reasons for this are many. The most compelling was the fact that the executive simply didn't want to be part of a system and had the prerogative to be excluded. The differences between the manager and the managed were great. The differences include intelligence, academic training, money, control, social class, and good old-fashioned snobbery. Another difference was the fact that the executive was cast in the role of father figure. Paternalism abounded, with programs instituted for the "children" of the organization, not for the paternal head. He was, in many cases, the owner of the business, and it didn't seem right for him to partake of the fruits of the same tree. These differences have largely disappeared. There are few entrepreneurs left today, and they usually assume the posture of being "just another employee."

The other differences have diminished or disappeared also—academic training is enjoyed by many, intelligence is widely shared, emphasis on family and social status has been reduced and most people have been put on a common plane. Taxes and other corporate controls have in many ways made all employees the same, from top to bottom. Prestige and ego needs remain the main distinguishing feature, and even these are diminishing as executive ranks are filled with younger persons.

There have been consultants who have played upon the theme of "exclusion," by selling the organization a plan for the masses but permitting the executive supreme exclusion from such a plan. While this approach has won engagements for prestigious firms, it hasn't served organizations well.

There are other specific reasons why executives want to be included in wage and salary programs. Perhaps the most immediate reason is the results of the Tax Reform Law of 1969. Prior to that law, executive compensation was given in several forms to permit the executive to derive tax-free or tax-deferred income. Cash was a less desirable form of income because of the tax rate used. The 1969 Tax Law changed all that, and as the many articles on the subject proclaimed, cash became popular again. Testimony to that change was the fact that before the 1969 law, executive salary increases were averaging 2 to 3 percent annually, and subsequent to it, executive salaries were increasing at an annual rate of 8 percent. Job evaluation plans helped executives dealing with sometimes obstinate boards to justify increases. Consultants have been hired more than just a few times by executives to show just cause why the particular executive should get a pay raise.

Another reason for executives wanting inclusion in wage and salary plans is to ensure more equitable treatment of the growing number of executives. Middle and upper management have increased so greatly that it has become a significant problem to pay these positions in a fair and equitable manner. However, the programs have improved to a point where the executive job can be evaluated using at least some of the systems in existence today.

The concept of the flexible compensation program, otherwise known as "cafeteria" or "smorgasbord" compensation, has prompted a need for evaluation stabilization. The concept of flexible compensation affords the recipient an opportunity to choose the makeup of his compensation, that is, to choose the relationship of cash to noncash compensation. What better way to determine total compensation allowable or to determine what options are available than by evaluating the worth of executive jobs and varying options at various levels of evaluations?

Many times in the past, compression has occurred, wherein the executives have gotten to a salary level that they deemed ample and they were content to remain at that level. The result was to compress all levels of the organization beneath them. An evaluation plan prevents that from happening, and the result is proper relationships of pay levels and employees throughout the organization.

Perhaps the most important reason for all concerned, however, is the acceptance of the plan when executives are included. Employees who perceive that an elite group has excluded itself from the exempt plan are usually disturbed. The obvious question is, "If the plan is so good, why aren't *they* part of it?" It's a difficult and embarrassing question to answer. There are so many ways to include executives in the system and yet not reveal their salaries that it's meaningless for executives to withdraw from the system. The result of that withdrawal is very damaging to the employee's perception and acceptance of the evaluation system. In publicly owned corporations and other public organizations, executive salaries are public information anyway. In private organizations employees often can guess the amount of money the chief executive makes.

Budgeting increases, bonuses, and other compensation planning are greatly aided by the establishment of parameters of executive salaries. Without ranges, it's difficult to plan the salary levels of any employees. Salaries for executives are not without their degree of motivation. Executives may be greatly in need of the esteem value of an extensive salary range assigned to their position. The executive is often overlooked as one who needs reassurance just as any other employee needs it.

The vagueness of the executive job is reduced when a salary range is assigned. The job lends itself to the establishment of goals and objectives when its parameters and results are outlined, if not defined. The exercise of executive evaluation is greatly enhanced when such goals are established and a salary range is assigned as a monetary measurement of that goal's value.

The growing number of younger people emerging in the executive ranks are professional executives rather than entrepreneurs. They are a mobile lot willing to give their all if permitted, but wanting to understand just what their rewards will be. The vague promise and dangling carrot of the past don't work with Challenger executives. They want concrete evidence of good faith. The executive job seeker is now counseled to seek a stable, high salary with a bonus option and not to be charmed into a low salary with a dazzling, pie-in-the-sky bonus offering. Challenger executives seek to understand the compensation program.

Challengers are cash-now executives. Their needs are prompted by the higher standard of living that they seek for themselves and their families. Unlike their predecessors who took many years to reach executive ranks, accumulating material wealth along the way, Challenger executives consider themselves already "arrived" and desire the "trappings" of success. They may have criticized their predecessors for their desire for material wealth, but the syndrome continues in each generation. The items and styles of those material trappings may have changed, but they're there nevertheless. The job evaluation program is perceived as a means to an end. Challengers are motivated to reach the higher levels of their salary ranges. They may aspire to satisfy self-actualization, but they are also constantly feathering their nest as well. This is the difference between the Challenger and the Senior Employee: whereas the latter was involved in trying to build and protect the nest, the former is busy adorning it.

Most organizations recognize there is nothing to be gained and much to be lost by perpetuating a caste system within. The inclusion of the executives in a total exempt plan reduces the caste grouping. Anyone who has administered the so-called executive payroll knows the pressures exerted by management to become part of that elite when it has been a separate group. That tremendous ulcer developer vanishes when all are included in one plan. The positive effect is that the one-group plan promotes greater team rapport.

The inclusion of executive jobs in the total exempt plan is to be sought by the compensation administrator. Nothing about executive compensation, as mystical and forbidding as some consultants make it, prevents executive positions from being included in the plan. The plan will make more sense when it includes all exempt positions.

• 8 •

Job Evaluation Systems

A New York socialite came into the salon of Walter Florell, mad milliner to movie stars and society, and announced she needed a hat at once for a cocktail party. Walter took a couple of yards of ribbon, twisted it around, put it on her head and said, "There is your hat, madam." The lady looked in the mirror and exclaimed, "It's wonderful."

"Twenty-five dollars," said Walter.

"But that's too much for a couple of yards of ribbon!"

Florell unwound the ribbon and handed it to her, saying, "The ribbon, madam, is free."

ERSKINE JOHNSON
Remarks of Famous People

JOB evaluation is the foundation for a sound compensation program. Without it, all else falters. My bias is that it is the basis for the entire personnel program. Most have criticized it and called it boring. Many have been correct in such appraisals. Job evaluation has earned the scorn directed at it. It has been done badly for so long that most want to gloss over it and "get on to more important things." Yet, job evaluation is the most important element of a compensation program. Do it right and the rest of the program comes into being logically.

It seems appropriate to define the term job evaluation to ensure a common stage for the total programs. To be effective, job evaluation must be a *systematic* method of appraising the value of each job in relation to other jobs in the organization. "Systematic" is the crucial word. Every policy serves the need of a presolved problem. When business problems arise, they need ready answers. The more answers and solutions available, the better

87

the enterprise, that is, so long as they don't stifle creativity. Job evaluation is a system for resolving problems about how much a job is worth. Under static conditions the answers are readily forthcoming. In dynamic conditions a flexible guide is needed for making continual decisions. The job evaluation program should be a living, dynamic system flexible enough to resolve problems yet to be encountered and specific enough to render discrete answers.

This leads to a second definitive nature of job evaluation. Job evaluation provides a *consistent* procedure that sets up and maintains a hierarchy of jobs, attaching to each job a pay rate commensurate with its status in that hierarchy. I once had a boss who said, "If you make a mistake in wage and salary, do it consistently." Obviously, this takes the concept of consistency too far. There are conditions and situations which dictate variations from a given policy. Nevertheless, an effective evaluation system must be perceived and operated as a procedure which is applied uniformly and consistently. The establishment of precedents, so important in labor relations, is equally significant in compensation. It is said that there are many labor relations programs in which there is a precedent for everything. Any way you do something can be shown to have a precedent. A faulty labor relations program is no more desirable than an inconsistent compensation program. If the program cannot be applied consistently, it may have been ill conceived and shabbily designed. It may need renovation. A deliberate design will produce a viable program.

One of the aspects of job evaluation that is difficult to comprehend is the fact that job evaluation is concerned with jobs, not individuals. Once when I was stressing this point to a group of employees, an older employee became quite disgruntled. When I asked him what disturbed him, he said that he was afraid that the company was getting so large that it was no longer interested in individuals. He had to be reassured that this was not the case, but that in job evaluation, in order to achieve objectivity the holders of the job must be considered to be identical in the execution of the job. Only then can the elements of the job be identified and the contribution of the job assessed. Once the program is designed, even conscientious evaluators encounter difficulty in distinguishing the job from the individuals. There is a common tendency to believe that the employee is the job. Only through diligent effort can the job be seen without the employee, and this must be done to see the job in proper perspective. The employee's influence on the job increases with the level of the job in the organizational hierarchy. Exempt employees frequently influence the scope of their positions, while nonexempt employees seldom do.

The two important functions in compensation programs are job evaluation and performance appraisal. The job evaluation program establishes the value of the job and the range within which the job holders may progress. The performance appraisal program establishes the rate of growth the employee can achieve through that range. (Performance appraisal will be discussed later in the book.) The *emphasis* in job evaluation is on the job or position itself, whereas in performance appraisal the emphasis is on the employee.

Job evaluation is the process of relating job to job, position to position. The *purpose* of job evaluation is to establish a relative value of the job and to assign a rate or range of pay. The purpose of performance appraisal is to provide individual guidance and assign individual wage or salary.

The *impact* of a job evaluation is broad and universally affects many jobs. Performance appraisal affects the individual and has very specific, individualized implications.

The *technique* used in job evaluation is the assessment of the job in terms of its compensable factors. In performance appraisal the employee is assessed in terms of more person-oriented standards.

The *scope* in job evaluation involves the contribution, or in some plans the content of the job, without regard for the job holder; it relates to the reason for the existence of the job. In performance appraisal the concern is the achievement of the job holder viewed against standards or stated or unstated objectives.

The *involvement* in job evaluation is between the employees whose jobs are evaluated and managers who evaluate and rate jobs. The performance appraisal is an intimate meeting between employee and supervisor.

The *frequency* of job evaluation varies with the plan. Usually, once the program is established in one great effort, reevaluation of jobs can occur at any time. The program should be as flexible and dynamic as the organization itself. Performance appraisal programs can be equally unstructured but rarely are. Appraisals are more likely to be made at regular intervals.

The *criteria* in job evaluation are objective and relatively static—the compensable factors, establishing internal and external equity with other jobs. In performance appraisal the criteria tend to be more subjective, since the principals in the matter are individuals with varying abilities and motives. Growth of the individual is key here.

The *communication* of job evaluation is usually of a general, pervasive nature since its impact is common to all. The performance appraisal session is best when it is a private exchange of ideas.

The principle of "Keep It Simple, Stupid" may be invoked here to establish the tone of the chapter. Few of the countless evaluation systems that I have seen have followed that principle. In the quest for accuracy and surrounded by a PYD bureaucracy, personnel technicians and consultants have devised complicated systems. The systems are complicated because what they attempt to measure is complicated. Most, if not all, systems seem to measure job content. They give lip service to measuring contribution, and proceed to describe and appraise job content. As mentioned earlier, job content is difficult if not impossible to define in a way that is complete, definitive, and yet flexible. The trouble with most plans is that they are misdirected in the object of their descriptions. The object should be to measure the contribution each job makes to the success of the organization.

Having thus identified what should be done, let us examine the four broad approaches that are taken in traditional plans. In selecting an approach which best meets the needs of the organization, let's establish criteria against which an approach may be measured for its acceptability.

Objectivity. The approach to job evaluation is enhanced by the degree to which it achieves objectivity. The question is, How objective is the measurement instrument? The job should be valued at a certain level regardless of the job holder. To that end the measurement instrument should be uninfluenced by the characteristics or traits of the person performing the job.

Simplicity. The approach should be as simple as possible. The costs of the programs are directly related to its degree of complexity. Sophistication is not necessarily a worthy goal if it merely introduces complexity. A simple program has its own rewards in sophistication. It requires a great deal of sophistication to simplify things to a common mean. The simple program will provide greater ease in its administration if not also in its development.

Understandability. The approach to job evaluation should be understandable to all concerned in order to provide a basis for motivation. The program can do much for motivation if the employees understand the rationale used to determine their pay. Healthy compensation administrators are those who have programs understood by them and by everyone who is affected by them. Although it is often taken for granted that an understandable program is desired by a compensation administrator, it is acknowledged that some compensation administrators would rather have a program only they understood. In such a position they can wield power of mysticism controlling the means to pay or not pay. The intrigue of such an unhealthy life style is self-defeating, and people who use power to sustain authority usually lose both often before they realize it. Hard-to-understand plans are selfdefeating. They not only cost more to administer but do a poor job in achieving equity. What equity they purport to achieve is contrived and is perceived by only the few who have dictated their parameters.

Meaningfulness. The program should be meaningful to the employees as well as to the employer. A plan which has meaningless compensable factors provides no basis for motivation. If employees cannot associate their pay with the compensable factors, they have no motivation to perform their tasks or to seek jobs at higher levels.

Ease in development. The approach should be one which doesn't require the addition of new people to the staff. There are approaches which require voluminous job descriptions and several people to write them. The problem many administrators find is that they simply don't have the time or the continuity of thought required by any program. The daily requests that flow over the desk of compensation administrators require immediate attention because they're usually at the end of an arm attached to an anxious supervisor who wants action. To develop a plan of any substance requires time and dedication to the task. Continuity of thought to achieve the plan's consistency is paramount to the success of the plan. One can't anticipate the countless details that will need to be taken care of in the development of the plan. It is therefore extremely difficult to plan one's time properly in the development phase. The plan should be as simple and easy to develop as possible. Developers should guard against the endless pursuit of accuracy because it will be ever elusive. In that pursuit they will have a tendency to introduce compound, though logical, intricacies which simply lead to a complex plan that few will understand.

Ease in administering. Most people live in the future, or realize that everything that's done today must fit the needs of tomorrow. The compensation administrator will live and die with the plan that has been developed and installed. As difficult as it is to develop a plan, the period of that development and installation is short when compared with the period of administration. Finding a plan that is easy to develop and easy to administer is a difficult if not impossible task. If a plan is easy to develop, look out, chances are it has been ill conceived and not carefully worked out. It will be a nightmare to administer. However, a plan that has been carefully and deliberately developed may be easy to administer, which is more important. It's doubtful that a plan can be found that is both easy to develop and easy to administer. Given this situation, the compensation administrator should choose the plan that is easy to administer no matter what pains it takes to develop it.

Flexibility. The plan chosen should be adaptable to changes in conditions in the organization. Growth and reorganization are the obvious changes. Vertical integration, the process of external growth through acquisition of input-output organizations, and horizontal integration, the process of external growth through acquisition of complementary products or services, are common organizational changes. An example of this is the company whose growth was tremendous due to the sudden demand for its product. The plan installed should need only minor changes to accommodate the new wealth. In another instance, a savings and loan company suddenly found itself the owner and operator of trailer parks and hotels. Modification of the plan permitted its continued use for this unusual growth. The plan developers should anticipate corporate changes when they design the plan. The plan should be flexible enough to accommodate foreseen and unforeseen changes.

Compatibility. The plan chosen by compensation administrators should be compatible with the management style of the company. This may seem obvious, but compensation administrators may be blinded by what they consider to be a good plan—even though it may be out of step with the management team that will have to approve and maintain it. For example, to install a plan based on Theory Y techniques in a Theory X management could be disastrous to the plan and the compensation administrator. Normally a dynamic organization will not choose the classification system used by the civil service because of the alleged bureaucracy that has developed in the administration of it. A company located in Washington, D.C., purposely adopted it, however. Its people did constant business with the government people who were covered by the civil service. This relationship was seen to be enhanced by the similarity of pay programs. Compensation administrators would be wise to analyze the management style of their companies very carefully before choosing a plan.

Contemporariness. As mentioned earlier, wage and salary has been done so badly for so long that most people are disenchanted with the whole practice. Contemporary approaches are needed to withstand the criticisms and challenges that will be put to the program. Moreover, the plan should be able to reverse the trend of criticism and start a new bandwagon of acceptance and motivation. Challenger employees demand that new practices replace those of old. Compensation administrators find themselves in the dilemma of the recruiter told to look for a person with a Ph.D., 22 years old, with 10 years of experience. The plan must be a proven one or have proven logic or merits, but should also be a new approach to an old but changing problem.

Cost. Probably the most ready reference for the value of a program at the onset is its cost. Most of the time, however, cost is what we make it. The short-term cost of a plan is not a good criterion for selecting the plan, yet budgets force that to be a major consideration. Administration costs are the really big costs, and most administrators don't appreciate that when choosing a plan. Compensation administrators should for their own edification, if for no one else's, get an idea of what administration costs will be incurred in the long run. Simplicity is the key to success. Keeping the program simple will keep the costs simple as well.

The selection of a program begins and ends with the same admonition: KISS. The program chosen should meet as many of the criteria listed as possible. Whatever program is chosen, if a simple platform is maintained, it will serve the organization well.

There are four basic approaches to job evaluation. Anything else is a modification of one of them: ranking, classification, point, and factor comparison.

All four attempt to do the same thing; they establish a hierarchy. The ranking and classification systems are nonquantitative; that is, they use no points or dollars to convert into grades. Further, both the ranking and classification systems look at the whole job; they do not dissect it and examine its several parts. The tendency is to compare the whole job to some subjective criteria or gradients and determine which jobs are more important than others. The point and factor comparison systems dissect the jobs and examine their integral parts. They assess them with points or dollars and thereby develop the values of the jobs. Each of the four systems will be examined in detail, and the advantages and disadvantages of each will be discussed. Keep the criteria mentioned above in mind and determine how many criteria are satisfied by each of the several systems.

Before doing so, let us discuss a term that has already been mentioned: compensable factor. A compensable factor is the basic reason for paying a job. It is the criterion for determining the value of the job. It can be considered to be a yardstick against which the jobs are measured. There are several characteristics of a compensable factor.

In order to qualify as a compensable factor, an item must be found in *all* jobs but in different amounts. Using the yardstick analogy, if an object were to be placed next to a yardstick and it registered no measurement because the yardstick was not sensitive enough to the dimensions, the yardstick could not qualify as a measuring instrument and another would need to be found. So, too, a job compared to a compensable factor that fails to register a reading suggests that the compensable factor is not truly a compensable factor.

Only the most important compensable factors should be used. Factors concerned with routine matters that have little or nothing to do with contribution ought not be used. The factors must not overlap because if they do confusion will result. Technicians, in their zeal for completeness, often come up with too many compensable factors and then find that their language overlaps. The number of factors appropriate to the plan is a function of that plan and of the design of the developer; there are plans with one compensable factor and others with 20 or more. In the discussion of the four approaches, this will become clearer.

The compensable factors should be meaningful to the employee as well as to the employer. It has already been stated that employees should know the reasons their jobs are paid what they are. Only then can they have a basis for motivation.

Compensable factors have been thought to be a consideration only when using point plans and factor comparison plans, but this is only partially true. The ranking method usually has some stated or tacit compensable factors, usually subjective in nature, against which the jobs are measured to determine the relative values. The compensable factor is important in the classification method also. The classification method uses one compensable factor with several degrees or variations of that factor.

Compensable factors are found, then, in all four of the approaches.

The ranking system. Every company has a wage and salary program and a job evaluation program whether or not they are acknowledged as such. A company that announces that it does not have these programs usually has an informal "pecking order" of job hierarchy. The company pays certain jobs more than it pays others, and someone has made that determination of job value. Such an informal system is the ranking system. The ranking system requires little development. All that is needed is to appoint some person or persons to develop a listing of all the jobs in the company and assign an order to them. As mentioned above, there may be tacit or stated compensable factors or criteria against which the jobs are rated.

Those charged with the task of listing and ordering jobs should be as free of bias as possible since the system is highly subjective. The person or persons should have broad observation of the several jobs rated and some knowledge of the interrelationships of the jobs and the organization. Job descriptions may or may not be used.

The methodology merely involves the placement of all jobs in a hierarchy from top to bottom, showing which jobs are to be valued higher and paid more than others. Usually a simple ordering process is all that is necessary. However, if grades are used, it is a good idea to indicate how much distance there is between the several jobs in the hierarchy. An example of this is the ranking of 10 jobs from 1 to 10. If grades are used, it should be determined if some jobs are in grade 4 for instance and if the next highest graded job would perhaps be two or three grades lower. It can be seen how subjective these comparison decisions can become—and how important it is to remain as objective as possible.

The advantages of the ranking system are:

◆ It is commonly believed that the ranking system can be instituted with little fuss and in a minimum of time.

◆ The costs incurred by the ranking system are minimal.

◆ Having no development to speak of, the ranking system's maintenance and administrative procedures are minimal.

◆ All jobs in the organization can be accommodated by the same ordering process. When a grading structure is used, this advantage is negated since nonexempt jobs will usually require a structure different from that used for exempt jobs. Nevertheless, a ranking system can put all jobs in the organization in a hierarchy.

◆ The ranking system introduces order into a disordered environment. If no plan exists, the ranking system is a semblance of order. If the style of the management is opposed to job evaluation, perhaps the ranking system is a start in the right direction.

◆ Job descriptions are not necessary in a ranking system. The ranking of jobs is a subjective process and can be done largely with titles alone. Job descriptions do aid the exercise when differences between jobs are unknown or nuances exist which the raters do not know. Generally speaking, for job evaluation purposes, job descriptions are not needed in the ranking system.

The disadvantages of the ranking system are many:

◆ It is difficult if not impossible to find a person or persons who are free from bias in evaluating jobs. The obvious person to do the ranking is the chief executive officer. But even CEOs may have some bias. If they have come up through the ranks, the area which has their path may be the favored one. CEOs who were engineers still think the moon was hung by an enterprising mechanical engineer. CEOs who were accountants still favor the person clutching the abacus, and so it goes. Frequently, CEOs have long ago forgotten the several jobs in their organization, if, in fact, they ever knew them to start with. Furthermore, the jobs have probably changed several times, and they would have little knowledge of those changes.

Sometimes they realize their own shortcomings, or they simply don't have the time, or they aren't interested or inclined to perform this task, or maybe they're smart enough to see the pitfalls and seek a way of getting out of doing the task. Whatever the reason, they may choose to have their assistants perform the task. That's when the real trouble starts. If with one person there is one bias, with several there are innumerable biases, some real, some imagined, some legitimate, all glaring. The conflict that can arise from a group performing an evaluation of jobs with nothing but subjective criteria dooms it to failure. The results are a compromised hierarchy and executives who bear memory scars earned in the "Battle of Evaluation."

◆ Job evaluation in most organizations is not a static situation. Its dynamics are the same as those of the organization. Jobs change and need reevaluation. The deliberation necessary to rank jobs is taxing and time-consuming. With only subjective criteria, the ranking can't be done well in a short period of time. It does not lend itself to a quick solution. Furthermore, the evaluator or evaluators can't be called upon at varying intervals to evaluate new or changed jobs without dredging up all the silt that covered the old ones. That takes time and executives have that in short supply. The ranking system is not a quick way to job evaluation.

◆ The costs incurred by the evaluators if they are CEOs can be tremendous. Count up the hours CEOs would have to spend through the year deliberating on the values of the several jobs. Multiply that by their hourly income. You'll find that it comes to quite a figure. Add to that the fact that while they are attending to job evaluation, they are letting some other task go, and the figure can knock the abacus right out of the controller's hands. The same problems exist when the job is done by a group of evaluators. Count up the hours necessary for them to deliberate, negotiate, and otherwise compromise in the values of the several jobs. Multiply that by their hourly incomes, and the figure is tremendous. Ranking is neither quick nor cheap.

◆ Acceptance is the key reason for performing job evaluation. No matter how respected the evaluators are, the response to the evaluation is often less than favorable. Challenger employees especially resent such dictates. Compensation administrators put themselves in a very vulnerable position and find that they have accomplished little when they announce the results of their evaluation exercise. If acceptance is not what it should be, the whole exercise in job evaluation can be futile.

◆ Compensation administrators using this "cigar box" approach also find themselves in hot water when trying to administer the plan. Without objective criteria, compensation administrators find they have few tools to work with in making daily decisions about job evaluation and wage and salary problems. The whole system can be bogged down, dragging the compensation administrators with it.

◆ Even with the best of systems, it can be tough to sit across from an employee, disgruntled or otherwise, and explain just how his job was placed in this or that category or grade. With the ranking approach, compensation administrators must rely on a "soft shoe" number such as Johnny Carson performs when his monologue is failing. Remember, though, that Carson has a 20-piece band backing him with "Tea for Two"; the compensation administrator may not even have Muzak.

◆ The subjectivity of the ranking system is its major failing. Job evaluation is a very sensitive process. To do it properly it must be done diligently, consistently, and with *objectivity*. If for no other reason, job ranking fails as a job evaluation tool because of its lack of objectivity.

There is a variation on the ranking system in which the organization structure is used as the framework for evaluation. Basically, the higher the job is on the organizational chart, the more value it has, and the more it should be paid. The scramble up the organization chart becomes a furious art, therefore. Line jobs are greatly favored in such a system since they are basically the ones that appear on the chart. Anyone working with organization charts can suggest several failings of such an approach. At face value, it is a simple approach, but this is just the tip of the iceberg.

Another variation is the guideline system. This is basically a two-part system. It was referred to earlier when discussing labor market sensitive approaches. The system uses key marketable jobs as guidelines. It "prices" these jobs on the open labor market, and assigns dollar values to them according to labor market dictates. All other jobs are ranked or slotted around the guideline jobs. Although the system is supersensitive to the labor market, internal equity is partially lost since it is achieved through the ranking process and all of the advantages and disadvantages peculiar to the ranking system are present. What's more, the system makes little or no use of contribution, since the basis for the key jobs is labor market value.

The ranking system is most applicable in a small organization, one in which the numbers of jobs and employees are few, trust is high, and little attention is given to administrative matters, such as compensation administration. In a company of fewer than 50 people a ranking system can work.

The classification system. The classification system works for the largest employer, the federal government. This system uses one compensable factor: skill. At one time the federal government employed persons through the "spoils" system. This refers to the old practice of victorious politicians rewarding their followers with jobs. Inefficiency and corruption led to efforts at reform in the 1850s, and in 1871 the first Civil Service Commission was established. The Civil Service System, using the classification method, has been adopted by most governmental bodies, state, county, and city. Although it has taken much abuse, it has continued to function. If stability was the aim of its founders, the system really is on its mark. It's very stable— just try to remove someone who is in it. What's more, it seems to be self-propagating. Surely, the Civil Service System using the classification method has had much to do with the great growth of the federal government, which now has 2.7 million nonmilitary employees and a payroll of $33 billion.

The development of the classification system for use in private industry could be quite simple. All an organization would have to do is adapt the public system, which would require a minimum of development time. If the organization wanted to modify the evaluative process it would be necessary only to redefine the one compensable factor used, skill, or to use one of its own choosing. The one compensable factor would have to be defined with several degrees or variations to be suitable to measure all jobs.

The methodology is simple enough. All positions are compared to the one compensable factor, and through a matching exercise of job description to compensable factor, it is determined which degree is the appropriate level for that job. Job descriptions are usually necessary since the matching exercise would be difficult with only little or superficial knowledge of the job.

Among the advantages of such a system is the one previously mentioned, its availability. Development time and the cost of implementation would be minimal. It has only one compensable factor, which limits the scope of the problem and enables easy communication of the plan to employees. The government use of the system is testimony to the fact that it can be used to cover the complete spectrum of employees, from the top to the bottom job.

It is not without its disadvantages, however, otherwise its use would be more widespread. Few organizations want to relate their system to the Civil Service. Correctly or incorrectly, there has been a certain stigma connected with the Civil Service. True, much of that has disappeared with the vastly improved pay scales. Nevertheless, quasi-government employees are quick to announce that they are not part of the Civil Service System. At any rate, this question should be posed by each compensation administrator: Would my organization and its style be compatible with the classification system used by Civil Service?

In choosing or not choosing this system, it should be determined if the one compensable factor of skill is really what should be measured. Does it necessarily equate with level of contribution? Because a position requires a great deal of skill, does it contribute more than a job requiring less skill? Whatever the conclusion reached, one thing is certain, there is too much dependence on the one compensable factor. To describe all the jobs in a company in terms of their various degrees of skill is quite a task. Extensive work is required to properly define the several levels in order to make the administration of the system feasible.

The development of the several variations of the one compensable factor involves much *subjective* analysis, which leads to verbosity, and thus invites all kinds of gamesmanship. The name of the game in classification systems is to know what "in" words to incorporate in the job description in order to get the desired level of skill relationship. The confusion found in such a system will lead to a multitude of people milling about trying to clarify the morass. This is the dilemma of the Civil Service. It has come to such a plight that in order to make the system work at all, the administrators "call the shots," that is, they are responsible for the interpretation and use of words and they dictate their findings. A Theory X environment prevails and authority is statutory. Hence the self-propagating nature of the classification system.

It follows that such a subjective system creates and furthers a PYD system and encourages voluminous job descriptions. The cost of such a system in the long run is tremendous, as any taxpayer knows.

The point plan. The vast majority of organizations that claim to have a formal job evaluation program have some kind of point plan. It is not easy to develop a point plan. The point plan is based on compensable factors, reasons for paying a job. Point plans usually have three or more compensable factors. The organization must decide on the number of compensable factors appropriate to its needs. There is an oil company in Oklahoma that has 21 compensable factors in its plan, but most plans have from 3 to 7. Simplicity dictates that the fewer the compensable factors, the better. The identification of reasons to pay jobs is the most difficult part in developing a point plan. Whether it is done by one person or by a group, the task of coming up with good, meaningful compensable factors is a real problem. Compensable factors can be developed before writing job descriptions.

Once the compensable factors are developed, job data is collected, and the jobs are compared against the compensable factors. Points, assigned to the compensable factors, are ticked off and accumulated. The more points accumulated, the more valuable the job.

There are many advantages to the point system.

♦ The first and foremost advantage is its characteristic of objectivity. Objectivity is probably the greatest reason organizations pursue a point system. Thus far we have discussed two plans, both of which are tremendously subjective and, therefore, lacking in the prime requisite of job evaluation. A plan which has objectivity has great appeal to the management of an organization because it is relieved of dealing with individual issues. The issues are "automatically" or systematically dealt with using an objective system. Objectivity also appeals to the employees. They seek the consistency that an objective program can give them.

♦ The objectivity of the point system makes it easier to administer the program. As stated earlier, even though a point system is difficult to develop, the development time is much shorter than the administration time. Obviously, then, ease in long-term administration is more important than ease in development. This reason probably accounts for the overwhelming prevalence of the point system in all kinds of organizations.

◆ The use of multiple compensable factors allows more facets of the organization to be represented, promoting greater equity. One of the failings of the classification system was its dependence on one compensable factor. This problem is overcome in the point system. There are several different reasons for paying jobs. The opportunity for recognizing the differences will be greater if there are multiple compensable factors.

◆ Stability in a point system is achieved by the weighting of the compensable factors and the points assigned. This stability also affords flexibility, since the point system relates the jobs to a common standard, whereas the previously discussed ranking system relates job to job.

◆ New jobs are readily integrated into the system. This is an advantage over the ranking system, which can be upset by the introduction of new or changed jobs to the hierarchy. Again it is the stable standards, compensable factors, which provide that ready assimilation.

With a minimum of training, persons new to the process can readily administer the point system, because of its objectivity.

The widespread use of the point system permits easy reference and job comparison in survey work. Because so many organizations use point systems, the surveyor and the surveyee can more easily discuss the integral parts of jobs being surveyed.

There are disadvantages to the point system:

◆ The most severe disadvantage occurs in the development phase in creating compensable factors. The factors have several characteristics or tests they must meet in order to truly be compensable factors. After identifying them, they must be defined, described, weighted, and diagramed. This is not an easy process. A point system will take longer to design than the plans discussed previously but not as long as the factor comparison system.

◆ Another disadvantage that has been alluded to but not really defined can be present in any plan but is frequently found in a point system. In the quest for greater accuracy and refinement, the point system designers may have a tendency to "overkill" the problem. Anyone who has written a policy knows this problem. It's like the engineer who never wants to release the blueprints because they're never quite ready. The designers of the point system often feel the same way. They want to try to clarify just a little more, to accommodate just one more possibility, and consequently may wind up producing garbled, complex plans that only they can understand. Simplicity, again, is the keynote of success in designing a plan. (Examples of point systems will be found in the next chapter. Since most organizations ultimately go to a point plan, this approach has been singled out for greater exhibit and study.)

The factor comparison system. This is the last to be discussed for a couple of reasons. To paraphrase the song from *Oklahoma*, we've gone about as far as we can go. If objectivity is attained by analyzing component parts from different vantage points, then the factor comparison system is the most objective of the four approaches. So rarely is the factor comparison system used, however, that it is only to be exhaustive in reviewing the subject that it is included here. The term "factor comparison" comes from the fact that the system is predicated on the comparison of jobs with other jobs to determine which jobs contain greater amounts of identifiable compensable factors. In a true factor comparison system, no points are used. Money, instead of points, is the common quantifiable denominator. This method uses a ranking procedure for classifying all key jobs in the company under each factor and establishing not only the rank order but also measuring the distance between each job according to corresponding elements in other jobs.

The development of the program is quite extensive. The first step in the development is to write job descriptions for every job. This is necessary in order to select key jobs and the compensable factors which are peculiar to the organization. Although the compensable factors are predictable, as they are in other systems, the factor comparison system is very specific to the organization, requiring each step to be done in a certain way. Key jobs are selected very carefully because the entire system is balanced on them. A series of charts and comparisons is made. First the key jobs are compared one to another against selected compensable factors. The key jobs are ranked according to the degree to which the compensable factors are present in them. Each key job is ranked against each compensable factor.

The next step is to estimate how much of the current wage paid the key jobs is allocable to each compensable factor. This judgmental calculation is very critical. It makes the assumption that all jobs are currently correctly paid.

Following this a chart is constructed showing the placement of the key jobs in relation to the amounts of money to be allotted to them. This job comparison scale can then be used to place all other jobs into evaluative relationships. Having all jobs thus placed enables immediate pricing. By comparing the rest of the jobs in the comparison chart with the key jobs, the rate paid is simply the accumulation of all rates in the several compensable factors.

The factor comparison system has a number of advantages:

 • One advantage to such a system is the deliberateness of the entire sequence. The painstaking process of selecting key jobs, comparing them, dissecting them, and cross-checking them suggests very careful scrutiny and meticulous results.

◆ Another advantage is the immediate pricing made possible under this approach. By simply picking up the amounts of money from the chart, the wage rate develops without the use of other conversions from points to money grade charts.

◆ The careful methodology restricts the use of the plan to only that organization for which it was designed. It is thus a custom-made plan, not duplicated anywhere.

The disadvantages of the plan are many:

◆ The process is very complex. It is so complex that even several readings of descriptions of the process in several sources don't make this plan as clear as other plans. If wage and salary experts encounter difficulty in understanding it, it will certainly not be understandable to most employees. Acceptance is predicated on either devout faith or understanding. Challenger employees rely more on the latter than the former. This presents a strong disadvantage to this system.

◆ Although there is objectivity in the process, the plan is nevertheless based on several subjective suppositions. One of these is the selection of key jobs. If the jobs chosen are not really key, the whole system is shaky. Another is the gross assumption that the rates currently paid the key jobs are correct. Usually this is not a "given," it is instead what is sought. Subjectivity again appears when the current wage rate paid is divided among the several compensable factors. How much money goes to one factor and how much goes to another are key to the success of the system and again challenge the integrity of the system.

◆ The system is very inflexible. The introduction of new jobs is virtually impossible since everything hinges on the key jobs and the other jobs' relationships to them. Similar to the hazards of the ranking system, the posture of one job is dependent on the status of all jobs at one time and place. If a new job is introduced it becomes a whole new ball game.

◆ Although it isn't impossible to use the system for jobs with a range of pay, it isn't conducive to use with such jobs either. The single rate developed as a result of the accumulation of money for compensable factors could be assumed to be the midpoint of the desired range. This would make the relationship of the several resultant midpoints rather haphazard, thus reducing the objectivity of the system even further.

◆ The very thing that is an advantage of the system is also its biggest disadvantage. I refer to the painstaking way in which the program is developed. The costs involved in establishing the program would be tremendous.

It requires several knowledgeable, reasonable persons working very closely together over a considerable period of time to make the system work.

◆ The use of the factor comparison system is very limited. Its complexity, cost, and inflexibility almost preclude it from serious consideration. It is a method of being fastidious in job evaluation and represents the extreme in technical attempts to analyze and quantify the worth of jobs.

·9·

Point Plans—An Opinion

Where all think alike, no one thinks very much.

WALTER LIPPMANN

POINT plans are found in the vast majority of organizations said to have formalized plans. Since the likelihood is high that a point system will be chosen, it is appropriate for us to delve into the several systems that exist using the basic point system approach.

One of the best examples of the typical point plans is that developed by the National Metal Trades Association. The NMTA recognized its members' need to have a plan that could be universally used, thereby avoiding expense in development time. Its intended use was for nonexempt jobs in the metal trades. However, it has been used as originally designed and, with modifications, in all other jobs, nonexempt and exempt. Its terminology is readily adaptable to nonexempt physically skilled jobs. When used in nonexempt areas including mentally skilled jobs, its validity decreases. With certain modifications, it became a hallmark in nonexempt technical and office jobs. With further modification, it has been used to assess exempt positions with mixed degrees of success. The basic plan has 11 factors:

Education
Experience
Complexity of duties
Supervision received
Errors
Contacts with others
Confidential data

Mental or visual demand
Working conditions
Character of supervisors
Scope of supervision

As shown, each compensable factor stands alone but has several degrees or variations. The variations of the factors are fairly standard in the several NMTA plans around the country. The explanations attempt to distinguish between the degrees. Words are used to describe the differences, and the wording can be varied to suit the needs of the specific user or organization. The plan offers a definite step toward objectivity, in that certain standards are established against which jobs may be compared and thus evaluated. The applicability of the system to numerous organizations has led to the system's use all around the country. It is so easily adapted that the technician might find it *too* easy to install the system as found. It is not necessarily the ideal goal of the conscientious compensation administrator, however. As one administrator put it, "It's worked out fine for us; it's as good as any system for distributing inequities among all jobs equally."

Even if the compensation administrator modifies the compensable factors to more nearly reflect the needs of the organization, the development time and costs can be minimal. Remember, however, the major truism of job evaluation programs: the program that is easy to develop is hard to administer, and vice versa. The NMTA program is easy to develop and hard to administer, although one could say, "It's easy to administer . . . if you don't insist on accuracy."

Let's discuss some of the compensable factors, beginning with *education* (Exhibit 1). Education may mean nothing more than the accomplishment of some level of academic preparation. It suggests literacy, but not necessarily wisdom. A person may have gained knowledge but not know how to apply it. It's been said that knowledge is learning how to take things apart; wisdom is knowing how to put them back together. Certainly all of us know of persons who have had limited education but have displayed remarkable prowess even in technical fields. The school of empirical knowledge provides much better preparation for the needs of life and business. This is true in many occupations. In Erica Jong's book *Fear of Flying*, the protagonist, Isadora Wing, laments, "I wasted two and a half years on an M.A. and part of a Ph.D. before it occurred to me that graduate school was seriously interfering with my education." *

Certainly there is a need for education and its measurement in a sound evaluation system. The point is that education has more meaning when it is

* *Fear of Flying* (New York: Holt, Rinehart and Winston, 1973).

Exhibit 1. Education.

This factor measures the basic knowledge or "scholastic content" (however it may have been acquired) essential as background or training preliminary to learning the job. The background may have been acquired by formal education, by outside study, or by training on lesser jobs. For convenience, the rating is expressed in terms of equivalent formal education.

1st Degree = 20

Knowledge of general high school subject matter. Ability to perform checking, posting, and counting; and to operate office equipment such as typewriter, adding machine, duplicating machines. *Equivalent to high school diploma.*

2nd Degree = 40

Knowledge of stenography, variety of office routines, or elementary knowledge of accounting. Ability to proficiently operate office equipment such as bookkeeping machines, calculating machine, mechanical tabulating equipment. *Equivalent to high school plus additional training up through one year of college, or business or secretarial school.*

3rd Degree = 60

Knowledge of specialized field such as cost accounting, data processing, statistics, advanced mathematics, shop practices. Equivalent to high school plus broad specialized training *equivalent to two years college.*

4th Degree = 80

Broad knowledge of a general professional field such as accounting, finance, statistics, or business administration. *Equivalent to four years of college and bachelor's degree.*

---

related to experience. Moreover, if the worth of the job is enhanced by the educational attainment of the job holder and the salary grade is thus influenced, it would suggest that the educational requirement had better be validated in order to satisfy EEOC dictates. Identifying education as a requirement for a job without correlating it with experience permits conscious or unconscious discrimination since not all members of society have had the opportunity to obtain a good education.

Only by inference does education relate to contribution. It is assumed that the higher the level of education, the more contributive the job will be. Although this may be true in some instances, it is certainly not true in every case. For the most part, education measures what the *individual* comes with; it is an input, not an output. When used as it is in the NMTA system and most other systems including the Hay system it is nonutilitarian. In an effort to upgrade the quality of employees, organizations frequently use education requirements of a job to screen out those who haven't attained certain levels of education. Yet many of the "dumb" jobs the employees do require little education. They are rote jobs which could be performed by persons with minimum education. Nevertheless, the first degree in most NMTA plans indicate high school completion as being a minimal consideration for a compensable factor. Even in exempt positions there are instances when the education level required is really not mandatory for the job. This is especially true when the education level is correlated with experience.

The *experience* factor (Exhibit 2) is not as offensive as the educational factor. Perhaps this is because experience is simply not as controversial as education. Experience prior to and since working for the particular organi-

---

Exhibit 2. Experience.

After determining the degree of education needed to perform the job, consider the degree of experience required for an average employee to satisfactorily perform the duties under normal supervision. In rating a job on this factor, consider the following:

    a. Previous qualifying experience on related work or lesser jobs, inside or outside the organization.

    b. The "breaking-in time," or period of adjustment, and adaptation on the specific job itself.

Both periods must be added together to secure the overall rating on experience.

1st Degree = 20

Up to and including 3 months of experience.

2nd Degree = 40

Over 3 months, up to and including 12 months.

3rd Degree = 60

Over 1 year, up to and including 2 years.

4th Degree = 80

Over 2 years, up to and including 4 years.

5th Degree = 100

Over 4 years, up to and including 7 years.

6th Degree = 120

Over 7 years.

zation are usually taken into account. The major degree of subjectivity in this factor is the use of the word "applicable" in reference to experience. Usually the job requires a certain amount of experience that must be considered applicable to the job under study.

The use of *contacts* as a compensable factor (Exhibit 3) is common both in exempt and nonexempt plans. Contacts made in the course of one's business activity can contribute to the success of an enterprise. It is also true, however, that if employees know their job grade will be enhanced by the number and even the quality of contacts made, they may be inclined to *increase* those contacts and get a higher grade. An increase in the quantity or

---

Exhibit 3. Contacts.

This factor appraises the responsibility for effective handling of any personal contacts that are essential for full and adequate performance of the job.

1st Degree = 5

Personal contacts limited to routine dealings (furnishing and obtaining information upon request) with other individuals in the *same department*.

2nd Degree = 10

Occasional contacts with other departments in the furnishing or obtaining of information or reports; requires some tact to avoid misunderstanding in contact where improper handling could affect results; however, the primary responsibility for harmonious relationships is assumed by immediate supervisor.

3rd Degree = 15

Regular contacts by telephone or personal meeting with other departments or outside the company to obtain or supply factual information; tact is required in these contacts, and the employee assumes the responsibility for harmonious relationships.

4th Degree = 20

Regular contacts with other departments and frequently with individuals in administrative or executive positions, consulting on problems; obtaining cooperation or approval of action to be taken; may represent the company to the public.

5th Degree = 25

Regular contacts of considerable importance, usually outside the company, and of such a nature that failure to exercise judgment in developing contacts and maintaining good relations may result in important losses to the company.

Exhibit 4. Direction of others.

This factor is intended to measure the responsibility of directing others. In consideration of this factor, the type of direction is primary and the number of people is secondary.

1st Degree = 10

No responsibility for directing others, but might train lower-graded employees.

2nd Degree = 20

Direction of the work of several employees, performing the same or directly related work most of the time, as those directed. No responsibility for costs, methods, or personnel.

---

quality of contacts for the purpose of increasing one's job grade could lead to more bureaucracy and wasted time.

What has been said about contacts could also be said about *scope of supervision* as a compensable factor (Exhibit 4). The difference between supervising and directing should be clarified, borrowing from the FLSA. If the job clearly means supervision is given, then consideration should be given to whether the job is exempt or nonexempt. If a job requires neither the leading nor the supervising of others, then this compensable factor is irrelevant. One of the characteristics of a compensable factor is that it must be found in all jobs in varying amounts. Often this factor is inapplicable to many jobs and therefore should not be considered. Perhaps a leadership differential should be considered for nonexempt jobs. Such a differential, expressed in money or as a percentage, could be issued to those in bona fide "lead" positions.

Supervision of others is really two-dimensional at least. Which job is more valuable, a supervisor of 5 technicians or a supervisor of 20 assemblers? Before making a decision, one needs to know how skilled the technicians and assemblers are. The numbers in the hypothetical situation may or may not be the ones that suggest an equation. The point is that there is some relationship between numbers led and skill level of those led. Presumably the higher the skill level, the higher the value of supervision. The more led, the more the need for supervision. Lower skill level, fewer led suggests reduced value of supervision. If supervision or leadership is to be a compensable factor, both aspects need to be taken into consideration. In exempt positions supervision may be better measured by simply measuring the budget. The budget, after all, is assigned to bona fide management people, suggesting true supervision. What's more, the budget is made up of the supervised people and the wages paid those people. The more people, the greater the budget. The more valuable those led, the more salaries or wages paid. The budget takes into account both numbers of people led and skill level of those led.

Working conditions are frequently a compensable factor (Exhibit 5). They have no bearing on contribution, but are a carryover from the Industrial Revolution, in which the conditions of work were frequently unpleasant, and to make people take jobs, systems were designed to allow for premium payment. Such a design is devoid of fiscal responsibility. Pay should be viewed from the perspective of the CEO. Does it make sense to pay for any reason other than to enhance profitability? To pay for working conditions is as sensible as to pay for other elements of employee need such as size of family, distance from work, or the size of one's belly.

There are few jobs which warrant any consideration at all for inclement conditions. The expression, "Everything is relative" is certainly applicable in this respect. What one person might consider inclement, another might feel is appropriate. David Belcher has said that a "contract" exists between employer and employee. Such a contract covers tacit elements of the job. Working conditions, tardiness, absenteeism are conditions of employment, and an applicant who does not want the conditions shouldn't take the job. Some people have very little opportunity for bargaining and are compelled

---

Exhibit 5. Working conditions.

This factor appraises the degree of physical effort and/or undesirable elements associated with the place of work.

1st Degree = 10

Usual office-type or very favorable lab-type working conditions.

2nd Degree = 20

Undesirable working conditions due to either (a) frequent physical effort involving handling or lifting of light weights, stooping, or standing for long periods; or (b) frequent exposure to one or more disagreeable elements such as loud noise, dirt, ink, grease, fumes, uncomfortable temperatures.

3rd Degree = 30

Extremely undesirable working conditions due to both (a) frequent physical effort involving handling or lifting of light weights, stooping, or standing for long periods; and (b) frequent exposure to one or more disagreeable elements such as loud noise, dirt, ink, grease, fumes, uncomfortable temperatures.

to take certain jobs. Some prefer to work indoors, others prefer to work outdoors. Analysts who work indoors project their own feelings on to other employees and presume that outdoor work per se means inclement conditions. There are many persons who wouldn't think of taking the analyst's job inside. What are "inclement" working conditions anyway? Certainly not necessarily the conditions of outdoor work. Should we measure variance of temperature? If so, how about lumens of light or decibels of sound? We select dark nightclubs and loud music. It's said that we frequently choose a mate in light darker than that in which we eat a steak!

How can anyone dictate the criteria for ideal or inclement? Is the controlled environment of an EDP center ideal or inclement? The atmosphere of such a room is carefully controlled, the lighting is usually excellent, and technology has reduced the noise level. Often, in outmoded job evaluation systems, in order to generate enough points for EDP personnel, this factor is used. How about the circumstances in executive offices? Should jobs in air-conditioned offices with soft music and pleasant lighting and colors have points taken away because of the "ideal" conditions? How about the inclemency of the positions of executives? They may have all the luxuries in their offices, but what about the stresses and strains? It seems that maybe there ought to be consideration for the inclemencies of being an executive. Such a system would measure manifestations of stress, such as nerve-ending irritations, ulcers, heart palpitation, and blood pressure.

Working conditions are just that—the conditions of the job. Employees accept or reject them just as they do other conditions of the work contract. No amount of money is going to change that in the long run. Rather than focus on the negativism or nonutilitarianism, why not concentrate on the positive side of contribution? I remember a utility company defending working conditions as a compensable factor on the basis of the hazards of being a meter reader. Evidently, meter readers have to fend off noxious weeds, barking dogs, and amorous homemakers in their pursuit of meter reading. Instead of paying for the negative aspects of the conditions, why not identify the invaluable task that is being performed? The contribution of meter readers should be emphasized. The readings they are making enable the company to charge its customers. That is pretty significant. The same attitude could prevail with linemen, those intrepid persons who hang wires on poles that enable the communication network to exist. Pay should be assigned to their jobs for this connecting link in communication, not the inclemency of climbing the pole. Steel workers who build buildings should be paid for their contributions to the erection of edifices, not for the hazards they incur.

Jobs in and out of doors in industry have become safe. OSHA and insurance companies have seen to that. There are few jobs today which have hazards over which the job holders have no control. Certainly no system should be a victim of extortion. Yet that's what is done when a lathe operator or a saw operator is paid to not lose a finger to the machine. This suggests that pay should be assigned to risk. If so, such a nonutilitarian approach should be used consistently. From machine operator to CEO, risk would need to be measured to determine the amount of pay assigned to it. Analysts are back measuring ulcers again, and, in the process, develop one themselves.

Probably the most disconcerting thing about the NMTA plan is the assignment of points. Both the weighting and the progression of points are a matter of mystery. Certainly they could be changed by the user of the system, but they seldom are. I've seen many administrators adopt the plan as is and use the points as given. The weighting of compensable factors is perhaps the most significant prerogative an organization should have in the establishment of a plan. In the NMTA we've already noted that few of the compensable factors relate to contribution. If those that did relate to contribution were at least greater in point weighting, this would provide some consolation, but, alas, this is not the case. The third degree of working conditions is worth more than even the fifth degree of accuracy. And so it goes—experience is worth more than all but two of the other factors. Education is worth less than experience and is equal to complexity. As given, the weighting of the several degrees defies logic and simply doesn't lend itself to meaningful dialogue with the employees whom the system is supposed to motivate.

If the weighting doesn't get to you, the progression of the points assigned will. At first glance the progression appears reasonable. Upon closer analysis, however, it is noted that the points increase at a markedly reduced rate. There is a tendency to increase by increments of 5 or 10 points. The second degree of the factor is twice the number of points of the first, a 100 percent increase. The third degree is half again as much, a 50 percent increase. The third degree is a third again as much, and so on. In other words, the more important the degree the smaller the amount of increase in points assigned to it! If the inconsistency of the point progression doesn't disturb you, its lack of logic certainly will. Consistency is the hallmark of a successful wage and salary program. The NMTA loses this quality in the point weighting and sequential development.

The NMTA plan was a good introduction to objectivity in job evaluation plans. It has served as a credible base upon which to develop better plans. The plan's failings, viewed several years since its introduction, include nonutilitarian compensable factors, confusingly worded compensable factors, factors that are less than meaningful when measured alone, factors such as education which may have some EEOC complications, factor weightings that are lacking in logic and reason, and point progressions that are inconsistent.

Probably the most popular job evaluation program in the country is that developed by Edward N. Hay and Associates. Hay conceived the plan when he was an employee in a bank in Philadelphia, and modified its concept several times before it emerged in the early 1940s in the form recognizable today. It was a great step forward in introducing new objectivity to job evaluation. Instead of single factor ratings, the Hay system uses grids or matrices to enable correlations to be made between compensable factors. Its popularity is due largely to the display charts which suggest order and direction. The point progression in the chart is a linear one in which the points progress consistently by 15 percent increments.

The three charts used are called Know-How, Problem-Solving and Accountability. Know-How measures the "smarts" required by the job, Problem-Solving the freedom to use those "smarts," and Accountability measures dollar impact.

One cannot look at the Hay system charts without being awed by the mass of data contained on them. The system's greatest weakness is its wordiness. Although many numbers are used, the system is highly dependent on the use and interpretation of its many words.

The first chart measures Specialized Know-How as it relates to Management Breadth and Human Relations. Level E on the K-H (Know-How) axis is basically college level, and like other entry points on all of the charts, once a level is assigned, all others become a matter of slotting. The terminology refers to levels of expertise *brought* to the job, an input measurement. The assumption is that the greater the level of K-H, the greater the value of the job. None of the levels relate to actual levels of academic accomplishments or experience. The chart merely alludes to the technical level of K-H, presumably the result of both education and experience. Without guidance, the reader of the charts does not find it easy to identify words on the K-H axis. For all its appearance of objectivity, it is quite subjective. The other axis, Management Breadth, without actually saying it, basically indicates that the higher the job is in the hierarchy, the more valuable it is. The rich get richer, the poor get poorer. The organizational location is the key to securing high points. If employees know that organizational placement enhances the number of points assigned to their jobs and eventually the money in their pockets, every effort will be made to secure higher and higher levels on the organization chart.

While we want to encourage ambition, we don't want to apply pressure to manufacture increased levels on the chart. This emphasis does have an effect of increasing organizational structuring and consequently bureaucracy. This chart keeps staff jobs from being too high in the organization. There simply are no points for the highly technical jobs to exist in the higher levels of the organization. The net effect in technical companies is to discourage any attempts at the dual ladder of approach, in which some employees can be paid highly without going into management positions, and to benefit top line jobs. This and other uses of the other charts lead to the conclusion that the Hay system benefits top jobs (occupied by the usual buyers of the system) and tends to favor line jobs at the expense of staff jobs.

The Human Relations axis is worthy of note also. It suggests that some jobs require more human relations skill than others. The degrees of measurement are Basic, Important, and Outstanding. Even if we overlook for the moment the fact that this is not necessarily utilitarian, that is, it is an input rather than an output, this measurement is risky. This system of assessing human relations skills assumes that these skills are greater in supervisory roles in which one needs to motivate and develop others. It seems to most persons when this system is explained to them that supervisors certainly have some need for human relations skills. It is quickly pointed out, however, that the people working for supervisors have strong but mixed motives for doing their bidding. Supervisors are, after all, the sources of increased salaries, promotions, and other opportunities. The expression "The boss is not always *right*, but he is *always* the boss," comes to mind. On the other hand, staff persons without statutory authority who must influence the actions of others have to muster all the interpersonal skills at their disposal in order to do this influencing. One can only speculate that the reason this factor favors line supervision is because the system is sold to high executives who may sympathize with the position suggested by the system's point assignment.

The second chart is Problem-Solving. It assesses the value of staff jobs, since problem-solving is the prime purpose of staff jobs. The chart relates the evaluation to mere slotting exercises, not job evaluations. The chart assesses on the X-axis the scope of the job from "Creative" to "Selective Memory." It correlates the scope with the degree of freedom or lack of guidance, suggesting that the more creative without guidance, the greater the value of the job. I take no issue with this. The points in the chart are expressed in percentages. The percentages are not very high and are only a function of the first chart. There is little opportunity for the staff position to come up with points to compare with those available on the Accountability chart which we'll see again favors line jobs. Being a function of the first chart, the percentage picked off the P-S chart compounds the error if the points off the first chart were incorrect.

The Accountability chart assesses the impact the job has on money and is again correlated with Freedom to Act. Of all the charts this is the most important in generating points and is the most controversial. The X-axis represents dollars, and the Y-axis represents the position's freedom to act with those dollars. Whereas the second factor, Freedom to Think, was not tied to the organizational hierarchy, Freedom to Act is definitely tied to the hierarchy. Simply, the higher in the organization, the more freedom to act. Dependence on the organizational structure, therefore, is the key to the success of this system. The name of the game is to succeed to higher and higher levels of the organization to enhance the "banana" points (as the Hay people call them). Again, line jobs are favored by such terminology.

The most confusing element of the whole system is this chart, not only the terminology of the Y-axis but the degree of impact on dollar volume. In an attempt to permit staff positions to register on this chart, the designers conceived the idea that jobs impact on dollars to varying degrees. Those degrees are "Primary," "Shared," "Contributory," and "Remote." Political pressure and one's ability to "communicate" are really tested on this chart. Each word is defined, but it still is up to the evaluator to make a guess as to which is appropriate for each job. Line jobs are relatively easily assessed because they have definite primary impact money. Staff jobs are not so fortunate. In order to permit staff jobs to register an impact, the chart allows a rather circuitous path to be taken. For example, a personnel manager hires salespersons and, therefore, has a "contributory" impact on sales volume. The system aids gamesmanship in looking for the best combination of dollars and degree of impact to go with the money. The purpose of the job is forgotten and gamesmanship abounds.

A fallacy that makes one wonder about the games people play with the chart deals with the assessment of the CEO's job. The most points will surely go to the CEO on this chart and to all other profit center heads as well. The most points will be produced by the volume of sales dollars with a "primary" impact. This suggests that the main reason for paying CEOs is their impact on the organizations in generating sales volume. This is ludicrous. CEOs and other profit center heads are held responsible for profit or net gain, not sales volume.

The inflexibility of the plan, with its limited compensable factors, each with wide variations in interpretations couched in confusing language, leaves a plan which has outlived its usefulness. It is marketed aggressively and by very capable technicians. It is well received by novice but bureaucratic organizations because it has the semblance of objectivity but permits a great deal of subjectivity in its administration. It is, despite all its faults, the most popularly used plan in the country.

· 10 ·

External Equity— Background

A man from the old country, uneducated in the world of business, developed a small hamburger joint. In time it grew. Soon he had several restaurants and a thriving business. He had advertising on all roads leading to them, hired his people well, gave good quality service and food. He had a son. He sent him to college to enable him to run the business. He majored in Business Economics. The son graduated and returned home. His father listened to his ideas. The son foresaw bad times ahead and advised his father to cut down in some areas of cost. So he did. He took away the signs, he cut back on his help, he doubled up the work assignments and reduced many of his expenditures in wages and benefits.

Sure enough, a year later, the business slumped.

EACH new design is an innovation on some older one. Seldom is something created which has no trace in something that has gone before. The expression "There is nothing new under the sun" is really quite true. Everything—devices, plans, programs, machines—everything has models to use as stepping-stones leading to that "ultimate" design. And as soon as it is designed, some modification or innovation will be made, contributing to a "new" design.

So it is with the evaluation plan to be discussed. It is the result of all that has gone before. NMTA, Hay, guideline—all have contributed to the design of this approach. It has been designed to remedy some of the failures of earlier designs. It has been modified many times by companies and employees. It was conceived to satisfy the need of multidivisional, multisized employee groups, varied product mixes, and diversely located divisions.

Through countless seminars it was tested, challenged, modified, and improved. Employee task forces designing their own plans refined the particulars of it and are responsible for the adequacy if not the validity of the plan. The flexibility and simplicity are prime facets. The universality of the compensable factors contributes to its wide use and acceptability. Having monitored its development during the last several years, I am satisfied that it is a successful, innovative approach to job evaluation. It is an attempt to get the best of all worlds: the external equity of the guideline approach, the matrix appeal of the Hay system, and the multiplicity of factors from the NMTA system.

The design and administration are simple. The plan is very objective and eliminates nearly all of the confusing language found in other approaches. Although its basis can be traced to other systems, it is a contemporary approach compatible with modern management techniques. Its simplicity and objectivity lend themselves to easy communication and understanding by employees as well as management. A careful, deliberate development will facilitate long-term administration and satisfaction. The compensable factors relate in a utilitarian manner to the business process and contribute to the success of the enterprise.

Once I was interviewed for a job in wage and salary. A question put to me by my potential boss was one that I later recognized had *no* answer. It was one of those moot issues which serves as a vehicle of discussion and permits insight into the thought processes of those involved. "Suppose you develop a sound internal evaluation process, secure integrity in internal equity, then when you go to hire for that job you discover you can't find anyone at that grade level. What would you do?" Sound familiar? It happens frequently . . . too frequently. These jobs are called "anomalies," and before long a whole structure of "anomalies" exists *outside* the regular structure.

When this happens, there are several alternatives—none of them easy and few palatable. The job can be reevaluated so that the number of points is high enough for the job to get a marketable grade. This compromise of the system destroys its integrity and comes back to haunt the compensation administrator. Or without reevaluating, the job can simply be put in a higher grade, thereby aborting, not merely compromising, the evaluation system. Or the total grading structure can be moved up so the original grade becomes equal to the market. Or just one grade can be moved so the job becomes marketable, but this destroys the system of grading. All of these alternatives have been tried. All contribute to the collapse of the system. Market compatibility is essential for the program to withstand the pressures of the market.

In response to this need, the guideline system says, "Why bother with internal issues? The outside labor market determines what the company should pay for a job. Why not just identify what the market pays and then set up the jobs in grades compatible with the market?" The question might better be asked, "Why have a system at all?" External equity, to some companies with many market-sensitive jobs, is the prime issue. In such cases where the guideline method is used, external equity is achieved permitting the company to hire with relative ease. All other jobs are placed in a ranking-comparison method about the market-sensitive jobs.

Such an approach has all the advantages and disadvantages of a ranking system. The internal relationship is dependent on the evaluator's perception of equity. The relation of the jobs to value is predicated on the labor market, not the product market or contribution. This can lead to runaway labor costs with detrimental effects on profit or labor cost control. Yet the external equity question must be dealt with in the evaluation of jobs. However, the question is usually left to the survey process and structure development. By this time, it may be too late. Why not include external equity measurement in the evaluation process? Measure the relative value of jobs in the evaluation plan as a compensable factor.

How is the market value of a job or a person usually measured? The two dimensions of assessment are academic preparation and experience—a maturity curve approach. The labor market value of every job can be measured using as criteria these two dimensions. Instead of using this measurement to the exclusion of others, let's integrate it into the plan as our compensable factor. See Figure 4.

Most employees and their managers in the recruitment process can assess the academic preparation and applicable experience needed to perform a job in an acceptable or optimal manner. Taking this input data and using it as an evaluative tool, we can measure its worth as an integral part of the evaluative process. It is not only a logical measurement, but it also will reduce the problem cited earlier in which a job sometimes was hard to fill from the labor market even though the system had evaluated it properly. By influencing the evaluation process with the marketability of the job, the administrator can more easily hire the necessary employees without having to compromise the integrity of the system. Furthermore, by integrating this factor with the rest of the factors of measurement, the criticism of permitting a carte blanche effect is avoided.

When discussing compensable factors, it is logical and normal that the elements of background emerge. Background assessment required by the job is usually identified by education and experience. Each is usually measured separately. Yet, we all know that the most able employees even in technical

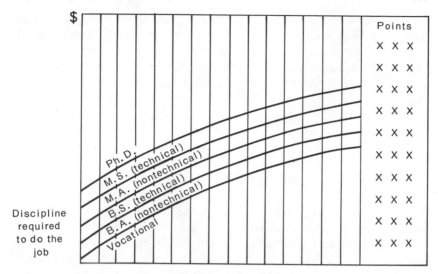

$

Points

X X X
X X X
X X X
X X X
X X X
X X X
X X X
X X X
X X X
X X X

Ph.D.
M.S. (technical)
M.A. (nontechnical)
B.S. (technical)
B.A. (nontechnical)
Vocational

Discipline
required
to do the
job

Years of Experience Required to Do the Job

Figure 4. Background.

jobs are frequently those who received little if any education. Their background is in the "school of hard knocks" gained through empirical experience. Further, it is recognized more and more that it is morally and legally improper to use education alone as a compensable factor, since not everyone in our society has had equal opportunities to get an education. The Hay system attempts to assess know-how gained from "whatever sources," which implies through education, training, and experience. Why not simply measure both education and experience required by the job in a straightforward manner in a grid?

Education—academic preparation—can be defined as that process by which we are formally trained in a classroom situation which may result in a completion of specific curricula. This definition excludes on-the-job training but not work in a laboratory setting. Since there are jobs even at the exempt level which do not require educational background especially when the person has applicable experience, the lowest level of academic preparation appropriate to the company or the industry should be used. This, too, is consistent with legal restraints on discrimination. What is sought for reference points are the various academic preparations the individual organization requires for its exempt positions. Some organizations will require several individuals with degrees; others will require very few. Some may require advanced degrees, including Ph.D.'s and M.D.'s, while others will not.

These levels of academic preparation can be placed on the Y-axis with good input data. For instance, College Placement Council, Endicott Surveys, and several other organizations provide readily available surveys of salary offers currently being made to students with varying levels of education and from various disciplines. These reportings establish the relationship that disciplines have with each other. Their placement on the Y-axis is done as a matter of statistical fact, not merely subjective judgment. While an accountant may not like the fact that a person who received an electrical engineering degree commands a higher starting salary, the person cannot deny that it is a fact of life.

Each discipline required by the organization is assigned a position on the Y-axis according to the amount of money each commands on the open market at zero years of experience according to one of the many sources, such as College Placement Council or Endicott. The X-axis is "Time" or "Years of Applicable Experience." Applicable experience may not be only that gained in the organization but outside as well. The word "applicable" may be a bit vague, but it is the best available. It should be used in its simplest form—experience which applies to the position under study. Whereas the Y-axis is limited to "Less than High School" on the bottom and the highest level of education required by the organization on the top, the X-axis will vary with the organization. It has been found that no organization has deemed it necessary to have more than 20 years on the X-axis. This seems reasonable. How many jobs can one think of that would require more? Even the highest job in the country, the presidency of the United States, requires only that a person be 35 years old, suggesting no more than 15 years since reaching maturity. The more mature the company, the greater the likelihood it will tend toward more years of experience, since such companies are influenced by the simple fact that their employees have that tenure. Younger organizations will tend toward fewer years on the X-axis since they generally do not consider many years of experience mandatory even for people holding the company's highest jobs. The time span can be divided into groups of years. For the sake of simplicity and because all of us don't develop at the same rate, such grouping is necessary and logical.

The organization must reckon with another consideration—the significance of education in their organization. In highly technical organizations where advanced and up-to-date technology can best be gained in school, the emphasis will be on education. Industries in which it is believed that experience prepares one better for the work will reduce the impact of education and increase the experience requirement. For example, the technical company producing sophisticated electronic gear will consider education to be twice as important as experience. That is, four years of college are worth eight years of experience. On the other hand, the organization for which no college program exists to prepare for its work will suggest that experience is equal to education or even that one year of experience is worth two years of education.

After establishing that correlation, the next step is to display all lines on the graph. What is desired is to show that every discipline plus its corresponding experience is worth a different amount than other disciplines and experience. This is not a salary administration tool, a maturity curve, or a recruitment offer guide. It is an attempt to show that different jobs requiring different disciplines are worth different amounts on the open market. There are three approaches that may be considered in designing the graph lines.

One approach would be to simply draw each line using a constant compound percentage. For instance, most persons develop an average annual percentage of income betterment over their careers, usually 5 percent. Some organizations and industries will vary from this, but this percentage will be found quite often. All points on the curve at zero experience could therefore be extended or extrapolated at a constant compound percentage. When this is done, however, the effect is a fanning of the data, the rich get richer, the poor get poorer. What's more, this is contrary to what actually happens. What actually happens is that most persons regardless of their academic preparation tend to converge or compress at greater levels of experience. If this is what actually happens, why not use this approach? One reason is that no analysis has been made showing at what point this phenomenon occurs. Does it occur at 5 years, 20, 40? Furthermore, at what point do the lines of career development begin to converge? In addition to this is the fact that instead of predicting actual salary patterns for salary administration or recruitment offers, what we are trying to do is to determine in a consistent manner that lends itself to easy understanding and communication the internal worth of each job with its characteristic education and experience combination. Another approach will be found to be the best. By simply extending each career line in parallel with the career line which is the most populated peculiar to the organization, more consistency will be achieved. For instance, an electronics company would have a preponderance of electrical engineering degrees. The electrical engineers degree (BSEE) would be the root career line, with all other lines parallel to it. In another company, a business degree might be the root line with all others parallel to it.

Reading the chart is easy. By merely reading the coordinates of education and experience, one can find the number of points that the job under study receives. It will be noted that the same discipline with varied amounts of experience yields different points. That is, the BSEE with three years of experience receives fewer points than the BSEE with seven years. Similarly, different disciplines with the same years of experience receive different points. The electrical engineering degree with three years of experience receives a greater number of points than the business degree with the same number of years experience. This is a fact of the labor market life. The labor market influences the evaluation of jobs. Those commanding greater salaries in the labor market will receive more points than those not commanding high salaries in the labor market. External equity has been achieved in the evaluation process without compromising the goals of internal equity and contribution.

Surely the amounts of money paid the several disciplines at zero experience will change from year to year. Usually, it will be found that each year the salary offers increase. In addition, the salary offers increase in a regular pattern, that is, they all go up in a regular manner. The cause of this is not our concern; the fact that they do this is our only concern. In boom years the salaries offered to developers and designers, those with technical degrees, go up at the expense of those with nontechnical degrees. In times of recession and cutback, the technical degrees go up less rapidly than the nontechnical degrees. This interplay is something to watch. Usually the difference between them does not vary too greatly. While the chart is not sensitive when disciplines rise uniformly, it is sensitive to changes between the disciplines in which the differences between them at zero years of experience diverge or converge by great amounts. Whenever salaries on such a chart are less than 3 percentage points apart, consideration should be given to include them in one index since very little difference exists. This is often the case with electrical engineering and mechanical engineering degrees. The virtue of the system, however, is its sensitivity to the market. If the changes become too pronounced, the chart should reflect this and the job be reevaluated. This will enable the system to remain current and sensitive to market changes. In practice it will be found that such pronounced changes will occur very infrequently.

·11·

Internal Equity— Responsibility and Expertise

The bureaucrat should—
"Phase words out" but never kill; *"opt" but never* choose.
"Sign off" but never clear, *"fall back" but never* lose.
"Draft up" but never write, *"staff out" but never* plan.
"Gear up" but never start, *"preclude" but never* ban.
                                    JAMES H. BOREN
                            When in Doubt, Mumble

THE word most often uttered by employees regarding what they should be paid for is "responsibility." "I have more responsibility than she has," or "I have more responsibility than I used to have." "Responsibility" is a very common word, yet there is little common understanding of its meaning. It means different things to different people. It certainly is a word to reckon with because it is so commonly used and because it is so often offered as a compensable factor. The dictionary provides no easy solution to the dilemma, giving such meanings as "answerable," "accountable," and "charged with." When responsibility is offered as a compensable factor, it must first be defined. It has been my practice to have employees and seminar students take a turn at defining "responsibility" as they see fit. Usually everyone can do it, but it takes some time, and definitions are often quite lengthy. The results from such an exercise can vary from: "The response to the hierarchical requisites of the functional organization and/or the political entity as perceived by the supervisor and/or the incumbent in relation to the

goals and objectives dictated by the exigencies of the mutually agreed char-
ter(s)" to "Doin' your thing."

Both of these are right, and I'm not convinced one is better than the
other. Words have a way of working against us sometimes. Numbers seem
to facilitate more universal understanding. Both line and staff jobs have responsibilities. How can they be measured and identified in such a way as to
mean the same things to each of us?

The engineering profession is often kidded about the way its members
banter about numbers and equations. Engineers are frequently critical of
personnel people for their verbosity. Personnel people would do well to heed
some of that criticism and to use numbers more than they do to express concepts and variations.

Every organization measures its status in numbers—numbers of dollars.
Dollars are a common denominator. We may have difficulty defining "responsibility" when we use words but not when we use numbers of dollars to
do so. The Hay system has done this for years. The problem with the Hay
Accountability chart is the language portion of it. Rather than cloud a
numerical common denominator with words, why not deal only with *primary* impact? Every job, particularly in the exempt category, has an impact
on *some* dollar figure in a primary mode. This is true whether the job is in
the public sector or private sector, a service- or product-oriented company, a
profit-making or nonprofit company, or whether it is a line or staff position.
The problem is that line jobs have a much more visible and therefore more
measurable impact on higher volumes of dollars because that is precisely
what those jobs are being paid for—the primary responsibility of a line job is
its impact on the dollar.

When given the task of developing a definition of "responsibility," a
group of employees or seminar students can produce individual definitions.
When asked to divide into groups and come up with a common definition,
they can do so with careful deliberation and compromise. When each group
offers its own rendition, it becomes apparent that each definition differs
from the others. After much discussion, frustration, and resolution, it becomes obvious that the only way to achieve a common understanding of
"responsibility" is to quantify the expression in dollars. It finally emerges
that a matrix in which dollar volume is on the X-axis is workable. The next
step is to deal with the Y-axis. See Figure 5.

Instead of taking the hierarchical approach of Hay's Freedom to Act, it
becomes clear that different jobs have primary impacts not only on different
volumes of money but also on different kinds of money. There is a hierarchy of types of money. In a product-generating company, the most important kind of dollar is net profit or return on stockholder equity, or return on

Type of Dollars	Volume of Dollars				
	◄——Thousands——►◄———Millions———►				
Net income	X	X	X	X	X
Financial	X	X	X	X	X
Revenue	X	X	X	X	X
Cost of sales	X	X	X	X	X
Budget	X	X	X	X	X

Figure 5. Responsibility.

investment, or some top-level, bottom-line measurement. The CEO has impact on this type of dollar. If there are profit centers in the company, each profit center executive would have an impact on varying amounts of profit. Clearly, this measure is very conducive to multiplant, multiproduct, multisite companies in which there is an emphasis on results in an MBO setting.

The next most important dollar in the life of a company is the cash flow dollar. Less visible, yet very important, is the financial control of short- and long-term loans, capital accumulations, and simply the cash flow transactions that keep a company afloat. Those that have primary impact on this sensitive dollar are a close-knit group usually performing the treasury function. There is some debate as to when this function is more critical: When a company is young and growing, the treasury function is critical to survival; when a company is mature and large, the treasury function is critical to continued growth and avoidance of stagnation. At any rate it is a critical impact and contributes greatly to the success of the enterprise.

The next most important dollar is a highly visible item, the sales dollar or revenue or gross income. This is the lifeblood of the company. Those with primary impact on the sales volume are and should be highly valued and paid well. Each level of sales management has an impact on the sales dollar. The dollar volume may vary depending on the level, but the emphasis is still there. The variations of dollar volume are the basis for identifying different levels of sales personnel. It is a natural process.

In a company producing a product, the value attached to that product is usually called "cost of goods sold" or some similar accounting term. This reflects the value-added concept of the company's product as it goes through the factory accumulating greater and greater value as material and labor and other direct costs are added. Finally as it tumbles off the end of the production line, it is called "cost of goods sold." The production line management has created this product and has primary impact on this value. The impact may vary from production line to production line; therefore this measure has good application in multiplant, multiproduct situations.

The next most significant kind of dollar is the budget dollar. Most executively exempt positions have a budget assigned to them or to the cost center they control. If line managers cannot relate in a primary mode to any of the dollars already mentioned, their positions will relate to the budget dollar. This, too, will be shown in varying amounts of dollar volumes. Larger departments will have larger budgets than smaller departments. The numbers and skill levels of those supervised are reflected in the budget dollar. The more people supervised, the more dollars in the budget. The higher the skill level, the more budget dollars. In this way, supervision is actually recognized as a compensable factor. The old question of who should be paid more, the supervisor of 20 assemblers or the supervisor of 5 technicians, is answered by this measurement of supervision; and it is done objectively, by using numbers.

The lowest level on the hierarchy deals with "expense" dollars. The nonsupervisory (FLSA) administrative or professional operative has impact on expense dollars. This, too, will vary. The more "responsible" the position, the more expense impact the job will have. Responsibility can be measured. It is measured in dollars.

Unlike other systems, this one does not favor line jobs over staff jobs, so the gamesmanship of the staff employee trying to come up to the grade of the line employee is avoided. The staff job is *not* paid because of its impact on the organization's money hierarchy. Certainly, it does impact on the organization's hierarchy of money, profit, sales, and so on, but not in a primary way.

What is it that the staff job is paid for? What is it that a line job seeks from a staff job? "Guidance," "advice," "expertise," "counsel" are the words that come forth when this question is posed. If this is true, then why not measure this very contributive impact? *Expertise* is the reason that staff jobs exist. Why bother with circuitous means of measuring the staff job's impact on money in a shared, contributory, or remote way? That just invokes gamesmanship. Why not recognize that the staff job is paid primarily because of expertise, just as the main reason for paying the line job is for impact on money?

Expertise is vital to an organization. Why, then, is it always ignored or reduced to second place? Expertise is to a company in the long run what responsibility in money impact is to the company in the short run. Without expertise, the organization will flounder, planning will be lacking, and costs will mount as bureaucracy eats at the heart of the enterprise. Staff jobs *do* contribute to the success of the organization and should occupy respectable positions in the organization's hierarchy. How, then, do we measure expertise? There are several ways, some quantifiable and sophisticated, others more language-oriented but still objective. See Figure 6.

The compensation administrator knows there are jobs in the organization that haven't lent themselves to traditional evaluation systems. Such was the case at TI. Problems arose around the legal counsel jobs in particular. It was known that they were contributive; this information was especially advanced by the vociferous attorneys! Market survey data supported their contention that they were underpaid and underevaluated in the system. Why didn't the evaluations come out high enough? Considerable stretching was done, and still the points wouldn't justify higher grades without just plain fudging. Pressures mounted and the attorneys' jobs were analyzed and reanalyzed. It became apparent that even though they were organizationally low in the system, their work was reviewed at the highest level of the organization. In other words, the impact of the attorneys' work was so great that their recommendations were viewed by top executive management before implementation. Furthermore, the duration of the study was quite long, going from inquiry to litigation in some instances. This was not the only job in the

Level of Review	Time Span on Assignment					
	Less than 6 Mos.	More than 6 Mos.	1 Yr. or More	3 Yrs. or More	7 Yrs. or More	10 Yrs. or More
Corporate		X	X	X	X	X
Executive	X	X	X	X	X	X
Directoral	X	X	X	X	X	
Managerial	X	X	X	X		
Supervisory	X	X	X			

Figure 6. Expertise.

company that "strained" or "fell out of" the system. All were staff positions, either nonmanagerial staff jobs or managers of staff functions. It became apparent that there were two dimensions that prevailed—the level of review of the staff work and the duration of typical staff assignments. In the process I remembered the teachings of Elliot Jacques. His book *Time Span Handbook* started to take on new clarity. Expertise was a function of the time span of discretion. The higher the job in the organization the greater the time span of discretion. Dr. Jacques defined it as "the longest period which can elapse in a role before the manager can be sure that his subordinate has not been exercising marginally substandard discretion continuously in balancing the pace and the quality of his work." * Jacques contends that for all intents and purposes all that is needed is to correlate pay and time span of discretion. As time span of discretion increases, increase pay.

Another facet that needs to be considered is the impact of that work. What better measurement of the impact of that work is there than the review it receives and level of the organization that makes that review? Expertise can be measured using these two coordinates, time span of discretion and level of review. Level of review, although stated in terms of organizational hierarchy—supervisor, manager, director, vice president—is not the same as level of organization. It suggests that even though a person, line or staff, organizationally reports to a supervisor, if that person's work has much impact, it will be reviewed by other, higher levels before implementation.

The test of such a system is to try it on several positions in any given environment. It will be found that this is the secret key that compensation administrators have been looking for but that has eluded them for years. Top executives have no difficulty in accepting the rationale of time span. "That's nothing new, I've been on that system for years," more than one executive has said to me. Personnel and compensation administrators do not enjoy the same ease in dealing with the concept, however, and frequently like to fall back on the less abstract, more traditional means of measuring expertise. Time span is abstract in a sense, and it forces compensation administrators to think in new parameters. Nevertheless, Jacques' ideas were the most refreshing concepts to come to the field in years. There are evaluation systems which have integrated this as one of the compensable factors and find it to be very satisfactory.

Expertise can also be measured straightforwardly as a bona fide compensable factor. This can be done by identifying the highest level of expertise found in the company. It seems reasonable that the job which is creative and also has wide powers of discretion has great impact. This can be mea-

---

* *Time Span Handbook* (London: Heinemann Educational Books, 1964) p. 17.

sured using a percentage or words describing succinctly the degree of guidance one has in the pursuit of his work. In any event the points in such a matrix should stand on their own. Usually, this factor which measures expertise is perceived by the organization as being every bit as contributive as responsibility; therefore, the number of points found in the matrix should be the same. These three compensable factors, background, expertise, responsibility, and their grids measure all that it is necessary to measure in establishing the worth of the exempt positions in the organization.

Background, for the first time, integrates the labor market consideration in the evaluation process and satisfies the objective established, external equity. Contribution, another objective, is measured by responsibility and expertise. The third objective, internal equity, is satisfied when contribution is properly measured. It may seem odd, but by measuring contribution, internal equity is also measured and satisfied.

These compensable factors have had almost constant exposure in the last several years. This exposure has been in real battlegrounds of actual company situations in various industries and in countless seminars with hundreds of analysts studying, testing, and challenging them. The use of these factors has been refined as a result of these experiences and incorporates the latest thinking in evaluation techniques. From these experiences, it can be said that there are no other compensable factors or considerations that are needed when these three are used. It is a universal system based on "simple truths," as one client has said. These three factors will permit a complete system which will withstand many changes in the organization before change is needed in them. They meet all the criteria established for testing a system.

The weighting of the compensable factors is a major consideration and attests to the flexibility of the system. Although most organizations will consider all three factors to be of equal importance and consequently weight them the same with regard to point count, some organizations may feel differently. The company which is very labor market sensitive, wanting to be able to be responsive to labor market shifts, may want to put more points in the background factor. An organization wanting to emphasize either line or staff jobs may want to give extra weight to either responsibility or expertise. Another organization wanting to emphasize contribution may want to weight the contribution factors, expertise and responsibility, heavily, at the expense of background. This flexibility is an advantage of the system.

The weighting of the factors needs resolution by the policy-making entity charged with the total development of the program. Usually, this decision is made by executive management. Or it may be the decision of the employee task force which designed the program, with the concurrence of top management. Whoever makes the decision should be aware of its importance.

The accompanying table shows all three factors with the same weight—the total points (100%) are spread in the grids equally (33.3% per factor).

Compensable factor weighting

	Background	Expertise	Responsibility	Grid
Equal weighting	33.3%	33.3%	33.3%	100%
Variable weighting				
Line position	20%	30%	50%	100%
(e.g., production	460 points	700 points	1056 points	2216 points
manager)	(21%)	(31%)	(48%)	(100%)
Staff position	30%	50%	20%	100%
(e.g., research	700 points	1056 points	460 points	2216 points
manager)	(31%)	(48%)	(21%)	(100%)

Note that the line job relates to all factors but in varying percentages. Because the line job is paid primarily for its impact on money, the number of points the line job receives will be greater for responsibility—perhaps as high as 50 percent. Certainly expertise is essential to the success of the line job and will receive about 30 percent. This leaves 20 percent to be received from background.

The staff job, paid primarily for expertise, will receive most of its points from the expertise factor (50%), and because that expertise was developed through extensive background training, it will receive many points from the background factor (30%). The responsibility factor will yield few points for the staff job (20%).

The table also shows that unlike most other systems, this system favors neither staff nor line jobs. The line and staff jobs may receive the same number of evaluation points from the system. Furthermore, the makeup of those points is different. This check on the evaluation process will be very helpful to the administrator. In some jobs there can be a balance between the points assigned for responsibility and expertise. The balance of points usually works out to be 40 percent for responsibility and 40 percent for expertise, with the remaining 20 percent for background. Oil company geologists are an example. These geologists have a highly technical job that contributes a great deal of expertise in finding oil, and they also have huge funds of money available to them for pursuing oil reserves.

· 12 ·

The Numbers Game

The animals were arguing about who had the largest number in their litter. Some talked about two or three. Some bragged of nine or twelve. Finally, they asked the lioness, who quietly replied, "Only one . . . but that one is a lion."

THE assignment of points to the grids is not a difficult task. Recall the inconsistency of the point development in the NMTA. It is important to develop the points in a more orderly manner. The advantage the Hay system offers is the means by which points are developed. It uses what is commonly called Weber's law of discrimination, or the threshold of difference perception. "In comparing magnitudes, it is not the *arithmetical* difference that one perceives, but the *ratio* of the magnitudes themselves." * Put another way, the "monk's law" stated that when 100 candles were lit in a monastery and others added to it, the human eye could detect no change until the fifteenth additional candle was lit. Thus, perception of difference is about 15 percent. Using this principle, the point progression in point plans is 15 percent, that is, each succeeding point is 115 percent of the preceding number.

The number of digits used in the system also becomes important. It must be realized that the chief advantage in using point plans is that they allow objective discrimination between degrees or variances in factors. The more these differences can be worked with, the better, until the numbers themselves become too cumbersome. To deal with six or more digits becomes difficult; to deal with only one digit fails to give interpolative discrimination. Therefore, the best scales have at least two digits, preferably three,

* *Journal of Applied Psychology*, April 1950, pp. 102–104.

and not more than five. Put more simply, start with 100 and increase the points on the scale to the higher-coordinate levels by 115 percent increments. On some grids the highest number on the scale will remain three digits. If the grid is larger and the numbers go to four digits, it must be realized that the accumulation of these numbers on higher-evaluated jobs could become unwieldy. This may make it desirable to have the scale on the grid begin at a two-digit figure somewhat less than 100.

The number of points for each grid is dependent on the weighting given each factor. If the factors are weighted the same, the total attainable points in the grid should be the same. If they are not considered to be of equal value, then the percentage of points governs the total attainable number of points in each grid. Under normal circumstances, it is better to have all factors of equal value and weight. This consistent treatment will be found to be more understandable and acceptable to all affected by the plan.

The pay rationales for exempt and nonexempt jobs differ considerably. Not only is there a legal separation in the FLSA, but logically the contributive impact of the exempt position is substantially greater than that of the nonexempt. The plan that works for exempt jobs will not work for nonexempt jobs and vice versa. The separation of exempt positions between officers and nonofficers such as that found in financial institutions is indefensible and illogical. The main reasons for the existence of this separation are tradition and status. By definition, officers are persons who can commit the institution to some act through the officeholders' discretionary action. Discretion is the key word in exemption status determination. Financial institutions which have wage and salary programs in which one program is for (exempt) officers and another one is for nonofficers who are a combination of nonexempt and exempt employees are simply incorrect in their groupings. If the employees are exempt, they should be grouped with exempt employees, some of whom may be officers. The nonexempt employees are a distinct group in job evaluation and structure and should have a program peculiar to their characteristics for pay determination.

The nonexempt jobs are those which are subject to the provisions of the FLSA. Most organizations have at least two groups of nonexempt jobs, those which manifest mental skills and those which manifest physical skills. Unless the organization has hundreds of nonexempt employees, one job evaluation program will suffice. The mental skill jobs (office and technical or O&T) are those found in the office setting and those rendering technical support to the engineering function. Stenographers, secretaries, and clerks are found in the office setting, and technicians and draftsmen are found in the technical support setting. The physically skilled jobs are those found in the production of the company's product and in the janitorial and maintenance functions. This group is frequently referred to as the production and maintenance group (P&M).

On occasion, with particularly large populations (thousands) it may be feasible to split these groups O&T and P&M into their separate parts: office, technical, production, and maintenance. The reasons which make such moves useful include differences in pay rationale and labor market differences and movements. It is also possible to further split these groups if there are bargaining units which represent various categories of workers. For instance, one union may represent the drivers and delivery jobs, another union the machinists, and so on. Labor market differences are discussed later. The concern here is job evaluation and pay rationale.

The problems of the NMTA plan include not only the weighting and points progression and assignment but the nonutilitarian compensable factors, factors that don't relate to contribution. Specifically, these include working conditions, work hazards, contacts, responsibility for safety of others, and responsibility for equipment.

Another difficulty in working with the NMTA system is the natural trend toward correlation of factors. Legal restraints have called attention to the use of education as a compensable factor since it permits unfair discrimination. This has prompted some companies to scurry about trying to validate the need for various educational levels and in other instances to abandon this criterion completely. Both are unnecessary courses. The first seldom can be done satisfactorily and then only after great cost. Abandonment eliminates an essential part of the evaluative process. In order to incorporate the concept of education in the evaluative process, it is best to correlate education with applicable experience in a grid. It has already been explained that not only is it logical to correlate these two ingredients of background for evaluation purposes, but this also permits the integration of market sensitivity as well. What's more, if education by itself is discriminatory, when linked with experience, it is not. The first factor that employee groups develop naturally is the education-experience factor.

There are several levels of education accomplishment which are preparatory to the nonexempt job. Few nonexempt jobs *require* anything higher than a bachelor's degree. If they did they would probably be exempt positions. Some jobs may be performed better if the employees have a college degree, but this degree is seldom necessary. A college education may produce high-level secretaries with a minimum of experience. Engineers and accountants who are given something less than technical jobs to do in their first few months out of college are nonexempt in most cases. The jobs they fill are paraprofessional in that they use background that is made up of either college education and a minimum of experience or less education complemented by considerable experience. At any rate, the possibility exists that a bachelor's degree is the highest level of academic preparation necessary for the nonexempt job.

The next levels of education can be enumerated and can be peculiar to the organization's need. For the technical company, military electronics training will be essential; for the financial institution, business schooling would be considered. Each industry has its own needs with regard to educational preparation. There are many jobs which require no high school accomplishment. This, therefore, would probably be the base level on the grid.

The experience correlative to education would express the company's need for the relevancy of experience. As in the exempt category, the older the company and its employees, the greater its tendency to want employees with many years of experience. It has been found, however, that five years of experience is adequate as the longest critical time required for nonexempt jobs. The area between zero experience and the maximum years of experience can be incremented as the company sees fit. It will be found in most organizations that the first increment for the lower-level jobs will probably be three months, the next six months, the next a year, and so on.

The correlation of education and experience is a natural compensable factor. Correlating the two elements of background permits the measurement of a critical element of evaluation for internal as well as external considerations and prevents unfair discrimination.

When given the chance, employees will offer compensable factors and concepts that can be readily used in correlative factors. Accuracy required is often cited as a factor. It is the key to success in the nonexempt position. Nonexempt employees are very conscious of the accuracy demanded in their position. If they aren't aware of it, perhaps an evaluation system will give them this awareness and improve their performance. If accuracy is vital to a company, it should be measured in its several dimensions—time, distance, and money. The consequence of error when measured in time, distance, and money impact brings new meanings to the incumbents and encourages greater proficiency.

The correlative to accuracy is determined by the company's needs. In some instances it may be the job's complexity. If the job requires great accuracy and is also of high complexity, the impact is great and the contribution high. In other instances, complexity may be correlated with guidance received. If the job is very complex and yet receives little guidance in its execution, the contributive impact is great and should be recompensed highly.

One of the most predictable expressions that will emerge from nonexempt employees when compensable factors are discussed is "pressure." Pressure is perceived as the responsibility they feel in "getting the work out." Pressure or responsibility is usually expressed in two dimensions, time and confidentiality. Nonexempt employees are more conscious of expediency than their exempt bosses. Often nonexempt employees are beset by work schedules that they neither control nor understand; they must merely react. The expediency with which the work must be done can be seen as relative to the contributive impact it has.

Different jobs have different levels of expediency, which will vary from job to job. For accounting clerks it almost is predictable; at the close of every month they are rushed for certain figures and reports. Sales clerks have little control over the arrival of sales orders, yet must process them immediately. Technicians, on the other hand, must work at a more even pace in setting up and testing design apparatus. The advantage of this system is that jobs may be paid differentially. The technician and the accounting clerk are a good example of this. In this compensable factor, the accounting clerk receives more points because of the greater contributive impact of his job. There are other compensating factors which yield higher points to the higher-paying job, thereby justifying the higher pay category.

The correlative to time in the responsibility factor is often seen as confidentiality. It was once a dilemma as to why the sales clerk should be paid more than other clerks. The traditional system didn't warrant higher pay, yet political pressure usually dictated it. There is logic to it as well. The sales clerk must expedite the processing of market and sales data, but the confidentiality is critical as well. The job processes information which cannot be compromised. Surely it is normal to expect all employees to be properly discreet in the use of information at their disposal, but that's just it, some jobs have more information at their disposal than others. The sales clerk has pricing information, delivery data, customer listings and other data. The accounting clerk works with sensitive financial data. The financial counselor in financial institutions deals with confidential data, as does the technician dealing with proprietary designs. Companies engaged by the Department of Defense have a heightened appreciation of security sensitivity. Many times employees are given leadership roles in addition to their other duties. These lead positions are valuable contributions and should be a basis for compensation. If leadership or guidance is an integral part of all nonexempt positions, it should be recognized as a compensable factor. Guidance given others is a function of two dimensions. The first is obvious—the number of persons led. Of equal importance is the skill level of those being guided. Few would deny that sheer numbers suggest greater guidance impact, but the skill level should be considered as well. The greater the skill, the greater the contributive impact and, therefore, the more valuable the guidance.

There are other factors that employees perceive as being compensable. The number of units processed in an insurance setting may be considered significant. In nonexempt physically skilled work where a production line is involved, there is a value-added concept which the employees know about. Basically it is predicated on the fact that as a product emerges from raw material into a recognizable, salable product, it is influenced or molded or developed by many production processes. The beginning of such a production process is vital to the formation of a product. The end of the production process is more significant, however, because the product at the end of the production process has many dollars invested in it in both material and labor. Furthermore, as a correlative to value added, the employees are aware of the marginal input each station makes to the formation of the product. This value can be expressed either in dollars in a relatively stable process or as a percentage of total worth in a more fluctuating environment.

Employees are a valuable source of ideas when designing a compensation program for them. Involvement has several advantages, not the least of which is the development of realistic compensable factors that they understand and accept.

· 13 ·

Data Collation

There was a systems analyst who almost had a nervous breakdown trying to apply scientific management principles to the Manhattan Project during World War II.

His first difficulty, the most traumatic, was that he found it impossible to describe the work. He couldn't even produce a job description. He went into the cubicle of a theoretical mathematician and said, "All right, what are your tasks, duties, and elements?" The fellow said, "What's that?" The analyst went through it again. The fellow finally answered, "Well, what I am trying to prove is that locally compact sets are not dense in themselves in Hilbert space." The analyst said, "That's a duty? Show me these things." The fellow said, "I can't because they don't really exist. They are just abstract ideas which we invent." The systems analyst exploded. "You are working with something that doesn't exist? Come on now, tell me your tasks, duties, and elements."

Eventually the analyst went to the second page in a book, published by the U.S. Employment Service, which tells how to analyze a job. It says, "If you don't make any sense of what the incumbent says, watch what he does." So he began to observe. Well, the theoretical mathematician did only three things. He drank coffee, he looked at books, and he wrote on the blackboard. That's all he did. Obviously, the analyst was getting nowhere.

He went to the man's boss, who really wasn't his boss because it turned out that the man really didn't have a boss. "What's this fellow doing?" he asked. The boss said, "We don't know what he is doing. If we knew what he was doing, we wouldn't have him doing it." Astonished, the analyst asked, "Do you mean to tell me that you don't know the tasks, duties, and elements of this subordinate?" The boss responded, "Hell, no. That's why we've got him doing it. He's the only man in the country who understands this sort of thing."

So the analyst went on to the next part of the interview form. "Now, tell me," he asked the boss, "how do you know when he is doing the job well? What are the criteria?" The boss answered, "I haven't the slightest

*idea." When the analyst persisted, the boss finally said, "Well, I guess
he is doing it well when he tells me so." "Do you mean to tell me,"
shouted the analyst, "that you depend on a subordinate to tell you when
he is doing a job right?" The boss stood his ground. "That's absolutely
true. He's the only person in the country who can understand the proof
of these theorems. If he says he's doing it right, he's doing it right. That's
why we have him doing it."*

THE section dealing with job descriptions in AMA's Job Evaluation Course
is entitled "Job Descriptions—Panacea or Pain?" That title covers the gamut
of the impressions people have about job descriptions. The intent of this
chapter is to explore this issue and to open the door to new ways of collecting information on jobs so that measurements of value can be made about
them.

First, it should be recognized that the term "data collation" is more appropriate to the discussion. It suggests the gathering and organizing of data
for study purposes. It suggests that there are more ways to gather job information than the traditional job description method. For that reason "data
collation" will be used to refer to the process of collecting job data for evaluation purposes.

It should be noted, too, that the discussion of job description or data
collation *follows* the lengthy development of job evaluation techniques. This
is done for a specific reason. The job evaluation plan should be developed
before the data collation process is begun.

The traditional method of beginning a job evaluation study is to have
job descriptions written. That *seemed* to be the logical starting place. Companies are still approaching the problem this way. The question in all of this
is, What kind of data should be collected and written? Without knowing
what they are after, how can analysts possibly get the information they need
to evaluate jobs? Collecting data on jobs before developing the job evaluation method is called the "shotgun" method. In this way job descriptions are
written with little direction or design, and the attempt is to cover as much as
possible in the hope that something will be relevant to the analysis. This
method is as effective as throwing mud against the wall and hoping that
what sticks to the wall will be important material. To collect data in this way
is expensive and grossly ineffective.

The better way is to develop the evaluation plan so that job data can be collected using the evaluation plan as a guide. This "rifle" approach zeroes in on the information that needs to be collected about the job and later studied and evaluated.

Opponents of this method claim that without knowing the elements of the job, they are unable to know what compensable factors are inherent in the jobs. Having written job descriptions, they develop job evaluation plans which use the same old NMTA factors as if they hadn't known they existed in the first place. Very rarely do new compensable factors emerge from the process in which job descriptions are written first. It is important to develop simple universal compensable factors, such as those suggested in earlier chapters.

The uses to which job descriptions are put influence the makeup and design of the program. In addition to their function as an evaluative device, they are used as a recruitment tool in letting the recruiter and the applicant know what is expected on the job and what qualifications are needed for successful placement. They may be used as a training vehicle to let the employer know the particulars of the job. They are used in making promotions to let new holders of a job know what the higher job contents are. They are used in job posting to let employees bid on jobs. Job descriptions are often the basis of exchange in salary surveys. They are even used in organizational dynamics and performance appraisal. They are used in organization analysis and structure development. They are used in financial and legal audits. They have been used in safety determination studies and in security checks.

In designing the job description program, it must be remembered that the more uses to which the descriptions are put, the *less* effective they will be for *any* of the uses. Job descriptions often collapse of their own weight. Job description programs are somewhat similar to skill inventory systems. Skill inventory systems have been seen as the panacea for getting the right person in the right job. In the design of the skill inventory system, many managers are usually asked what they want to see and retrieve in the system. Everyone seems to want something different and the system becomes overloaded and many fail, collapsing of their own weight. A job description program can also collapse if too much is asked of it.

The job collation device, the job description, should be designed primarily for one use, job evaluation. If, as a byproduct, it can serve other uses, that is fine, but it shouldn't be encumbered with other demands or it will fail in all of them. Does this mean other documents will be needed for training, recruitment, performance appraisal? Yes, it does if the need is really there. It will be found, however, that when it comes to developing a special form for the other uses, few will really be needed. The requisition form can be used for recruitment specifications, the organization chart for analyses and audits, and procedures and reports for training purposes. Performance appraisal does need special attention and more is given in Chapter 12.

Job descriptions have become known as the onerous part of the wage and salary program. Wage and salary programs have been ill conceived and have produced bad job description formats. The descriptions get the heat, but it has been the job evaluation programs that have created the fire. Employees criticize job descriptions because they work with them. What should be criticized are the job evaluation programs that have created the bad descriptions.

Job descriptions have been assailed for being too long. This is a problem with verbose evaluation plans. Anyone who has written a policy knows that the more the writer tries to clarify, the more confused the policy becomes. The job description suffers from the same malady.

Even though the description is too long, it is often incomplete. It's difficult if not impossible to include all that is necessary in a job description. This is especially true in a job content program in which the intent is to capture all the activities done in the pursuit of the job. This, of course, is another point against a job content program. In a contribution system, it is necessary only to identify what the results of the activities are. In an attempt to make job descriptions complete, analysts are faced with writing too many particulars about the job and thereby setting up myriad jobs, each with its own details. The other approach is to write about the jobs too generally. Probably the most ludicrous thing that wage and salary analysts do to make sure the whole waterfront is covered is to write the description and then at the bottom put the all-encompassing line, "And all other duties assigned." While this "Ha, gotcha!" line seems to be the supreme act of ensuring that everything is covered, it should be noted that this one-liner negates all that was covered in the description! Either the description details everything done in the job, or the one-liner is all that is needed. The basis of pay could be altered considerably by this line.

Because the name of the game in job content systems is to snow the evaluator, job descriptions tend to be too wordy. The wordier the descriptions, the more likely it is that they will include the magic words which may make the difference in grade. The simplicity of the job evaluation program, the freedom from confusing language, the emphasis on objectivity rather than subjectivity, the quantification of concepts—all lead to a more effective wage and salary program with succinct data collation techniques.

Many are in awe of the job description. Management sees it as a vehicle which will do all it hasn't been able to do in achieving efficiency and productivity. Analysts see the job description as that magic vehicle which will once and for all capture the true worth of the job. Employees see the job description as that great and wondrous god which will either put money in their pocket or take money out of it. All realize that the job description must be carefully and deliberately developed, a very time-consuming task. As an analyst at Univac, it was my job to interview management people about their jobs for evaluation purposes. The result of the interview would be a four-page document which would cast their jobs in one grade or another. When I would come for the interview, the managers would duck out, hide, and generally do all they could to avoid the exercise. They knew the significance of this visit. They dreaded it because of the time involved, and because they knew they had to be very sure that everything about their job was covered.

Since time is money, job descriptions are very costly documents. They require the analysts' time, the employees' and the supervisor's time away from their jobs, and the time of all others who process the descriptions. They are not only costly in time. It costs money to print them, mail them, and store them.

Management people, having had bad experiences with costly job descriptions, usually want no part of a "new" job evaluation program because they see the specter of cost involved with job descriptions, three R's— "readin', writin', and writhing." Administrators could dispel this distaste by assuring management that a new, simpler program will *reduce* cost because of its simplicity and succinctness.

Even with the best-intended data collation program, the information is dated before it is printed. At best it is a snapshot of a moving vehicle in a rapidly changing scene—all the more reason to invest as little as possible in the process. The dynamics of industry today have seriously challenged the validity of the job description as a viable reflection of the job. Less subject to change is the result of those activities; therefore, a contribution-based program is again preferred.

Too often the job description is seen by both management and employee as a meaningless document which was conceived by an unholy ghost, born of a political necessity, and suffered under countless harangues, the result being a useless vehicle which never served a worthwhile purpose. It frequently becomes an object for trying to win political battles and settle illogical disputes. It is so carefully written as to cause little concern because of its generalities and vagueness. To ignore it is to love it. What's worse, it becomes an element of demotivation. As Robert Townsend has said, "At best a job description freezes the job as the writer understood it at a particular instant in the past—they're morale sappers." *

From the ashes of old descriptions, what can be salvaged to build a via-

---

* *Up the Organization* (New York: Alfred A. Knopf, 1970), p. 42.

ble program? Job data is necessary to job evaluation. What is needed are
new approaches consistent with the dynamics and economies of the decade.
Let's build a new approach.

Who should write the description? As the internal consultant, the administrator should be able to view as many sources as possible as the means
of developing and collating job data. Such job data is dependent upon the
type of job evaluation plan that will be used in determining job value and
the uses to which the job data will be put, once obtained. There are several
people who could develop job data: members of top management, a wage
and salary analyst, the supervisor of the job, or an outside consultant.

Some programs are done in such an aura of secrecy or mysticism that
sometimes only top management should develop data about the jobs. The
disadvantages of such an avenue of job data collation is the time it takes, the
expense of involving highly paid executives, and the lack of visibility to
them of the several jobs. If top management collects job data, redundancies
will be reduced if not eliminated, organizational structuring may be solidi-
fied, and such dictates with regard to job content are accepted as the "final
word."

The wage and salary analyst has been the most likely one to collect job
data. Large organizations employ squads that do little else but collect and
audit job data. Consistency is probably the greatest advantage of having the
analyst collect the data. It would be nice if efficiency and cost could be
listed in the advantage column, but I'm not at all sure that this can be done.
Like so many things, the process becomes an institution in which self-
preservation and perpetuation of the system become all-important, and bureaucracy wins out, negating efficiency and making the process expensive.
The analyst as data collector has been criticized as lacking adequate knowledge of the elements of the jobs and not being in a position to capture the
salient elements of the position in question.

Supervisors are a source of data, but visibility of jobs is a problem. Too
often they do not know the jobs they are supervising. Frequently they are
politically motivated as well and may have a tendency to build things into
the job that will inflate the evaluation.

Job holders are criticized for the same reason. It is frequently felt that
they will purposely inflate the job description because they know it influences their pay. Employees are in the best position to know what is going on
in their jobs. The trick is to get them to report it candidly. To think that
they will not be honest is drawing from Theory X experience. It is always
amusing to observe a person who professes to a Theory Y attitude when the
prospect comes up of employees writing their job descriptions. The Theory
Y person suddenly becomes Theory X, assuming the worst of all possible

things that the employees will do. In a Theory X environment, employees will probably react in a Theory X manner. They'll play games with the system and try to fool their evaluators. In a Theory Y environment, employees will probably react in a Theory Y manner, being rational and candid.

Outside consultants are available to write job descriptions. If consultants can't bring expertise about the jobs, they should be able to bring objectivity to the process—but at what a cost! Many consulting firms recognize this money-making opportunity, and a part of the firm's program bid is to have the consultant write descriptions of a number of the "executive" jobs to demonstrate "objectivity and integrity," not to mention to earn a handsome dollar for it. Although it is ego-inflating for executives to have the consultant write their job descriptions, it is an expensive perquisite and if quantified, the executives would probably rather have the money used elsewhere.

Which is the best way? The best of all worlds, of course. The root of the system has to be the employees. Their perception of the job may not be the best, but it is the way the job is performed. If they are incorrect, their perception should be altered, probably by their supervisor and also by top management. The analyst should monitor and guide the whole process with an assist from the outside consultant. The validity of the program and its acceptance are predicated on the employee's involvement to some extent; why not all the way?

This naturally brings the discussion to the several means of collecting job data—observation, interviews, questionnaires, and so on.

The observation of a job is revealing and has been the most typical way of learning about a job and developing job data. The economy has changed, and the jobs with it. No longer are the jobs purely physical activities. As the economy has changed from product-oriented to service-oriented, the jobs now involve a great many mental skills rather than only observable physical skills. Moreover, job evaluation used to concern itself with the lower-level jobs. Now job evaluation pervades the company's structure, and observation can no longer be relied on as the means for collecting job information. While a machinist can still be observed and job data developed, the same cannot be done with the executive who sits at a desk. Observation is no longer a valid means of securing job data.

The interview is probably the most popular means of obtaining job data. It supplies firsthand knowledge from the job holder and/or the supervisor as to the content of the work. It is limited only by the ability of the participants to communicate. And although this may seem to be an oversimplification, the interview is an excellent means of securing job data. However, it is expensive. The time away from the job on the part of the interviewees is costly. In addition, certain issues must be dealt with when using this means.

Which employee should be selected, if all are not interviewed? Who should select the employee to be interviewed, the analyst or the supervisor? If the supervisor selects the best employee, the job may be overrated due to the bias introduced. If the supervisor's selection is predicated on who is available at the time of the interview, the job description may also be faulty. The "typical" job holder is the best representative if only representative interviews are to be made.

The questionnaire is also a very popular technique. This was introduced as a timesaver in large populations when employees became more communicative. Even at that, the employee needs guidelines. A piece of paper which says "Tell me about your job" and then confronts the employee with a page to fill in is a poor excuse for a questionnaire. What's more, it may also be discriminatory because it requires a certain amount of verbal and writing skill that not all members of our society have had the same opportunity to obtain. Even in a homogeneous group, the open-ended questionnaire is still a questionable technique. What results from such a technique are many nonstandard replies about the writers' perception of the job. It is a wasteful and expensive technique. To be useful, the questionnaire must be structured. Many structured questionnaires still play games with the employee. The employee, so encouraged, will play games with the analyst, and nothing of value emerges. What is meant by playing games is that the questionnaire will ask questions about the *content* of the work in the hopes that the response will in some magic way lend itself to analysis and evaluation. The results do not bear this out.

There are other means of gathering job data. One is through old job descriptions of the same job. Caution must be exercised in using some of the data found in them because of technological and other changes. Another source is job descriptions from other organizations. As an analyst, I established contact with other companies and swapped job descriptions with them and developed a library of job descriptions. They proved to be a continuing source of good information. Reports, equipment specifications, organization charts, policies, procedures all help in giving information on the contents of jobs. The accumulation of job-related data is an invaluable source for writing good job descriptions. Such data should be filed with the job description (the method of filing will be discussed later).

The more of these techniques that are used the better the job data will be. The least expensive and most effective means of collecting job data is the structured questionnaire. The questionnaire, developed and communicated in a Theory Y manner, specifies the compensable factors in simple, quantifiable terms. In so doing, it permits employees to respond about how they perceive their job to relate to the compensable factors. As has already been discussed, the factors must be developed with care, so there is a minimum of opportunity for inflated responses. Asking employees to justify their responses further safeguards against inflation. The form identifies the several compensable factors in the system. Employees check off what they consider to be the relation of their job to the factors. This is usually reviewed by the employees' supervisor and a balance is achieved. Such checks also prompt good dialogue between supervisors and employees, which contributes to better mutual knowledge of the job's expectations. This process is so effective and timesaving that all employees can be involved in it, which leads to greater credibility of the data and greater acceptance of the system by the employees. It also reduces discrimination, since respondents do not need to write extensively about their jobs. In most instances, when given the opportunity, employees will respond in an honest, straightforward manner. There will be some modest replies and some inflated ones, but most will form a believable pattern. Responses that are either too inflated or deflated need special attention. Some employees will be found to be simply lacking in information about their job or the system, some will be deliberately trying to beat the system, and others will simply be in different jobs than was thought. This system is by far the best, but it is predicated on a simple but contributive set of compensable factors.

No matter what system is used, analysts have to make a decision about their attitude set. In the role of data collector, are they reporters or innovators? Should they report data just as it is gathered, or should they identify problems of organizational duplication and try to change them? Should they record what a job is now, or how the employee and/or the supervisor intend it to be? Each of the above possibilities will be appropriate in a particular situation. The key to success is consistency. With mature and large organizations, chances are analysts are playing the role of reporter. They should consistently report jobs as they are currently structured. With small and growing companies, chances are analysts have the role of innovating and helping to formulate new jobs. To be inconsistent, that is, to collect job data as jobs are now in some instances and to formulate other jobs as they will be can be disastrous.

There are several ways of collecting data. The choice depends primarily on the use to which the data will be put. For job evaluation purposes there are these means of organizing the approach:

⋄ duties and responsibilities
⋄ chronological sequence
⋄ organizational or functional groupings

⋄ percentage of time allocations
⋄ objectives, strategies, tactics
⋄ compensable factors

The most typical method is to develop the data by the duties performed and the responsibilities held. This usually involves such questions as Where does the work come from? What does the employee do? Where does the work go? Obviously this method attempts to capture the *content* of the work performed. It can be as succinct or verbose as the compensable factors and the parties involved permit. In the attempt to gather information about job content, this method strives to gain sufficient data for use in the subsequent evaluation process. Although it is the method most often used, it is probably the worst. It has little direction, and offers no assurance that the information gathered will be sufficient to render a successful job evaluation. But because it is the traditional process, its use goes on and on.

The collection of data in a chronological sequence is a technique that might be used in assisting lower-skilled job holders to organize their thoughts. It must be remembered that not all employees are proficient at writing and speaking. Analysts must never talk down to job holders or patronize them; they must, however, achieve a level of communication which is compatible with the particular interviewee. Employees in lower-level jobs frequently are "doers," not talkers or thinkers. Their thought patterns are related to the job to which they are assigned. The chronological sequencing merely asks them to recite the activities performed in a period of time. "First I do this, then this, then this." This means of information collecting is appropriate for routine jobs in which the same activities continually recur. In some companies there are several jobs for which this technique is appropriate, in other companies, very few if any.

When analysts discuss the scope of a job with a management employee, they may find it helpful to use the organization chart in obtaining job content information. Managers' jobs are revealed in the functions they manage. By learning of those functions, analysts get to know what managers' jobs entail. Probably the easiest means of collating job content data about *relatively sophisticated jobs* is in terms of the percentage of time spent on each function.

Many persons cannot conceptualize a percentage allocation. Employees are not to organize their thinking to conform to the analysts'. In fact, it is the other way around. Analysts must modify and customize their style to suit the interviewees. Usually the percentage of time effort is a good means of collecting data from most exempt positions and certain technical and administrative nonexempt positions. But analysts must be alert to a dilemma that frequently occurs. In most cases, employees itemize their activities in order of importance, from most to least important. If, when percentages of time or effort are assigned to these activities, it is discovered that they spend a very small percentage on the most important one, the question arises, What are the employees being paid for? Are they being paid for doing the most important item, even though they do it in a small percentage of time? Or are they being paid for what they spend most of their time on?

A clue to getting the answer is the "pilot question." What are airplane pilots paid for—the critical moments, which take a small percentage of time, or when the plane is on autopilot, which takes the greater percentage of time? Usually the basis of pay is the critical element, no matter what its duration or percentage of time—which somewhat negates the benefits of using this method even though it is revealing.

The listing of objectives, strategies, and tactics can be used in both a job content system and a contribution system. A listing that is succinct and specific would be used in a contribution system. One that is general and verbose would be used in a system based on job content. Both instances suggest tentative descriptions. They must be viewed as subjective, thus making many individual descriptions necessary, all of which are temporary, or good only until the objectives are met, altered, or reassigned. This system is more a personalized MBO system conducive to small organizations or to large analyst staffs.

The best, but alas least used, method of collating data is by the use of compensable factors. Probably the reason it is little used is that companies frequently gather job data without first having a job evaluation system. Another reason is that the company which does have an evaluation system doesn't want its employees to know the compensable factors. (After all, if they know them, what secrets remain to keep management people in the business of people management—and, what's worse, if employees learn what they're being paid for, they may be motivated by this to try to earn *more* money!) Still other managements feel that if employees knew the compensable factors, they would inflate their descriptions, thereby getting overrated evaluations. This logic is not only Theory X, but is the result of projection, that is, that's what management would do if given the chance.

The gathering of data based on the compensable factors is the most efficient method and gives the greatest assurance that the data collected will lend itself to evaluation using the compensable factors. As mentioned before, the compensable factors need to be simple, quantifiable, and objective, and the company setting must tend toward Theory Y. An old tenet of child psychology is if you tell a child he is good, he lives up to it. If you tell him he's bad, he'll live up to that too. This tenet has similar applications in the organization.

Because the interview is an important means of collecting job data, it would be appropriate to spend some time on the makeup of a good interview. There are several steps.

◇ Preparation and research
◇ Location, notification, and selection
◇ Building rapport
◇ Developing support and cooperation
◇ Title and summary data
◇ Collecting data
◇ Identifying qualifications
◇ Summarizing and concluding

Preparation and research. In order to perform the interview for collecting job data, it is best to research the job as much as possible. This can be done through organization charts, department charters, current job descriptions, job titles, reports generated by the area, equipment used in the area, and the jargon peculiar to the job area. All of these make analyst-interviewers more informed, permit them to ask their questions more adroitly, and reduce the possibility of their being "snowed" by the interviewees. Analysts should not overlook other companies' job descriptions in similar job areas. Sometimes they'll render the terminology, setting, and particulars that may otherwise be overlooked.

Location, notification, and selection. The question of where the interview takes place is important. "Your place or mine?" is vital to the success of the operation. If analysts conduct the interviews in their offices, they must remember that this may be a strange setting for the interviewees, who may be emotionally concerned about it. Obviously, these interviews are not "ego trips" for the analysts. Hopefully, they can put aside their egos long enough to conduct the interviews in a location that will yield the best results. If they are conducted in the analysts' environment, interruptions must be kept to a minimum. To conduct the interview in the environment of the employees may be all right if employees are not intimidated by their peers or by the exigencies of their workplace.

The managers of the employees to be interviewed must be notified of the event. At least one level of management of the interviewees should be permitted to see the results of the interviews. The managers should also select the interviewees. Managers should be given guidance on the desired characteristics of the person chosen, but the actual selection should be left to them.

Building rapport. Some will say that one way to build a rapport with interviewees is to research their background and learn something about them in order to establish some commonality. Although this may work if time permits, employees may feel threatened if they believe they have been specially selected for the interview. Caution must be used; not all employees regard this exercise as a privilege. They may be antagonistic if they think it may be a "cover" for another purpose.

Developing support and cooperation. The degree to which analysts can disclose the intent of the program should be clarified before the entire program begins. The reason for this is that in the interviews, analysts must have a clear understanding as to how much information may be given to the employees in order to conduct an effective interview session. If employees are not permitted to see their own descriptions, which is still the practice in some companies, this would influence how much analysts could talk about the purpose of the interview.

Title and summary data. Because of the many interviews conducted and the frequently confusing organization structures and titles, it is wise to elicit a summary statement about the job from the employees at the outset. Such a response may be forthcoming when this situation is posed: "Suppose you were standing at a bus stop and a friend tapped you on the shoulder and asked you what your job is. Your bus has just rounded the corner and is pulling up to the stop. You have only until the bus stops and the door opens to respond. What would you tell your friend?" When the question is put in this manner, employees can usually summarize their jobs easily. Similarly, ask employees what title they would use to succinctly and descriptively identify their job. Such preliminary information provides the setting for what is to follow.

Collecting data. The next step is to gather data using one of the methods identified earlier (duties and responsibilities, chronological sequence, etc.).

A guide will be very helpful to analysts in soliciting answers. Without one, they may forget some important area, and the value of the interview will be reduced. It should be decided before the interviews which techniques will be used—consistency is vital. It should also be decided in advance which alternate approaches will be tried if the original choice is not successful. Note-taking is essential, unless the analyst has an exceptional memory, and is usually preferred to tape-recording, which is still considered somewhat intimidating. Before concluding the interview, wise and courteous analysts ask the interviewees if they would like to add to what has already been said. Some employees feel better if they can depart from a rigid sequence and offer some data, which may or may not add to that already given.

Identifying qualifications. Analysts need to assist employees to view the qualifications for their jobs as objectively as possible. The bias of the employees is manifested in three ways. (1) They may project their own qualifications as being the best—they succeeded in the job with their qualifications, therefore, those are the right qualifications. When hiring wage and salary analysts, I would purposely seek persons who had been teachers because my work at the University of Minnesota was in education. Teaching involves the measurement of an intangible, learning. Wage and salary also is involved in the measurement of an intangible, that is, worth to the organization. It was natural, it seemed to me, that a teacher was ably qualified for wage and salary work.

(2) Employees who are trying to show how well they are doing may state that although they have only high school training, their job could be done better by a college graduate. What they may be saying is, "Look how good I am, I did it without a degree." It is possible, however, that they are being very candid and suggesting that they would have done better had they been better equipped.

(3) Employees who want to get ahead may say, "I've got a college degree, but anyone with a high school diploma could do this job." What they're saying is, "I'm much better than this job, get me a better one." Again, it must not be overlooked that this may be a candid reply in an honest effort to restructure the job or have someone hired who is more appropriately prepared.

Objectivity may be achieved just by asking the questions in a certain way. For example, the analyst says to the interviewee, "Suppose you have been promoted out of this job, and your boss has asked you to help select your replacement, what combination of education and experience would you seek in the applicant?" With this phraseology, the employee gets two positive reinforcement strokes—the suggestion of promotion and the opportunity to participate in the selection of a successor—and is encouraged to give an objective response.

Summarizing and concluding. Employees should be thanked for their time, cooperation, and input. If appropriate, they should be told that they will see a draft of the results of the interview and research. Their supervisors will probably also be keenly interested in the interviews. If communication channels have been approved and if time permits, having supervisors and subordinates go over the interviews together is an excellent way to handle this. However, it may be tremendously time-consuming. Both employees and their supervisors know the importance of these documents and may want to spend a long time going over their contents. Time limits and due dates must be assigned to the viewing of these documents and monitored to move the program along.

· 14 ·

Writing
Job Descriptions

Officialese is a form of bureaucratic writing in which you can under-
stand only the words but none of the sentences. There are two kinds of
officialese: one is hard to understand and the other is easy to misunder-
stand.

L. J. PETER
The Peter Prescription

PERSONS charged with writing job descriptions are truly blessed. It may
not seem like much of a blessing, but the writers of job descriptions have an
opportunity that few persons get throughout their business careers. This is
the opportunity to get paid for learning many facets of the business world.
Many people go through their business careers never knowing what's on the
other side of the fence, never being permitted to inquire. The best times to
inquire are when one is charged with the responsibility and when one is new
to the business world. The writers should view the task of writing job descriptions from another angle, too. Often interviewees haven't really thought
about their jobs until the task arises to describe them. They will learn about
their jobs, possibly for the first time. And if not, they will at least see them
or aspects of them from completely different viewpoints. The company
gains, too. The company needs guidelines to make value judgments about
jobs, and the writers can help. The company needs help in identifying inconsistent work assignments, duplication, and unnecessary workloads.
Through this whole process in which the analyst-writers are learning, both

151

the company and the employee benefit because they are all contributing to the continuing success of the organization. Writing job descriptions may not be all fun, but it is a tremendous opportunity for the writers to make a significant impact on the organization and to build a memory bank that will serve them well throughout their careers. In writing the job description, there are many things to keep in mind.

A good job description will take time to write. Like anything else, the first one will seem like a never-ending task, but once a technique is routinized, the writers will find they can complete several descriptions in the same amount of time it took to write the first one. Therein lies a danger. There may be a tendency to become too glib and efficient at writing the descriptions. Planning and timing become very important. It will probably take about four hours to collect data, analyze it, and develop the several drafts into a final one. Budget the time accordingly. If the time spent on the process falls off sharply, it would be a good idea to review the work done. See if it stands the check of consistency. Do all the sentences or phrases hang together, or are they scattered, random thoughts that do not form a picture of the job?

Descriptions must be updated. Some companies take very deliberate steps to ensure that job descriptions are up to date. Obviously the dynamics of the organization dictate the need for such accuracy. Certainly compensation administrators have an interest in maintaining current job descriptions, but it seems impractical for them to establish actual review dates for determining the relevancy of the data. Time doesn't alter the content or expectancies of the job, circumstances do. Part of the circumstances are the job holders and their supervisors. Instead of spending time auditing job descriptions, it would be better to respond to employee/supervisor requests for updating. In other words, the responsibility for updating a job description should rest with the persons holding the jobs and the supervisors. They have the most to gain or lose in terms of accuracy of the data. Furthermore, employees and supervisors will definitely keep compensation administrators informed of job description changes if they believe that the pay assigned will also change.

Management must be serious about a good job description program. The time spent on the development of job descriptions is costly. Management should be apprised of how costly it will be in hours away from the job for the interviewees and in hours of concerted effort and attention of the analyst staff; they should also be apprised of the significance of the findings. When duly apprised and shown a reasonable, efficient, and professional approach to job descriptions, management can be counted on to support the program.

The filed job description should be accessible to the appropriate people.

That statement may not seem very meaningful, but no one can dictate what persons should see job descriptions in any given environment. Each organization has to decide who is going to have the right to see the descriptions. Some companies keep descriptions hidden from the employees. That is tantamount to the situation in which the librarian insists that all books remain on the shelf so they don't get dirty. The descriptions should have wide visibility. If the company has a job-posting program where employees can bid on openings, the job descriptions will have high visibility. The problems of reproducing and updating the descriptions should be the determinants of how widely distributed they are.

Quantitative job descriptions should be used whenever possible. The extent to which numbers can be used depends on the compensable factors. The simpler, more objective the compensable factors, the more quantifiable the description can be. The success or failure of the job description lies in the design of the compensable factors. One caution—the compensable factors to be quantified should have enough flexibility to allow for reasonable variances before the description needs to be redone and the job reevaluated.

Analysts should keep in mind the uses to which the job descriptions will be put while they are writing them. Remember that the job description should be used primarily as an evaluative tool. To encumber it with other applications may render it useless for many of its intended purposes and accelerate its obsolescence.

A job description program should be undertaken at the proper time. When a job description is composed, it should be an accurate reflection of the state of the job. This suggests that the job description is best developed after the job itself is developed and occupied. Every job changes, some grow, some recede. The job description should reflect the content or expectations of the job at a particular time. If the company is going to consolidate jobs due to a cutback, the job description program should be postponed, to be undertaken during a more stable period.

Job analysts must gain and keep the confidence of the employees. Writing a job description is a serious task. Analysts are charged with representing a job in its true form as best as they can understand it. Their attitude must display their sincerity in serving employee and company needs as well. Employees will take the attitude they see displayed by analysts. If analysts are diligent, employees will be diligent. If they are careless, employees will be careless. Analysts must display by word and action that they are committed to their task. Only then will they secure the proper response from employees.

Descriptions should be understandable. They should be written in a clear and simple style that is as free of technical jargon as possible. The purpose of the descriptions is to inform persons other than the job holders and their bosses of what the jobs are comprised of. Achieving this purpose will ensure that a proper evaluation can be made. Some say the descriptions should be understandable even to persons who know nothing about the jobs. This seems a little farfetched. Describing today's jobs does involve the use of "shorthand" terminology for processes, techniques, and equipment. In order to avoid such language, analysts would have to use many more words to describe the jobs. This would result in totally nontechnical but very verbose pieces of work that would be clear to no one.

Descriptions must not be interpreted too rigidly—they must be flexible. How general should job titles and descriptions be? The more specific the titles and descriptions, the more of both there will be and the greater will be the tendency toward rigid evaluations. The more general the titles and descriptions, the fewer of both there will be, but the less accurate the subsequent evaluations. At one extreme, each employee would have his own title and job description; at the other, all employees would be covered by one general classification and description. Somewhere in between these two extremes, the organization must find the position that best suits it.

A problem common to large companies with multiple plant or office locations is the equity of job size. Many jobs with similar titles found in several locations may not all be equal in value to the organization. Yet because of the similarity of job title, it is assumed they are of equal value. An example might be accounting clerks found in large divisions compared to similarly titled positions in small divisions. Accounting clerks in the small divisions handle a wide variety of accounting functions: payroll, accounts receivable, accounts payable, cost accounting, and so on. Although these clerks have great breadth in the accounting activities, they have no depth in any of them because the data is sent to the home office. Accounting clerks in large divisions may handle only one aspect of accounting, such as accounts payable or accounts receivable, or possibly only those accounts from A through L. Are the jobs equal? Which accounting clerk should be paid more? Does the breadth of one equal the depth of the other? Only the well-developed job description will reveal the value difference, if there is any. A contribution-based system reduces the problem since it is not the value of the activity that is measured, but the value of the output or result of that activity.

Another problem that perplexes the writer-analyst occurs in times of recession or depression when, because of a cutback, three jobs, for example, are combined into one. Does the resultant job warrant more pay? There is a tendency to believe that it does, especially on the part of the employee. In a job content approach, where activities are measured, the new job may appear to be of greater value, but how about output? It is conceivable that the grouping of all three jobs results in less output than the three single jobs produced. With the job content approach, it is difficult to reckon the problem, and more pay is usually given. With the contribution-based system, the true value of the job can more readily be identified and the appropriate action taken.

The format of job descriptions will vary widely depending on the uses to which the descriptions will be put. The following steps and discussion can serve as a guide for job descriptions to be used for evaluations and general wage and salary administration.

Job title. As already mentioned, titles can be a problem. There are jobs in the company which need special or extra titles, primarily for customer edification. It's natural for employees to choose titles they like—and quite difficult to keep them from doing this. If the sales representative calls himself marketing director and gets in to see a purchasing agent and makes a sale as a result of that title, would it be correct or even wise to strip him of that title? By developing a classification system which serves as a basis of pay determination, companies can permit, if not necessarily encourage, employees to call themselves whatever they want to on their correspondence, desks, business cards, and pajamas. As a CEO once said to me, "Look at it this way, you're not going to stop it, so why beat your head against a wall? *Classify* them however you want to, but let 'em tell their friends anything!"

Another titling decision that must be reached is whether the functional adjective should precede the title or follow it. For instance, which is the better listing of a job, "Accounting Manager" or "Manager, Accounting"? There are advantages and disadvantages to each. Each organization will need to determine the better approach for its needs. Remember that the title should be succinct and descriptive of the job. The more distinct, the better. Titles do cost money, contrary to general belief. There is a tendency to *pay up* to the title. The title should be realistic and bear some relation to the organizational structure.

Summary. After the description has been written, a brief summary that catches the full flavor of the job is written. In some cases, readers will get all the information they need from the summary; in others the summary will lead them to read the description in greater detail.

Job data. This is the major portion of the description, and it should be arranged for easy reading. It is not an entry in a prose contest, nor is it a product specification. It should have life, but it must be succinct. The method by which the data is obtained will determine the format of this section. For example, if the compensable factor technique is used, each compensable factor will need to be identified, with a corresponding paragraph or line indicating the manifestation of that compensable factor in the job.

There are certain rules for writing effective job descriptions:

List duties in a logical sequence. Avoid numbering them. Numbers alongside points have little value. They suggest that the first item is the most important, and the last item least important. This is not necessarily the case. Moreover, if the points are numbered, there may be a tendency to have the same number of points for all jobs, even though some jobs may require fewer points and some may require more.

State separate duties clearly and concisely. Some jobs will have a number of similar activities or responsibilities. Even though they are similar, these items should be mentioned as separate points so that they will be noticeable to the reviewer.

◆ Begin each sentence with an action verb. By doing this, the style will not only be consistent but the tone of the job will become evident.

◆ Use quantitative terms where possible. Such a technique lends itself to greater objectivity and clarity.

◆ Use specific rather than vague terms. There is an urge to resort to vague generalities in an effort to be all-inclusive. The writers need to examine everything they have written and to see if they have really said what they intended to say. A good test is to have an associate read and review the description to see if the information is properly communicated.

◆ Answer the questions of how, what, who, when, and why. This will make for a complete job description.

Job data files. The retention of job collation data can be as important as the initial phase of gathering it. The data should be retained as carefully as an attorney or an accountant retains background information. One way to turn an accountant's hair white is to tell him that his backup data has been destroyed. Similarly, an attorney needs the data preparatory to a suit in order to review the evolution of the issue. Many times analysts will look at an old job description and find that parts of it seem curious in light of what the job makeup is. If they have background information, they may find the answers to why the job description is the way it is.

The retention of the data begins with the request for the job description. If the description is the result of a start-up of a program, the reason for this is obvious. Let us instead concern ourselves with jobs introduced after the program has been installed. The request for a job description and/or job evaluation may be in official form, or it may be simply a note or a telephone call. At any rate there should be some evidence of the transaction. It can be a handwritten note, dated, and saying, "M. T. Noggin, head of accounting, called and wants his clerk's job rewritten and reappraised," or this information can be put on a special form, which some companies provide. Each is effective for establishing the need and the date of that need.

The data which resulted from the research of the job should become part of the file on the job. Later, such data will help the analyst to recall the situation in which the job was located and the type of reports that were generated.

The first draft of the description will be the most spontaneous reflection of the job as perceived by the writer. After the first draft, there will be many influences which will alter the subsequent versions. It will be interesting to see what was included in the first draft that was deleted in later copies. It will be found that the first draft reflected the best account of the job. Frequently, the final draft and the first draft bear a great resemblance to each other, with interim drafts varying considerably. This curious phenomenon simply shows how many persons will become involved, influence what's going on, but eventually the original facts will surface. The monitoring of the description through its several drafts is a lesson in patience. Each draft should be kept in the file, even after the final copy is approved by whoever is charged with that responsibility.

Pricing action. The final item in the file should be the pricing action taken. The form reflecting the pricing action becomes a vital document for completing the story on the position status. Such a form will contain a record of the evaluation points, by compensable factor, the total points, the conversion into the grade structure, job holder's average salary data, market data, participants in the evaluation process, cognizant management approvals, and the date of action. This data becomes very critical to the successful maintenance of a system. The filer should get into the habit of fastening these several items securely in the file. A loose file permits data to be lost or released inadvertently.

It will be found that the manila folder in which this data is secured will serve the analyst and future analysts in good stead in the continued administration and maintenance of the wage and salary program.

· 15 ·

Surveys

It is more important to do the right thing than to do things right.
PETER DRUCKER
The Effective Executive

WITH a great deal of effort, based in logic, the analysts have produced a job evaluation system in which there is internal integrity. The environment in which it was conceived and nurtured is a controlled one, in the sense that the forces that influence the development of the system are known and understood. Now, having lived through the adventure, the analysts raise themselves up to look at the outside world. There, they find forces which are not readily understandable. In the outside world, supply and demand rule with an iron hand. Cold economics dictate policy and much of what happens in the labor market. These forces must be reckoned with, and some semblance of order must be introduced so that the internal scheme of the evaluation system can be integrated with the scheme of the outside world. How to do it? The answer is to conduct surveys to obtain labor market data.

There are three types of surveys: job comparison, maturity curve, and evaluative projection.

The job comparison is probably the most frequently used survey, and yet it is the worst of the three. Survey data is costly to obtain. Therefore, analysts must try to maximize the data validity they get with a minimum of expense. There are three ways to obtain labor market data in the job comparison method: secure data from other sources, conduct one's own survey, or have a consultant conduct a survey.

The first, securing already published survey data, is probably the cheapest but also the least satisfying. The labor market and related survey data are divided into at least two groups—exempt positions found in the national market and nonexempt jobs found in the local market. At least two grade structures are necessary to accommodate these two major groupings of jobs. Although the exempt employee is primarily a product of the national (and international) market, there are some jobs at the lower end of the exempt categories which are more locally oriented. Such jobs include foreman, first-line supervisor and various administrative jobs. The total grade structure for the exempt jobs should reflect the pay practice of the total labor market, since it is to the total labor market that the employees look for growth, opportunity, and equity. By the same token, although the labor market for the nonexempt job is the local market, the term "local" has different meanings. Production and maintenance jobs may be restricted to a neighborhood market. Holders of such jobs are inclined to consider jobs in close proximity to their living quarters, usually in order to keep commutation costs to a minimum. Office and technical employees, because of their pay patterns, will consider the entire metropolitan complex as their labor market. Technicians and draftsmen have been considered to be part of a regional labor market, but studies show that salaries paid nonexempt technical jobs *do not vary* among regions, and these workers are becoming more mobile within any region.

The advantages of job comparison surveys are numerous. There are many surveys available that do not require participation in order to obtain the data. Those that require participation tend to be more valid for the surveyee's purposes. Job comparison surveys are a traditional survey method, and so they meet with little resistance. When a surveyor approaches a surveyee, the normal pattern is to exchange data based on job descriptions. The surveyor needs very little training to elicit the relevant information from the surveyee. Even without job descriptions to refer to, data on job content can be exchanged and understood. The format and techniques for collating and computing job comparison data are fairly simple and require minimal use of statistics.

The disadvantages of job comparison surveys are few but overwhelming. The basis of job comparison surveys is that data is exchanged on like jobs, yet job comparability is rarely if ever achieved! When job descriptions are used for the basis of exchange, each participant has a job description that is peculiar to that organization. Very few organizations have similar job descriptions. Furthermore, each job description is written by a different person with a different job in mind in a different organization with different employees. It really is a wonder that any comparability occurs at all! When jobs are compared, each analyst tries to reckon with the subjectivity of job con-

tent found in the others' job data. Some compromises are made, acknowl-
edgments of differences are offered, and concessions suggested. After these
subjective negotiations are made, each analyst dutifully reports the salary
data. Salary data must be reported very objectively. A salary is not reported
as about $950 per month; it is reported as exactly $952. Yet the basis of that
objective report is some very subjective data. The humorous thing is that the
surveyor who arrives at that figure treats it as if it were sacred. The figure is
there in irrefutable, uncompromisable black and white—Engineer,
$952. But the very basis of the job comparison survey is job comparability,
and since this is seldom achieved, the data resulting from such a survey is
not valid.

There are many sources of job comparison data for exempt positions.
The granddaddy of them all is the AMA Executive Compensation Service.
The data contained in these books is valid but conservative. If you want to
show employees how overpaid they are, show them the AMA data. Realize,
however, what you are doing. AMA data is good data, but if your salaries
don't compete with AMA salaries, your company may begin to lose some of
its employees to higher paying organizations. The AMA data is relatively
easy to read because it is not highly technical. The analyst can pick out specific salaries paid in durable or nondurable goods, by size of organization
and by geographic region. General job descriptions also are available for
easy comparison.

The Labor Department publishes considerable data for a number of key
jobs. The data in its *National Survey of Administrative and Technical Positions* has been the standard for many years. The data in these sources have
led to public positions being paid more than their counterparts in private industry.

Various consulting firms collect salary data as an adjunct to their client
work. Hewit, Inc., has Project 777, an elite survey of executive positions.
TPFC has a new survey competing with ORC's SIRS survey. A. S. Hansen
produces the Phillip Weber survey, which is primarily for use in electronic
data processing jobs. Robert Sibson compiles executive salary data, as does
McKinsey & Company. Various consultants specializing in serving specific
industries have salary survey data available. Cole Associates serves the financial community, the U.S. Savings and Loan League has data for the savings
and loan industry. The insurance industry is served by the Life Under-
writers' Survey.

Professional associations also compile salary data for their members. It is
this data that is plunked down on the analyst's desk to show how underpaid a
particular employee is, compared with survey data from the employee's association. Although much of the data of the professional associations is a valid

reflection of the market in which their members compete, there are certain biases that may exist. The members polled by the association are those that not only remained in the field but have been successful enough to retain membership in the association. Knowing the use to which the data will be put, it's conceivable that some of the members polled will exaggerate their responses or in some instances misrepresent the data. For instance, they may report total compensation instead of salary, when it was salary that was requested. Others may simply misunderstand the questionnaire and complete it incorrectly. Association data is usually on the high-pay side of survey data. It cannot be overlooked. But it must be remembered that in dealing with employees, we are dealing with their perceptions, right or wrong, no matter what the rationale or logic was that produced them. If a little information is dangerous, then compile all the information possible to get a much more realistic picture.

The nonexempt job market also abounds with data. Here, too, surveys are available that do not require participation in order to obtain the data. In addition, the AMA has one of the best sources for nonexempt salaries paid in many locations in the country. The Administrative Management Service (AMS) has for years published good data for many of its chapter cities around the country. The Bureau of Labor has published inexpensive though dated data on many metropolitan centers around the country. The Federal Reserve Bank has had considerable experience in publishing valid data. When nothing else can be found, the Chamber of Commerce in a town usually has some pertinent data. The reason that the Chamber of Commerce collects and distributes such data is to entice prospective industries to come to that town. Therefore, the data reported may present a lower rate of pay for labor than is actually to be found in that town.

Employment agencies in both exempt and nonexempt recruitment delight in reporting salary survey data. Since their revenues are based on the salary of those they place, the information that is reported may be biased, and must be used with caution.

The National Labor Relations Board ruling which declared that survey data used at the bargaining table must be shared by both sides of the table has changed the way many companies gather survey data. If the company collects the data, it must share all of it with its union negotiators. Such disclosure destroys the confidentiality under which most surveys are conducted. In view of this many companies have third parties perform the survey and report only the results. Such surveys have the advantage of being specially designed and done with no time lost on the part of the company. The cost incurred may even be less than the cost the company might have incurred by having its own employees compile the data.

The following is a comparative listing of the advantages and disadvantages of securing data from other sources, having a consultant conduct the survey, and conducting one's own survey.

A. *Using surveys purchased and/or participated in*

ADVANTAGES

Relatively inexpensive
Work involves only supplying own data and interpreting survey results
Companies less reluctant to provide data for top management and certain other jobs
Large number of participants
Easier to get statistically sound sample size (randomness may be a problem)
Professionally conducted and summarized

DISADVANTAGES

Not able to choose benchmark jobs
Not able to choose questions
Not able to choose effective date of data
May need to age survey data
Not able to choose time the survey is conducted
Not able to choose companies surveyed
Not able to identify individual company data
Not able to weight data according to relative importance of participants
May need to resummarize data tailored to own company's requirements
Need to interpret survey data

B. *Using a consultant*

ADVANTAGES

Consultant does most of the work
Consultant picks or helps pick benchmark jobs
Consultant chooses or helps choose questions
You choose effective date of data
You choose time to conduct survey
Consultant chooses or helps choose companies to survey
Easier to get companies to provide data for top management and certain other jobs
Easier to get statistically sound sample size (randomness may be a problem)
Able to identify each company's data
Able to weight data according to relative importance of participants

Professionally conducted, analyzed, and interpreted survey

Benefit from experience consultant has gained working with other companies similarly situated

Salary structure and job slotting recommendations more acceptable to top management

Implemented salary structure and job slottings more acceptable to employees affected

DISADVANTAGES

Cost

C. *Conducting one's own survey*

ADVANTAGES

You pick benchmark jobs
You choose questions
You choose effective date of data
You choose time to conduct survey
You choose companies to survey
Able to identify each company's data
Able to weight data according to relative importance

DISADVANTAGES

Time-consuming
Need to contact each prospective participant
Difficult to get companies to provide data for top management and certain other jobs
Difficult to get statistically sound sample size
Difficult to get random sample
Need to compute and summarize the data
Need to interpret data
Need to distribute the results

"When all else fails, read instructions," seems to be appropriate in discussing doing one's own survey. Conducting a survey takes much time, constancy of thought, perseverance, and continuity of action. When analysts decide to conduct their own labor market survey, there are several issues to be addressed at the outset. They are discussed in the following paragraphs.

♦ Determine manpower needs and availability in relation to the general economy. Don't go blindly into the market without first appraising through manpower planning and analysis. Such deliberation will prepare the surveyors to know the number of new employees, the types of new employees, and sequence of bringing in new employees. All bear on the type and urgency of the ultimate survey. Much attention has already been given to the need for awareness of the economy. The relation of GNP, unemployment, and supply of personnel to salaries are key to understanding of the data.

♦ The labor market cannot be defined simply as "our industry," "our size," or "our locale." The labor market, like the participants in it, has become much more cosmopolitan and even universal. No longer will a survey of salaries paid in one industry necessarily identify the market's going rate for all jobs. Surveys must be conducted in the companies, locales, and industries in which the organization's resources are located. Determine the company's resources of talent. All that may be needed to do this is to review the application files.

♦ Although companies from which an organization attracts employees are frequently identified, perhaps the more critical organizations are not identified, through simple defaults. This reference is to the companies to which an organization *loses* employees. These organizations are more critical, and yet they are frequently omitted. This is probably due to the fact that their names are not so obvious. They can't be found in some easy reference, such as on application forms. They are known by the managers of the departed employees, however, and also by the peers of the departed. This is invaluable input, and it is waiting to be tapped.

♦ Determine the dimension compatibility of the companies you intend to survey. In general, larger organizations pay higher salaries. This is truer, the higher the job is in the organization. Managerial and executive pay are a function of volume expressed in sales, assets, or premiums.

In larger organizations it will be found that similarly titled jobs have reduced breadth and greater specialization. This makes job comparison more difficult, and suggests another drawback to the job comparison survey, since it's difficult to "factor" such jobs to make the exchange of salary information meaningful. To reduce this distortion, job comparability surveys are best conducted in organizations that are similar in size.

♦ Determine the mobility and geographic scope of the labor market. Do not assume that your organization's employees can be recruited from any specific market. More and more jobs are becoming mobile with the changing life styles and greater mobility of the labor force. One company contended that draftsmen were a statewide market because they had "fallen in love with the license plate" and wouldn't move out of their state for any reason. Such an inane statement reveals the provincialism that still abounds in small-minded compensation administrators. A technical company was convinced that it could satisfy its total needs for accountants with graduates from the local college. It recruited for other exempt jobs on the national market, but strictly on the local market for accountants. It was pointed out to the company that even if it got all the accountants needed from the local college, it might get better candidates if it searched a little more broadly. As an aside, it should be noted that the company's financial department was a mess. This blind spot can occur in any organization.

The exempt job is a function of the national market, and therefore a national survey should be done to determine a rate structure. There are some practical exceptions. Some parts of the country are naturally more pleasant to live in than others. When the economy goes sour in those Edenic places, the people are compelled to support their habit of eating and are forced to accept employment elsewhere. When economic conditions improve back in Eden, these newly acquired employees hop the first "want ad" back, and the company has lost lots of money in the process. For some companies in areas that are deemed less desirable by the outsiders, the labor market is really a confused one. Such organizations make a practice of tracking native sons and daughters as they go through college and into employment. Native sons and daughters frequently like to return home. The salaries paid back home must be competitive, however; otherwise, these children won't be so homesick. Often the "home" company will err and consider that "native" is spelled n-a-i-v-e. Going away from home puts more than just the "t" in the native son and daughter. They come home with new expectations, and the "back home" organization had better live up to them.

In identifying the labor market, the socioeconomic considerations offered by the organization must be taken into account. Many organizations pay less than the competition because of other factors that make up for pay. Location near a college or cultural or recreational facilities may be compensating factors. Obviously, economic conditions are important. Rapid transportation and the rapid exchange of information have reduced the differences in cost of living around the United States. In fact, some lower cost of living areas are experiencing accelerated increases in living expenses as they catch up with the high-cost areas. Salaries are competitive with other salaries, not with cost of living. Do not be unduly influenced by the supposed cost of living that exists in the organization location. Employees moving to low-cost areas still experience increased costs because they inevitably increase their own standards of living, often without their even knowing it. Salary competition is the only valid means of basing salary structures, not cost of living.

◆ Determine industry relevancy. Traditional surveys are run constantly and have become institutions unto themselves. In many instances they have outlived their usefulness because employees are no longer bound by industry ties. More and more employees are switching from private sector to public sector, and vice versa. Change is much more universal. The product market has a more meaningful influence on industry surveys, in that no company can afford to price itself out of the product market by paying inordinately high salaries and increasing labor costs. Try to achieve a balance between industry participants and nonindustry participants.

◆ Determine management's position regarding "competitiveness." Just what does "competitiveness" mean? The word is like motherhood, apple pie, and the American flag. Its meaning is in the mind of the individual. To some, it means paying the *same* as the market dictates. To others, it means paying *less* than the market and taking into account the several "intangibles." To others, it means to lead the market and be a leader in pay practices. Management itself seldom knows what it means by this term; it needs to be told. Don't be like one compensation administrator who sat on his hands and waited for "management" to determine what competitiveness means. The compensation administrator *is* management and should advise other levels of management of what positions they may take regarding the labor market—with strong recommendations as to which position is right for the organization. Compensation administrators should not wait for such direction, they should be able to give it.

◆ Determine the expectations of the survey, its goals, and its objectives. Compensation administrators usually have a féeling about the market in which their organizations compete. These expectations should be identified so that the survey will either confirm or deny them. Should compensation administrators feel that their organizations are paying less than they should but that there are compensating factors, they had better identify these factors and attempt to survey them. If benefits are lagging, they had better survey benefits. Compensation administrators should determine just what they're trying to accomplish through the survey.

◆ Determine the format, reporting techniques, and extent of disclosure to management, employees, and surveyees. At an early point, compensation administrators have to determine how they are going to ask for data that will lend itself to good presentations. Further, they should determine how much is enough data to report to management, how much can be revealed to employees, and what data will be returned to the survey participants. They should know the formats of such reports so that the turnaround time is kept to a minimum. If the surveyors are lucky, they'll be swamped with data that needs organizing. Panic can be avoided if surveyors organize the formats of questions and duties of the staff in handling the data *beforehand.*

The greatest advantage in conducting your own survey is that you will be able to obtain salary data stated in terms of your system. The format for the survey is pretty much up to you. Remember, however, that by getting data from other companies, you are imposing on companies and their administrators, and they don't have to cooperate. Be emphatic, design the format for greatest usability, but keep in mind the needs of the surveyees as well. Keep the survey as short and simple as possible while still meeting your objectives. If you permit your survey to be too long, you will have difficulty in getting participants. You'll find that they have planned to be out of town on the day that you're coming. It's not your mouthwash, it's your survey!

The heart of the survey is the selection of the jobs themselves. There is frequently a mention of key jobs or benchmark jobs. These are jobs which are common to the marketplace or are of significant impact in your company to warrant market status. Usually, a survey will concern itself with exempt positions or nonexempt positions, not both. If data for both groups is not handled by the same person, completion of the survey may be delayed. Other differences in labor markets for exempt and nonexempt jobs, discussed earlier, also make it preferable to limit a survey to one of these groups.

·16·

Conducting the Survey

A minister, a doctor, and a consultant, adrift on a raft, sighted a distant island. There were signs of human habitation, but no persons in view. Since the drift was away from the island, the consultant volunteered to swim ashore and bring help. Just as he was about to dive into the sea, the minister urged a word of parting prayer, so a brief religious service was held.

Eagerly the two remaining voyagers watched their companion. Presently they were horrified to see a huge shark making directly for the consultant. At the last moment, however, the shark veered away and the swimmer was saved. Later, another shark came into view and he, too, veered sharply away when he came close to the struggling man.

"There!" said the minister triumphantly. "Observe an answer to our prayers. Because of that service we held, the Lord has preserved our friend from the hungry sharks."

"Well, that may be," said the doctor dubiously, "but personally I'm inclined to think of it as professional courtesy."

THE selection of survey jobs is always a challenging task. The validity of the whole survey may depend on them. They must satisfy employees and management alike that the survey and its findings are credible. They should be found in the surveyees' organizations in sufficient numbers to yield good, substantial data. They should provide facts for a distribution of data from low-level jobs to high-level jobs. They should also be representative of the several jobs found in the surveyor's organization, so that most if not all segments of the company can be satisfied. The jobs should reflect the several skill levels found in the organization. For ease of review, the jobs should be grouped according to job families and other useful groupings.

These are the guidelines to be followed in selecting the jobs. Now, who should make the selection? The natural response from dedicated compensation administrators is that they should. It does seem reasonable to have such jobs selected by the persons responsible for conducting the survey. Consider something else. Suppose the survey has been completed. The analyst has used good judgment in selecting the jobs. The data is abundant and relevant. It lends itself to good display and suggests useful conclusions. Upon review of the results, management and/or the employees find fault with the jobs surveyed. They may refute the entire survey and its results, and jeopardize the whole program. Instead of reason and logic, their perception of "what should have been done" prevails. How can this dilemma be avoided? Simply by having the key jobs selected by the management and/or employees in the first place. Armed with guidelines for key jobs, they can do as well or better in selecting key jobs, and there is one overwhelming benefit. They will be much more accepting of the resultant data. This is worth a great deal in the sensitive area of salary surveys. Does the compensation administrator give up something by permitting others to contribute in this way? The answer is a resounding no. In fact, the administrator gains in personal authority, the stuff good administrators are made of. The involvement of others in sensitive issues will enhance the success of the program and increase its acceptance, and everyone gains from the experience.

The number of jobs selected is important. Surveyors must be mindful of what they're trying to do. They want to determine the pay level of the labor market in which they compete. They are going to need enough data to make such a judgment. They know that the judgment is the result of statistical reasoning; that is, they must have enough data which reflects the market. The larger the sample surveyed, the greater the validity of the information collected. This fact might prompt them to include all or most of their jobs in order to obtain a large sampling of the market. They must be influenced by another consideration. If they approach surveyees with too many jobs to compare, they'll find the surveyees unwilling to participate. Too many jobs take too much time, and the surveyees are responding primarily to help the surveyors. What's more, if the surveyors covered all jobs, they would probably wind up with too much data to handle. Statistical needs and feasibility dictate that the number of jobs be large enough to render enough data points and small enough to encourage surveyees to participate. Is there a magic number? No, there is not; each situation dictates the best number. The least number of data points from which to draw any conclusions is 12. If there are 12 jobs, each with sufficient numbers of employees and salaries reported, surveyors can make some conclusions.

Also critical are the particular organizations to be surveyed. The inclusion or exclusion of organizations in the survey as decided by either employee or management may lead to a lack of acceptance of the data and the program. To prevent such dissatisfaction, both employees and management should be involved in the selection of surveyees. Both management and employees are well aware of the labor market competitors. A manager may have lost two employees just recently to a particular company that must be offering something. What is it? Include the company in the survey and find out. Employees can be asked not only from which organizations they come, but, more important, to what organizations they are attracted.

Whether the organizations are chosen by the compensation administrator, the management, or the employees, there are some guidelines for the selection process. An obvious must is that the surveyee have jobs which are either similar to those found in the surveyor or require similar skills. Each surveyee must have sufficient numbers of jobs for comparison in order to make his participation worthwhile. This precludes heeding the request of special interest groups. For example, accountants in a manufacturing company might ask that surveyees include some of the "big eight" CPA firms. However, while there would be accountants to survey in such firms, there would be few, if any, other exempt jobs to survey. A trip to a firm with so few jobs to compare is not feasible. The surveyee must have data available to share.

One of the most troublesome choices for survey is an up-and-coming employer that either has no personnel person with whom to compare data or that has data that is so unorganized as to be meaningless. The surveyee representative must have access to and authorization for sharing survey data. Too often even in these times administrators or their management are unwilling to cooperate in surveys. The development of contacts among surveyees is vital to the formation and continuance of a compensation system. The more similarities that exist between the companies, the better the results. Such similarities include size, population mix between long-time versus short-time employees, old versus young population, with similar pressures and problems. If a surveyee is different in any of these particulars, it shouldn't automatically be excluded. The critical issue for inclusion is, Is this company competing with us for labor? If the answer is yes, the company must be included.

All other considerations are just that—considerations. If companies are inordinately large, their numbers can be factored to reduce their impact through the modified weighted average discussed in Chapter 17. Some arguments are heard about companies with high turnovers or with aged populations or with employees who have long tenure and who therefore are likely to be highly paid. These differences between companies will always be found, so many analysts factor this data to reduce the bias. This is the main issue: if these companies with old population, young population, short tenure, high tenure, or other dissimilarities compete for the surveyor's labor, they must be taken into account. They represent the market, and to discount them or exaggerate their influence reduces the credibility of the survey.

Compensation information, whether it be wages, salaries, benefits, or whatever, is sensitive. Jobs have been lost because of careless handling of the data. The compromise of the data is intolerable in most organizations, yet the surveyor must try to exchange this highly sensitive data. The day may come when there is universal posting of this kind of data, but until then the exchange must be done with care. The contacts one can develop are crucial. They may be local administrators or those found in the industry around the country. The more contacts, the more opportunities to exchange compensation data. Meetings, seminars, visits—all contribute to the development of contacts. The more data that is exchanged, the better salary structures will be. It has been said that such an exchange is inflationary and that as a result of such an exchange, salary structures go higher. The movement of structures is not inflationary, it is the distribution of pay within those structures that causes inflation. Inflation results from pay being issued where productivity gains are lacking. The performance appraisal program is the culprit behind inflation, not structure movement. In a free economy structure movement must remain the device to enable organizations to attract and retain productive employees. The means by which such productivity is rewarded is another issue (see Chapter 12).

The exchange of salary structure information must also continue to be one of the means for companies to compete in a free economy. It is doubtful that collusion on the part of companies to keep pay down will ever occur in a free economy. Companies are too competitive to permit this to happen. Each organization wants to be a little better than its competitor, in quality or price. This is gained through better-quality employees who usually demand greater compensation, and thereby sustain the company's competitive urge.

In some industries, obtaining and supplying data have practically become institutionalized. Such a state of banality can contribute to a meaningless survey in which comparisons are not valid. It must be remembered that the validity of this type of survey is predicated on job comparability; without it, the survey is meaningless. When a survey exchange has reached the point of being a rote procedure, it behooves the participants to review the situation carefully before perpetuating it.

At the other extreme are industries in which the exchange of compensation data is unheard of. This is usually found in old industries in which the heads of the organization are complacent about such matters or in industries in which there is no one assigned to handle such an exchange. In these instances, a communication to the surveyee's CEO may be in order. Protocol suggests that such a letter come from a peer in the surveyor company, but this is not always necessary.

There are still some compensation administrators who don't have license to exchange data unless specifically authorized to do so. One would think that persons selected for the delicate and worthy task of compensation administration would have been chosen for their good judgment and objectivity. These qualities are essential for the position. Along with the position should come full access to the pay information about all jobs in the company and the authority to deal with that data. A company that authorizes less is not getting its money's worth. And compensation administrators who accept less will feel their freedom to do their best job severely limited.

It behooves every surveyor to develop contacts to further the exchange of compensation data. Depending on the data and its formality, requests can be either by phone or by letter. Although the former is quicker and cheaper, the latter is generally preferred, especially if there is a large quantity of data to be exchanged or if the contact is not well established. The quantity of data to be exchanged also dictates whether the survey questions should be sent to the surveyee ahead of the surveyor's visit, or whether the surveyor should present the questions at the time of the visit.

Sometimes, the survey questions may be left with the surveyee after the surveyor has explained them. The problem with sending the questions to the surveyee before the surveyor's visit is that they may remain in the surveyee's "in" box until the surveyor arrives, which cancels out any advantage that may have been gained by sending the material in advance. The problem with leaving the material with the surveyee after the surveyor's visit is that follow-up visits, phone calls, or letters may be needed to get the data returned to the surveyor. The success of the study often depends on the degree the contact has been developed before the survey is made and the simplicity of the survey. If the survey is long, it may never be completed. There is often a tendency on the part of the surveyor to include many items on the survey "as long as I've got the opportunity" to get some data. The survey can collapse of its own weight, and caution should be exercised in the design of the survey. The surveyor should be sympathetic to the needs of the surveyee. Only the data necessary to the success of the program should be solicited. The surveyors should not be greedy or too academic in their approach.

What is essential data? Very little has been said about the "benefits" portion of the compensation package. A survey of the several benefits and their myriad differences is interesting, but it is very cumbersome. Such data is relevant to the design of the benefits, however. If the interest in benefits is more than just academic, surveyors would better spend their and the surveyees' efforts by asking a summary-type question such as "What percentage of total payroll is your benefit package?" The response to this may complement the "cash" portion of the wage and salary information obtained. If this approach is used, it may be necessary to make a list of the items to be included in the benefits portion. The surveyor may make the list or use as reference the list of benefits included in a standard survey such as that published by the U.S. Chamber of Commerce.

For recall, collating, reporting, and display purposes the *title of the corresponding job* surveyed is essential. More than just a reference point, it serves as a guide for nomenclature and structuring. It may also be helpful in the establishment of new titles in the surveyor's organization.

Of all the data obtained, the *average pay* assigned to the surveyed job is the most important. While some may like to use median pay, the average is more universally used as a measure of central pay tendency. However, the median pay is extremely helpful to have because averages do have a way of being influenced by a few inordinately high- or low-salaried employees.

The *number of employees* in the job surveyed is useful in weighted average computations the surveyor may wish to make.

The *highest and lowest pay* is also useful information because it establishes the degree to which the surveyee is putting the pay range into actual practice. The *pay range* with the corresponding minimum, midpoint, and maximum suggests the value the surveyee has placed on the job surveyed. With the data above, the extent to which the pay practice is controlled can also be determined. The surveyor should never be content to receive only pay-range data. Pay-range data is not very sensitive, so surveyees tend to offer it freely while they withhold other, more useful data. In fact, pay-range data may be largely irrelevant in that the employees may be paid with little respect to the range to which they are assigned. What employees are actually being paid is the crux of the matter, not what the surveyee thinks they should be paid. Actual data, not opinion, reflects the market.

Helpful information includes the *compa-ratio* of the jobs surveyed with respect to the range to which they are assigned. The compa-ratio will be discussed in greater detail in a later chapter.

Although not essential to a survey of exempt jobs, the *normal workweek duration* is essential to a nonexempt survey. It can no longer be assumed that the normal workweek is forty hours. There are many variations, and there is a tendency for greater flexibility in the number of hours in the workweek. Pay reported on an other then standard workweek can easily be arithmetically factored to be compatible with other data.

Especially in the lower, entry-level jobs, the *starting pay* or the hiring rate may be of interest to some surveyors. This would be especially true if an employer was creating a structure for a new labor market and needed information on prevailing starting rates.

On occasion employers have *special or unusual compensating factors* which influence the pay practice. Technically "fringe benefits," such factors may include housing, free meals, company product discounts, and other intangible privileges. Knowledge of such perquisites may help the surveyor to understand the pay practice of the surveyee.

The *age and tenure* of the employees are frequently a major consideration in a survey. If pay data reported is high, it may be explained by the fact that the surveyee's company has an aged population. Highly paid or not, the employees are a part of the labor market, and so the pay data is valid as is. How much would surveyors factor it if they thought it did present a bias? What age of the employees warrants special treatment? The same question can be asked about tenure considerations. Even with these questions, surveyors may find it useful to know the age and tenure of the surveyed company's employees.

Turnover data is of similar interest. If the turnover is high, the pay may be too low; if the turnover is very low or nonexistent, the pay may be too high. The analyst has no means of factoring the information, but such information augments the statistical data received.

The *date and amount* of the most recent or expected pay structure change are indicative of how the surveyee perceives the structure in relation to the company's labor market. Such clues are helpful in the design of the surveyor's ranges.

The practice in the surveyee's company regarding *average percentage annual increase* and also the number or *percentage of employees receiving that increase* will help the surveyor to draw up salary administration guides.

The initiation of the survey communication is vital in securing the cooperation of the surveyee. Whether it is done by phone, personal contact or written message, the following items should be stressed: Be sure to state *why you want the survey data*. For purposes of developing, a compensation program is a worthy need, and most respondents will be willing if not anxious to render assistance. Further, indicate that you are in the process of *developing a structure* and you need comparisons with the labor market. This should allay the fears of the prospective surveyee that you are trying to set up a means of pirating his people. The number of jobs that you will survey will be of significance to the surveyee. *Keep that number reasonable.* Remember the surveyee is doing you a favor. If the number of jobs is too large, the surveyee will not be as eager to help. Let the potential surveyee know the organizations that will be asked to participate in the survey, explaining that they will be similar to the surveyee's company in size and industry. Furthermore, the data will be carefully collated and a report of its contents will be sent to each of the participants. Assure the surveyee that the data submitted will be kept in the strictest confidence, and that no company will be identified with individual data in the report. Whether the survey is sent ahead of time and followed with a visit from the surveyor or the information is left with the surveyee to complete is up to the style of the surveyor. Monitor the progress of your survey data collection. Make follow-up letter or phone requests for data that is late or still outstanding. Establish reasonable but firm due dates and acknowledge the receipt of data promptly. Most important, compile the data diligently and carefully. Report your findings to the surveyees promptly. This is a normal courtesy, and if you ever intend to knock on their doors again, it behooves you to be prompt, professional, cordial, and forthright.

· 17 ·

The Maturity Curve
and the Evaluative
Projection Approaches

Chauncey M. Depew confessed that he warned his nephew not to invest $5,000 in Ford stocks because "nothing new has come along to beat the horse."

THUS far we've discussed one type of survey, the job comparison method. It is the most frequently used but has the serious drawback of being dependent upon the degree to which job comparability has been accomplished. Without job comparability, the data exchanged is suspect, if not downright worthless. The problem is that while the salary data exchanged is expressed in discrete values or numbers that are perfectly understandable, the basis of that exchange is one of subjectivity, job descriptions. No two jobs are exactly alike, especially in different organizations. Organization structures, products, and employees all differ from organization to organization.

The maturity curve survey. The engineering profession, known for its predilection for quantification of concepts, has developed the maturity curve survey, which is quantifiable not on one axis, as with job comparability survey, but on both axes. One axis reports dollars, similar to job comparability, but the other axis, the X-axis, reports an element of time, usually years since acquiring bachelor's degree. Both axes are quantifiable. The objectivity of such a method appeals to the scientific natures of technical personnel.

The maturity curve system became very popular in the fifties and sixties primarily in companies that handled defense contracts due to the large numbers of technical persons. The proponents of the system hail its simplicity and quantifiability. The opponents feel it is too easy. They point to the time axis and state that time is not a worthy component of a person's worth. They do not feel that just by getting older, one is worth more. They add that the maturity curve is not specific enough to help them price out the engineers in their particular organization. A retort to this last comment is that engineers of a certain discipline are equipped to work on many if not all jobs that require that particular discipline. For instance, they maintain that electronic engineers working on electronic components in a missile system can transfer their knowledge to work on electrical components in toys. What's more, the electronic engineer is competing in the labor market with all electronic engineers. Maturity curves can be found for most of the disciplines in several industries and by areas of the country. Should an organization become too enamored with the maturity curve system and use it for establishing specific pay rates for individuals, it need only recall the law on age discrimination. Pay becomes a function of age on the maturity curve and therefore is illegal. Two sources of maturity curve information are the Battelle Memorial Institute, an Atomic Energy Commission organization, and the Engineering Joint Council. Both distribute maturity curves. The obvious limitation of the maturity curve approach as a survey device is that it can only be used with technical jobs. A similar survey of nontechnical persons was once done. The vertical axis was salary, the horizontal axis was age. There was little acceptance of the survey, and it disappeared. There is no maturity curve approach used for nontechnical jobs. One reason is that there is no common level or discipline for nontechnical jobs. Whereas for technical maturity, engineering is the base discipline, there is no common discipline for nontechnical jobs. Even in the field of accounting, for which there is an obvious preparatory discipline, there are many practitioners who don't have the basic college degree and, therefore, it would probably be difficult to use a maturity curve approach to survey the field. One of the difficulties of the maturity curve is in placing practitioners on the curve who do not have the basic college degree. What is equivalent to four years of college? Some companies using this system use a 2:1 ratio. That is, one year of college is worth two years of experience. Even in technical circles, this ratio doesn't hold true. If it can't be done with the technical fraternity, imagine the difficulty in arriving at some conclusion with the administrative employees throughout the country.

The maturity curve approach has disadvantages, as we've seen. These include its limitation to technical jobs, the age discrimination component, and the equivalency problem. The main advantage of the system is the objectivity and quantification of both axes. In that aspect it is far superior to the job comparability approach.

The evaluative projection survey. Developing something which takes advantage of the good points of previous designs is the way of progress. The evaluative projection approach to surveys is just that. It has the quantification advantage of the maturity curve approach, but it is not limited to technical jobs nor dependent on time or education for one of its axes. It has the advantage of the job comparison survey approach because it can be used for all jobs in an organization, but it is not dependent on achieving job comparability.

The evaluative projection approach reverts to the basic premise of pricing in relating internal equity with external equity. The common denominator for such an integration is the evaluative system. The point evaluation system, developed to achieve internal relationships and equity, can be used or projected into other companies, the surveyees, to achieve external equity. Both axes are objective and quantifiable. The vertical axis, the Y-axis, is quantifiable in dollars. The horizontal axis, the X-axis, is quantifiable in evaluation points.

The process is obvious, and yet even though it establishes a great deal of integrity, it is an approach seldom taken. The reason for this is that the evaluation plan must be simple and have universal compensable factors. It must be simple enough to enable a surveyee compensation administrator to use it with a minimum of instruction. The system will evaluate the jobs in the surveyee's company, which is why the compensable factors must be applicable. The compensable factors for both exempt and nonexempt jobs discussed in Chapter 9 lend themselves to the evaluative projection approach. Data is gathered, a scatter diagram is created, and a line of central tendency reveals the labor market. The factoring of job content that is sought in job comparison surveys is done through the process of evaluation in evaluative projection.

The procedure for such a survey is simple. The surveyors inform the surveyees that they would like to exchange salary data based on evaluated points for the surveyors' jobs using the surveyors' system. No job descriptions are necessary, but they may be used to assist the surveyees in evaluating the jobs. It is not necessary to exchange job descriptions. It is suggested that a number of commonly found key jobs be used, but the job descriptions and their variations are not critical to the successful exchange of data.

The surveyors show the surveyees how to use the surveyors' evaluation system. If it is simple and universally based, the learning process is short. Once the surveyees are fairly competent at using the evaluation plan, they can proceed to use it to evaluate the jobs found in their organizations. The more jobs evaluated, the larger the sample and the more valid the survey. As the jobs are evaluated, the salaries paid for those jobs can be shared. Whereas a job in the surveyor organization may be evaluated at 1,000 points and paid, for example, $900, a similarly titled job in a surveyee organization may be evaluated at 1,050 points and paid $1,000. The dissimilarities have been factored by the evaluation system. The latter job, evaluated higher than the other, is paid higher than the other. By plotting this and other cumulative data on a scatter diagram and submitting the data to a line of central tendency, the market will be identified and the relationship that each surveyee has to it will be determined. At any point on the line of central tendency it can be determined how much should be paid any job with its corresponding points.

Should a surveyee require complete confidentiality, positions can be evaluated without being identified by more than job A or job B. In this way key, single incumbency jobs can be evaluated and salary data shared with utmost secrecy maintained.

Because differences result from the evaluation process, the number of positions or data points will be more than just the minimum number of points sought. For instance, in an attempt to evaluate 15 common key jobs, it is likely that 100 data points will result, due to the differences identified through the evaluation system. Such an increased sample increases the validity of the survey and its findings.

If there is a continued desire to match job for job, the process accommodates this because it makes it possible to discern the differences between the jobs. Job comparison is an optional adjunct to the process.

Data compiled in this way lends itself to the important decision-making process involved in competitiveness. The line of central tendency *is* the labor market. By comparing the company's pay line to it, the competitive status can be determined in quantifiable terms. It would be a coincidence if the company's line were perfectly parallel to the market line, but percentages can be computed at any point along the line to determine the difference.

Because of sensitivity to the labor market, most companies will choose to develop their line superimposed over the labor market line. Under certain circumstances, such as with fringe benefits, a company may elect to lag behind the market line. If the company wants to lead the market, it can elect to exceed the market line. Whatever seems appropriate for the organization will become apparent through the evaluative projection approach to market surveys.

One last comment on this approach. The reason that organizations haven't used this approach is that (1) they have not developed a plan simple enough to use the surveyee's organization, and (2) they have not developed universally applicable compensable factors.

The Hay system survey is an evaluative projection method. It uses the Hay system points as the common denominator. The Hay Company collates the data submitted by its client companies, displays it by industry, and reports it back to its clients. The survey is limited to those companies using the Hay system and presumes that all Hay client companies have used the Hay system in a consistent manner. Herein lie two disadvantages. The surveyor may or may not want to limit the surveyees to Hay Company clientele, it may not want the data reported, or it may want to exclude some but not all companies reported in the industry survey. The other disadvantage to the survey is the vast presumption that the Hay system, a semantic system, is applied consistently by all compensation administrators in Hay client companies. The data is as good as the input to it, and although the survey report is beautifully presented, these are drawbacks to its use.

· 18 ·

Developing the Structure

He who does not tell the truth is likely to be found out, as the congregation of one country clergyman discovered.

"Folks," he said to his flock, "the subject of my sermon this evening is 'liars.' How many in the congregation have read the sixty-ninth chapter of Matthew?"

Nearly every hand in the congregation went up immediately.

"That's right," said His Reverence. "You're just the folks I want to preach to. There is no sixty-ninth chapter of Matthew."

THE analysis of data and the building of the structure are probably the least liked parts of compensation administration. Yet they needn't be. It does take time and careful deliberation to handle the data consistently and to make the necessary computations. For the most part, there are few difficult computations, but all require careful attention to details. Because of the similarities of the numbers worked with, it is easy to become confused and to make errors. When beginning this part of the program, it behooves compensation administrators to literally clear their desks of all other work. It would be ideal if they could escape to some hideaway for a few days while they worked on the data.

For the market-sensitive organization, there is a need to develop a trend line indicating the labor market around which to build a pay structure.

There are a few instances in which the organization would want to build its structure not about the market line, but about its own pay practice. This is called the "ostrich approach" because it is the equivalent of the ostrich sticking its head in the sand. This technique uses wages and salaries paid one's own employees on the Y-axis, against the evaluation points on the X-

181

axis. This ignores the market influence, although an organization's own employees are part of the market, and assumes that the company's pay practice is correct—often a grossly mistaken assumption.

One technical company took this approach because it couldn't afford to match the market. The president stuck his head in the sand and thought he'd save lots of money by building a structure around the salaries paid his own people. They were grossly underpaid by market standards, and he knew it. The result was that good employees were constantly leaving, the older employees were content to stay and remain at low productivity levels, and the few energetic ones that remained realized the way to beat the system was to have their jobs overclassified and so get into higher grades with higher salaries. Money was lost, productivity was low, and employees learned how to beat the system. The president who sticks his head in the sand does not have to see the changing world around him, but he makes his rear end a conspicuous target.

An instance where the ostrich approach may be appropriate would be the organization for which no labor market data is available. The only company in town or a truly unique set of jobs that cannot be matched would be such a case. Most of the time an organization wishes to be labor market sensitive and can locate labor market data. This is the situation dealt with here. Some terms that will be used in the discussion follow.

Grade/range—the parameters of dollars paid for an evaluated position. This suggests a minimum and a maximum worth. The midpoint of the range is halfway between the minimum and the maximum and normally relates to the market value of the jobs assigned to that range.

Range spread—the percentage depth from minimum to maximum. In exempt ranges this is usually 50 percent, that is, the maximum is 150 percent of the minimum. In nonexempt, nonbargained-for office and technical ranges, the range spread is 20 to 30 percent.

Midpoint progression—the difference between one midpoint and the next midpoint. The variance is usually from 5 to 15 percent with 10 percent being most typical.

Range overlap—the amount of the next range covered by the preceding range. A 10 percent midpoint progression will produce a 67 percent overlap, that is, two-thirds of the next grade will be covered by the preceding grade.

Conversion chart—the allocation of evaluation points to grades/ranges. A certain number of points will assign the evaluated job to a certain grade/range.

Before constructing the line, let's identify and define the terms to be used. All the terms reflect the typical or central tendency of data.

Average. The average, or mean, is found by totaling all items and dividing by the number of items. It is frequently called the "simple" average.

Median. The median is that number which is greater than one-half of the items and smaller than the other half.

Weighted average. The meaning of this term can best be conveyed by an example: Say you know that the average salary of a computer programmer in private industry is $16,000 and that the average salary of a computer programmer working in the public sector is $14,000. You cannot therefore conclude that the average salary of all computer programmers is $15,000. You must develop a weighted average, based on the number of programmers in each sector. The calculation would be made as follows:

$$\text{Weighted average} = \frac{(\$16,000)\begin{pmatrix} \text{no. of} \\ \text{programmers} \\ \text{in private sector} \end{pmatrix} + (\$14,000)\begin{pmatrix} \text{no. of} \\ \text{programmers} \\ \text{in public sector} \end{pmatrix}}{\begin{pmatrix} \text{no. of programmers} \\ \text{in private sector} \end{pmatrix} + \begin{pmatrix} \text{no. of programmers} \\ \text{in public sector} \end{pmatrix}}$$

Since there are more programmers in the private than the public sector, the weighted average would come out closer to $16,000 than to $14,000.

Modified weighted average. This is similar to the weighted average except that the data has been factored, or qualified, to reduce the influence of unusual populations. Again, an example should prove more enlightening than a definition. Suppose your survey (see the table) includes seven companies with varying populations, one of which (Company A) is unusually large.

COMPANY	EMPLOYEES	AVERAGE PAY	TOTAL PAY
A	55	$1.00	$ 55.00
B	11	1.10	12.10
C	9	1.50	13.50
D	9	1.50	13.50
E	7	1.60	11.20
F	7	1.20	8.40
G	7	1.20	8.40
	105		$122.10

The first thing to do is to calculate the average population of the seven companies, which is 15 (105 divided by 7). Because Company A's population is well over that average, it will be *factored down* to the average figure plus an arbitrary percentage (usually 10 percent) of the company's excess population. The excess population is 55 minus 15, or 40. Since 10 percent of 40 is 4, the factored population of Company A is 15 plus 4, or 19. The entry for Company A will now be changed to read:

Company	Employees	Average pay	Total pay
A	19	$1.00	$19.00

Of course, in surveys with unusually low populations, the data can be *factored up* in much the same way.

First-degree least-squares line. This line—often called the line of central tendency, regression line, or line of best fit—is arrived at either through trial and error or through a complicated mathematical procedure. The line represents an approximation of the central tendency of a group of scattered data, usually shown in graph form. When completed, the line is often referred to as the trend line around which the grade structure is developed.

The development of the trend line or policy line using the least squares method is about as much fun as filling out yearly tax forms for the IRS. If you have access to a computer, you will probably find a subroutine already worked out that requires only the input of the coordinates. Unless you really enjoy working with mathematical formulas, gaining access to a computer is suggested. There is another way to compute the policy line, however. In his book *Compensation Administration,* David Belcher refers to the freehand method.* Belcher, the "dean" of the wage and salary field, suggests that the freehand method approaches the accuracy of the formularized method to such a degree that it is perfectly workable. To make this point, Belcher would give his students data with which to compute the policy line using the formula. After doing so, he would give them the same data in a scattergram, not mentioning that it was the same data with which they had struggled the day before. He would ask the students to study the data and trace the central tendency of it visually. Then he would direct the students to freehand draw a line through the data. The lines drawn in this "eyeball" method very nearly approximated the lines developed the day before. Thus, his point was made. Under his tutelage, the "eyeball" method won many advocates. The analyst will find it very helpful to develop a trained eye to visualize the central tendency of data. It will become as easy as riding a bike and usually as accurate as working through the formula. Lines of central tendency become the hallmark of the analysts' work, and they need to acquaint themselves

---

* *Compensation Administration* (Englewood Cliffs, N.J.: Prentice-Hall, 1974), p. 262.

with techniques in working with data. The "eyeball" technique gives them another skill, informal perhaps, but a skill nevertheless.

Another means of developing a line of central tendency is used by some who feel it lends a little more professionalism or credibility to the establishment of the line. This method uses arithmetic. By finding the median point of X-axis data and plotting it with the median point of the Y-axis data, there is the beginning of a line. By finding the median point of the top half of the data on both axes and the median point of the bottom half of the data, two more points can be plotted on the chart. All of these should be in a straight line, indicating the central tendency of the data. This method should produce a line very similar if not identical to the trained "eyeball" line and that developed by the formula. Compensation administrators must exercise their judgment, and they will develop a line of central tendency that will be compatible with the needs of their company, employees, and management. Some may think it scandalous to submit objective data to the subjectivity of the eyeball technique. Others may feel the formula is too rigid and time-consuming. Acceptance of the data is the key issue. The method that enhances the acceptance of the data is the one that should be used. A highly technical group might not accept it if the "eyeball" technique produced the line which determines their salaries. Another, less fussy group might consider the "eyeball" technique good enough. Other than the development of the line itself, the only "heavy" arithmetic is in the design of the structure and its grades. This is a "recipe" kind of methodology which requires continuity of thought and a little arithmetic. The policy line will have been established. The organization through its management process or dart throwing (which may be one and the same) will have determined the degree of competitiveness desired.

The first issue to be addressed is, At what point in that line does the grading system begin and at what point does it end? It may be recalled that there is a policy line for the exempt positions and at least one for the nonexempt positions. The bottom "anchor" or beginning point on the exempt line is either the long-test (FLSA) salary requirement or the lowest marketable salary if it is higher than the FLSA long-test salary. The top "anchor" for the exempt structure will be the CEO's grade or the highest job that is to be included in the structure, both of which are established by market survey information.

The lowest point on the nonexempt policy line is the federal minimum wage or the lowest marketable job if it exceeds the minimum wage. The highest point will be determined by the highest marketable job. The analyst shouldn't be surprised if there is an overlap between the low end of the exempt scale and the high end of the nonexempt scale. In recent years this phenomenon has emerged. That is one reason why one structure will not accommodate both exempt and nonexempt jobs.

The low ends of both structures have grades lower than the lowest-paid or evaluated jobs. There is no harm in this. This permits a job grade lower than anyone in the organization, a psychological plus. Similarly, grades at the high end of the structures in which there are no jobs or job holders suggest opportunity and growth. In both instances, these grades provide slots into which new jobs can be entered at some future date should the need arise.

It will be found that the interplay between depth of range, midpoint progression, and the labor market itself will dictate the number of grades in the structure. The nonexempt structure may have as few as 5 and as many as 20. It is usual to have 12 grades in the nonexempt structure, using the typical design mentioned. Similarly, the size of the company will dictate the number of grades in the exempt structure, as well as the depth of the range and the midpoint progression. The exempt structure could have as few as 15 and as many as 30. It is typical to have 20 to 25 in a medium-sized company using a 10 percent progression and a 50 percent spread.

The arithmetic of the structure development involves only addition, subtraction, multiplication, and division.

There are several ways of computing a salary range. One method is simple and can be used to accommodate any range spread. In it, the establishment of the first midpoint is an arbitrary decision. It is hoped, however, that there some rationale contributed to its choice. This could be a percentage over the minimum of the first range or some other logical point. The chosen midpoint is divided by 100 percent plus half of the desired range spread. For instance, if the range spread is going to be 30 percent, then the midpoint is divided by the sum of 100 percent plus 15 percent or 115 percent. This produces the minimum of the range. Dividing a midpoint of, say, $920 by 115 percent produces a minimum of $800. Next, subtract this minimum from the midpoint ($920 − $800 = $120) and add that difference to the midpoint in order to produce the maximum ($920 + $120 = $1040).

In a 50 percent range there is yet an easier way to determine the minimum and maximum of the range. The midpoints are developed as described earlier, using some means of progression technique. The minimums and maximums in a 50 percent range can be found by multiplying the midpoint (considered to be the 100 percent or "whole" position of the range) by 80 percent to find the minimum and by 120 percent to find the maximum. Although this technique can be used for other spreads, the figures are not nearly as easy to work with.

The next grade is a function of the preceding grade. The midpoint is calculated by a percentage increase over the preceding grade/range. For instance, if the first grade/range midpoint is $100, then the next midpoint, using a constant midpoint progression of 10 percent, becomes $110. The minimum and maximum of this new grade/range are calculated the way those of the preceding grade/range were calculated. This process continues until all market-related jobs have been accommodated.

The market has determined the slope of the line; the midpoint progression is computed on that line. Grades are computed in other ways as well. Sometimes an increasing or decreasing midpoint progression is used. Other structures have no regard for midpoint progression and develop grades around natural job clusters and groupings. With such structures, the consistency has been lost, and they don't lend themselves to easy explanation. Analysts should always keep in mind that they want to design something that they will be able to explain in detail to anyone. This is enhanced when common sense, logic, and consistency are applied.

Another means of developing the grade/range is from a completely removed source, the conversion chart. The conversion chart is the means by which the determination is made as to what jobs are assigned to what grades. It is a table or chart which coincides with the total number of points in the system.

One approach to the design of the conversion chart has already been alluded to. When jobs are seen to be clustered about a certain number of points, they can be grouped into one grade. Such assignments are likely to develop rather inconsistent point groupings, however. One grade may have 150 points, the next grade 80 points, the next grade 110, the next 113, and so on. Such inconsistency is difficult to explain. The cluster approach is a response to a visual grouping which occurred at one point in time but which may not occur again.

Another popular approach to the design of a conversion chart is to assign the same number of points to each grade. This is consistent but not too logical. The way it works is to simply divide the total number of points by the number of grades and put a constant number of points to each grade.

Another approach is to use the market data which produced the structure in the first place. This is referred to as the natural data method. In developing the midpoints along the line of central tendency, a 10 percent progression from midpoint to midpoint is used along the full length of the line. It begins at the minimum wage or lowest marketable salary and ends at the highest marketable salary. In most nonexempt structures there will be from 9 to 12 midpoints along the line of central tendency.

To find the point conversion, simply go along the line of central tendency and split the difference between the now established midpoints. Drop from this point on the line directly beneath to the point scale, and natural break points will emerge. The number of points going into each grade will increase, but this is to be expected since the line upon which the structure is predicated is a constant 10 percent along an increasing base. This increase accommodates constantly increasing complexities of the jobs. Moreover, this process is logical and consistent and lends itself to greater equity and to explanation.

The numbering of the structure is relatively arbitrary. The typical approach is to begin with 1 for the lowest-level job and to continue consecutively up the several grades. For ease in computerization, it may be a good idea to group the nonexempt jobs in a block of numbers, say from 1 to 20, and to start exempt jobs at 21 and go as high as necessary. If there are several groups in the nonexempt grade structures, it may be necessary to assign blocks of numbers in groups of, say, 15, which may necessitate beginning the exempt group at, say, 45. This numbering process facilitates retrieval of information from the data bank. Some systems use letter designations instead of numbers. Both ways are adequate. The letter sequencing has the drawback of being limited to 26 letters and then requiring a double-lettering sequence. This appears to be a little more cumbersome.

There may be an advantage in numbering the grades in reverse order. The top job would then be number 1, not an illogical situation. Numero uno is frequently thought of as being the best or the highest. This would make the lowest job the highest number. Such an approach makes it somewhat difficult to add jobs at the higher end, since the top job is already number 1.

In order to add higher grades, the whole structure needs to be raised. This is not an impossible task but does suggest some lack of ease. This may be an advantage in negotiating with the union. The union frequently wants to add another grade at the top. It is easy to do this if the number 1 is at the bottom, but if it designates the top job, the whole structure needs to be moved, and jobs juggled. This is a minor point, but it does have some psychological advantage. One company was clever in making the top job number 1. It negotiated with the union and indicated the difficulty in adding another job—a whole new numbering sequence, juggling of jobs, confusion, and so on. The union was about to buy it when they forced the company to designate the new grade above number 1 with the letter A! When last seen, the structure was up to H, and still climbing!

There are occasions when it becomes necessary to have multiple structures. This occurs when an organization competes in more than one labor market, and those labor markets differ in how jobs are paid. Although this is usually unnecessary and not recommended for the exempt jobs, it is frequently necessary and recommended for nonexempt jobs.

When organizations became aware of differences in local markets around the country in which they had nonexempt jobs, it became a common practice to divide the country into regions or zones. There was the Northeast, around New York City; the Southeast, with Atlanta at its hub; the Midwest, which included several states located near Chicago; the Southwest, with several states around Texas; the Northwest; and the Pacific Coast. While it was recognized that the wages varied between these regions, it was assumed that within these regions the wages were similar.

As survey data became more available within the regions and analysts became smarter, they realized that each region was far from homogeneous. A structure for any one region was found to be inadequate for high-paying metropolitan centers and too adequate in low-paying centers. This pattern emerged all over the country. It became evident that the wages paid in one metropolitan center did have comparability with the other metropolitan centers but not necessarily with other areas in the same region.

Enter the Metro-Cluster concept. The Metro-Cluster concept recognizes that metropolitan centers around the country relate to each other in the wages paid nonexempt jobs. By identifying the several levels of pay practices, different structures can be used in different metropolitan areas to accommodate that labor market. In a large retail company that had various-sized stores and offices in 400 cities around the United States, it took only five nonexempt structures to satisfy the needs of the many locations.

The administrative burden increases geometrically with the number of structures. If line managers have nonexempt employees assigned to them in a particular region of the country, they may not pay these nonexempt employees, located in different metropolitan areas, according to the same rate structure. The use of several different structures can create problems for line managers and certainly increases their administrative load. Compensation administrators have that many structures to control and survey as well. The need is to develop rate structures which reflect the tenor of the market, but not to develop so many structures that the pay program becomes cumbersome to administer or manage. A logical grouping process of metropolitan cities is a matter of the compensation administrators' judgment. A cluster of markets is as good a means of grouping as any other. When a metropolitan area varies from the average of the cluster by 10 to 15 percent, this suggests that a different structure is needed.

By using multiple structures, the company can be more responsive to local market conditions by neither paying too much and adding needlessly to labor costs, nor paying too little and creating discontent among employees. Through the use of multiple structures, all jobs can be evaluated with the same evaluation system and slotted into the appropriate job grade and paid according to the dictates of the local labor market in which the jobs compete. Equity and ease of administration are the balancing forces on the Metro-Cluster teeter-totter.

The continuum approach in structure development is a system which uses no grades. It uses a policy line developed in the manner already described. Instead of having grades, the continuum approach has the potential of having as many grades as there are employees and/or jobs. The maximums and minimums in a 50 percent range (as in most continuum ranges) are computed as 120 percent and 80 percent of the midpoints. These three lines—the midpoint or policy line, the minimum line, and the maximum line—describe the parameters of the salary range.

Every job has a salary range according to the number of points assigned. If the number of points assigned is different, the salary range will be different. While the system suggests a great deal of individuality in its design, that is, every individual has his own range, it also increases the administrative load. A change in job, no matter how minute, can change a person's evaluation and thus the salary range. In programs in which position in the range is critical to getting more pay with regard to performance, this becomes a real motivation to employees to get their jobs reevaluated. This supersensitivity of the system prompts frequent reevaluations. Administrators using the system find the increased workload necessitates a larger staff. They also find that the system may cause more, not less, discontent. While change may be good, it can be seen here that some employees might push for changes that are essentially groundless. When linked with a confusingly worded, long-winded evaluation system, the continuum approach can become a nightmare. Some administrators using the continuum system will group jobs as often as possible so as to reduce the administrative load. If this is done, the prime advantage of individualizing the grades is reduced, if not negated. The continuum system may succeed in small organizations, but in large ones, it takes added staff to maintain it.

· 19 ·

Communicating the Program

A New Yorker, pointing to a hillside field, complimented the New En-
glander on his corn. "How do you plow that field? It looks pretty steep."
*   "Don't plow it; when the spring thaws come, the rocks rolling downhill*
tear it up."
*   "That so? How do you plant it?"*
*   "Don't plant it really. Just stand in my back door and shoot the seed*
in with a shotgun."
*   "Is that the truth?" asked the New Yorker.*
*   "Hell, no! That's conversation."*

THE communication of the compensation program is frequently one of the most sensitive issues of the program. How much information should be communicated? To whom should it be communicated? In what form? How often? Why communicate it at all? Can it be overcommunicated?

Whether or not money itself motivates, the scheme of the distribution of pay must cross the threshold of acceptance in the perception of the employee if any motivation is to occur. Although the issue of communication was up for debate once, this is no longer the case. Today's employees are not the robots of yesteryear. There is no longer the wide difference in literacy or intelligence that there once was between the managed and the management. The employees demand to know what forces are affecting them and are fully capable of understanding them. It behooves management to tell the employees about the program, for what management does not tell them, they make up for themselves. And what they make up is usually worse than the truth. Borrowing from the Bible, "The truth shall make you free."

To what extent can a compensation plan be revealed to an employee group? The answer depends on how sound the program is. The sounder the program, the more about it that can be released. If a person has a high level of confidence in something, he will tend to talk about it. If he doesn't, he will not talk about it. It's that simple. If there are elements of the program in which the management has little confidence, they will not disclose information about it so as not to subject themselves to criticism or ridicule. If the job evaluation program is makeshift or nonexistent, not much can be said about it because there is very little in it that is concrete enough to communicate to employees and discuss with them. And what is said will probably be suspect, which will make the program worthless anyway.

"Soundness" is a perception, and it must be remembered that communication is an attempt to influence a perception. The employees' perception will be enhanced if the employees have participated in the program. If they have actually designed it, their perception of its soundness will be enhanced. That perception is heightened further if the communication of that program is done by their peers rather than by an outside consultant or the administrator, or by management itself. Naturally, if an employee group has been involved in the design of the program, all lines of communication, formal and informal, official and grapevine, have been opened and much is known about the program. The main advantage in employee involvement is communication and acceptance. The flexibility of employee involvement permits employee involvement to cease whenever it is deemed appropriate by management for this to happen. Employees being involved in the design of the compensable factors does not necessarily mean that they must be involved with any more than that part of the program's development. Employee involvement is a communication process itself and offers many advantages.

Often a program is designed by management or consultants or the compensation staff. Communication may then become a political issue. Because not all minds react to the same stimuli, there is no single means of communication which will transmit an idea with equal effectiveness. The organization must examine and utilize several means of communication and not depend on one technique to reach all employees. While some respond favorably to information transmitted in a face-to-face meeting, others prefer reading information—just as some prefer to get the news from the daily newspaper, while others prefer to get it from a telecast. The organization must appreciate these differences and use all media at their disposal to communicate the message of the compensation plan.

Holding a general meeting in which the message is introduced to the employees is a good method. Whether the meeting is conducted by the peer group that developed the program or by management personnel, it has definite merit over the printed word. It permits immediate feedback, which is important to both parties. The acceptability of the data is influenced a great deal by the manner of the presenters. If they are perceived as slipshod or not believable, the program they present will be so judged, no matter how good it may be. The contrary is true too—a professional explanation of a weak program can gain more acceptance than it may warrant. Remember that it is hard to fool employees. Management people can be fooled into accepting a program because they're playing the management game, and often their own success depends on how well they "accept" a management program. Not so with an employee group. They're all from Missouri, the "show-me" state. They must be convinced of the program's credibility, and that sometimes takes a great deal of convincing—especially in the sensitive area of money in their pockets.

A bad track record on the part of management in prior programs is a hindrance to acceptance of a new program. It takes a great deal in the way of a program, competence, and sincerity to overcome the past. Communication with any track record is risky, which probably explains why management refuses to communicate. If the program can stand the light of day, if it is well intended and sound, the potential response of the employees warrants the risk of communicating it to them.

The general meeting will be more effective if those who attend are permitted to ask questions. This means limiting the meeting to about 30 persons. It is not necessary for it to be a homogeneous group. There are many advantages to having a mixed group of employees from various departments. Whereas a homogeneous group may be less intimidated because there are few strange faces, and their concerns can be more localized, they may also suffer from myopia in that they may not be able to appreciate the needs of employees from other departments. A mixed group, then, can introduce a greater variety of concerns which can help the speakers show the universality of the program and result in more cohesiveness in the group's acceptance of the program.

The purpose of the general meeting is not only to convey information about the program, but to secure the employees' understanding of its various elements. The responses given by the presenters to the questions from the audience will be judged not only on content but on the manner of their presentation. Answers that are straightforward and complete can greatly enhance acceptance of the program.

If the presentation precedes the completion of job questionnaires or descriptions, those tasks will be facilitated when employees have a better appreciation as to the "whys" of questionnaire or description completions. The overall effect of the general meeting is to open channels of communication and to improve employee relations. Communication is a key to success in employee motivation. Without communication, the employee will frequently be demotivated and seek a third party to restore some flow of communication. General meetings are time well spent and should be viewed as a normal business expense with a return of high productivity.

Organization newspapers should augment whatever communications are used. They should not be used *instead of* other means. No matter how well written, the company organ is not read by everyone nor is its message understood readily by everyone who does read it. It is a helpful means and should be used often in the development of the program and certainly at the final presentation of the program.

Memorandums are also auxiliary devices and should not be used in lieu of meetings. Memos have a way of being written in less than informative ways. Their use frequently has fallen to merely reciting the official "company line." The reader is often leery of such a communiqué and tries to read between the lines, no matter how well it's written. To some, the company memorandum tells them exactly what they want to know and for them it's the best means of communication.

The success or failure of the program really rests on a more intimate exchange. The exchange between employees and their supervisors can restore confidence in a badly presented program and likewise can destroy confidence in a program well presented. As always, the link in the communicative network is every supervisor. General meetings should be held hierarchically; the "word" should be disseminated through the hierarchy, letting the top people know first, then the next level, and so on down the pyramid. To abrogate the hierarchy is to place the kiss of death on the program. The supervisors are key people in employee acceptance of the program. That acceptance or rejection will be revealed in the relations between the employees and the supervisors. The balance is touchy. If the supervisors are convinced and convincing, the employees will accept the program also. The employees' acceptance is the real test of the program. With their acceptance, other forms of motivation programs can be introduced. If they don't accept the compensation program, there is no way of motivating them.

Communication is essential to higher levels of productivity. Games only increase bureaucracy and idleness. Straightforward communication will enhance a company's profit and productivity, but it must be built upon a sound program in the first place.

Generally there are some items of interest to the employees. The employees are interested in the consistency of the program. They want assurance that favoritism will not prevail in the new system and that all positions were examined and appraised against the same criteria. Further, they want to know that these criteria are logical, rational, and complete. When the employees know the basis of the pay relating to their job, they can better direct their efforts. A great deal can be gained by clarifying what the compensable factors are in the system. The employees want to know that performance, seasoning, and other pertinent factors will receive proper consideration. They want assurance that management in the development of the program has examined all outside forces which bear upon the compensation issue—the economy, competition in labor, competition in the product market and other costs. The employees want to be assured that the program, no matter how well based, will be reviewed regularly to ensure its continued equity, competitiveness, and applicability. Finally, management needs to reaffirm that the program is flexible enough to adjust to internal and external changes.

There are several items that may or may not be revealed to the employees. The first of these wage/salary items is an employee's salary or wage itself. It is possible to confuse and cloud just how much pay a person is actually getting. Takeouts, deductions, and the format of the paycheck or statement itself can conceal this vital information from the employee.

Job descriptions or job questionnaires are other items that have been concealed from the employees. The advantage of this is not known, but it remains a fairly common practice to not permit employees to see their own job description. Maybe one of the reasons is the state some of these descriptions are in!

The evaluation method and its compensable factors are frequently not revealed to the employees. A company would not want to reveal what it was paying for on the theory that this would only tend to increase the employees' attempts to pursue those factors in order to get more money. As mentioned earlier, without knowing the basis of one's pay, one has little cause or direction for increasing one's productivity.

Many times executives claim that they don't want to reveal the salary range to which individuals have been assigned because they feel it will demotivate them to see that their salary has a limit. Even without showing employees their salary range, all employees know that there is a practical limit to how much they are going to be paid for the jobs they are doing. To think otherwise is foolish and unrealistic. "The sky's the limit" is swallowed only by the naive, and there aren't too many of them around anymore.

One reason executives don't want to show employees their salary range is that they don't want to be asked to explain why a job has been assigned a particular range. Another reason is that from the executives' point of view, they know all the "players" in their "game," and they know that each and every one of them will gain an increase. This "privileged" knowledge makes the executives feel powerful. Employees, on the other hand, looking up into the organization, feel quite helpless and dislike the uncertainty of not knowing the range. At least with a range, they know there's more to be had. Employees are seldom concerned about the raise they have already gotten. Their attention is directed toward whether or not there are going to be more raises. With no salary range information, there is a question as to whether the salary they currently receive is the highest they will ever attain. This is a very negative motivator. A salary range gives the employees a sense of order and suggests that there definitely is an opportunity for them to enhance their earnings—if not in their present job, then they know they must prepare themselves for some higher-evaluated job in which there is more room for advancement.

Very good employees are never stalemated at the top of their salary ranges. Good employees, maybe, but not the very sharp ones. The very sharp ones move to higher ranges before they've reached three-quarters of their present range. Every job has a limit; there is only one CEO's job, though there may be several persons in the organization who are qualified for it.

Few companies reveal all salary ranges to the employees. This is perhaps the cutoff of disclosure for most companies. The reason for not disclosing the structure has to be based on the fact that the ranges cannot be justified. A sound program could justify the ranges and the jobs assigned to them. One that is not sound will cause its designers and administrators (or are they manipulators?) to conceal the ranges from employees.

In an attempt to open up the salary range issue, some companies consider giving members of management those salary structures in their purview. Of course, what happens is that the smarter ones will compare notes, and before long all ranges will be known. What has been lost is time away from the job, hardly an efficient resolution to a touchy problem. Others maintain that salary ranges can be given to employees, based on the jobs in their likely career path. The problem then is, Who is going to say which jobs are likely for this or that employee to pursue? Much time and effort can be put into such an exercise, and although it may go under the guise of career development, the smarter employees will huddle and swap ranges, and before long the grapevine has released the entire structure. Secrecy is quite a motivator. Employees will often spend much time and energy in uncovering a secret. Such time and energy could be better utilized toward higher productivity. Companies considering a job-posting program are compelled to post grades and, therefore, must reveal the entire system. Before developing a job-posting system, a company should have a fairly carefully worked out program that can withstand the challenge that job posting will present.

When survey data is compiled and collated properly and honestly, it can be shown to employees. Such data must be displayed in such a way as to preserve the confidentiality under which it was procured. Given this limitation, however, salary survey information is good, logical data to share with the employees. The management must be prepared to act on the data presented or to show cause why it isn't acting. Generally, survey data is more favorable to a company than the rumors about its competitiveness. It has been said that an employee tends to overestimate the salary of a peer. If this is true, then mystery, intrigue, conspiracy, bureaucracy, politics, and other games people play might be eliminated by revealing the salaries of all employees. If the salaries thus reported are the result of a sound program, they will stand firmly. The story is told of a president of an oil company who found out his employees were playing "payroll poker" with their paychecks. He was afraid that the disclosure of salaries in this way would create chaos. He wrote a note which was enclosed in every paycheck. It read, "Your pay is secret information, and you are not to reveal it to anyone." Upon receiving the notice, one petroleum engineer appended it, signed it, and sent it back to the president, saying, "Don't worry, I won't tell anyone my salary; I'm as ashamed of it as you are!"

Employees have a tendency to underestimate the salaries of their superiors. If this is true, the degree of motivation might be enhanced by knowing how "juicy" the "plum" really is in the executive suite. If employees feel that their superiors are not making very much more than they are, they have little reason to be motivated. By knowing what may lie ahead through growth, opportunity, and promotion, employees could be greatly motivated. While some companies are experimenting with the revelation of all salaries, it will be some time before this is a universal practice.

Job evaluation systems have been developed which lend credibility to the salary ranges assigned. Such programs permit the revelation of salary structures. Performance appraisal programs have a long way to go before individual salary information can be disclosed. When that happens, the mystery will be over and the employees will talk about other things.

Once the decision is made about how much information to disclose, the method of its disclosure must be decided upon. Is it to be posted like so much dead data? Should it be sent to the employees at their homes? If it were, the changes in data would necessitate constant updating of the program and result in a great deal of administrative work.

To whatever extent an organization chooses to reveal its program, from descriptions to structures, it might consider the practice of the public library. The library has reference books which are kept within its confines. They are there for any citizen to use, but they cannot be checked out. Copies can be made of some of the data but not of all data contained therein. The situation of the reference books is analogous to wage and salary program information. If the updated program were kept in reference manuals in the compensation department, it could be viewed by all who cared to see it, but there wouldn't be countless copies all over the place. Reasonable and just safeguards could be applied which the employees would find acceptable. When first in use, there would be a "run" on the system to see if it really works and if the information is really available. After this, the rush for the data would abate, and only occasional use would be made of the material. The system could remain intact, with all parties' needs satisfied. Such a controlled reference station permits updating when necessary and, therefore, reduces the typical problem of out-of-date information.

To be sure, there is data that needs to be distributed to management, perhaps in the form of memos or policy manual addenda. Such information is more easily disseminated when the numbers are held down and a central reference area is maintained.

The degree to which information is distributed is a very key company and personal issue. It reveals the style, character, and integrity of the management and the regard it has for its practices and employees. It is a vital issue that must be settled even before a program is designed, since the program must be designed with the integrity which will permit disclosure compatible with the style of the organization.

Surveys of policies and practices are funny things. Not the data necessarily, but the actions taken as a result of such data. Some management people will do something *because* other companies are doing it, others using the same data will *not* do something because *other* companies do it. Such is the case with the practices of companies with regard to their communication of compensation data. An article reported the findings of an extensive survey on the subject.* The survey revealed the forefront of "progressive" thinking on disclosure of information about salary structures. And even that data was held pretty close to the chest.

The survey included 184 companies, and the surprising thing was that 69 percent of the companies reported they still do *not* give wage schedules to employees. All of those employees don't know how much they can make in their jobs. What motivation can they have? Is it any wonder that there is a lack of productivity in the country? Just think of all of those compensation

* *Personnel Journal*, February 1974, p. 131.

programs that are so weak, so bad, that the managements won't reveal salary data on the jobs. Another surprising statistic was that only 48 percent of the companies tell management personnel their own salary structures. It's difficult to imagine management people tolerating that glaring illustration of lack of confidence.

There's a long way to go to disclosure!

· 20 ·

Control Techniques

In a world where quantity, wealth, power and size are valued over quality and self-fulfillment, there is a tendency to mistake escalation for satisfaction.

L. J. PETER
The Peter Prescription

THE most important part of the development of the compensation program is the generation of maintenance and administrative procedures. Too few, and the program developed is useless, since it is directionless. Too many, and the program becomes a burden to everyone—especially the administration. Compensation policies are like babies—easy to conceive, but difficult to deliver and develop. The monument to oneself that triggers the collapse predicted by Parkinson's third law, the ridiculous word games that Laurence Peter cites in his books, and the treatment that policies receive in *Up the Organization* by Robert Townsend all suggest an awareness of the perils of writing cumbersome policies. The policy can be an instrument for guiding action and for preanswering oft-repeated questions and conditions, or it can be the device that cripples the organization by reducing its flexibility and promoting mediocrity and conformance. While the design of the compensation program is vital to the success of the company, its development is of short duration. The maintenance plan goes on forever—or so it seems.

The successful policy is the one written in simple, straightforward language in an attempt to help rather than constrict its reader. While the short policy is not always the best, the best policy always seems short.

200

Anyone who has written a policy knows that the more writers try to clarify a point, the more complex they make it. There is a place for the policy, but it must remain a simple, flexible device which provides answers to repeated questions. It will not answer all questions or solve all problems, but it will cite the parameters of good logic. The purpose for having the policy is critical to the administrators' understanding and execution of the policy. If the intent of the policy is understood, the administration of it will be effective even in instances not directly covered by it.

Of all the management processes fulfilled by the compensation program, the control function is the most prominent. The compensation system itself is a great means of control. "Control" here does not mean holding down wages, it means *directing* the payroll dollar effectively. This is not an attempt to couch a negative thought in positive terminology. It is a whole new attitudinal set. Payroll will increase no matter what happens—whether a compensation program is installed or not. The direction of that compensation dollar is the key to the organization's success.

The payroll dollar must be viewed as an investment in human resources. As with any investment, management should expect and receive a reasonable return. This is the contract between an employee and the organization. The return on that payroll investment is measured in productivity of the employee. The measurement process is the function that the compensation program fulfills—first, through an effective contribution-based job evaluation program which assesses the value of the jobs, and, second, through the performance review program which assesses the value of each individual's performance.

Control, then, means directing the payroll dollar to those jobs and those job holders who are contributing to the success of the company. A recent example of this is Japan, which increased compensation and profit by increasing productivity.

The job of the compensation administrator is to see that wages and salaries are correctly directed to the contributors. This direction can be accomplished by the staff function if it is done with the proper emphasis. That emphasis must be on a positive perspective toward your objective. Remember that administrative polices often serve as a powerful *de*motivator because of their bureaucratic and restrictive nature. They often come from a Theory X posture in which the authors and administrators assume the worst on the part of the employees and also assume a strongly authoritarian approach to the administrative role. Obviously, this is the wrong way to go about it. The policies should be guidance devices that will assume the best in employees and contribute to their flexibility, integrity, and higher productivity.

A recent article in *Personnel Journal* * identified the three postures assumed by the staff function. While the first two, the service function and the control function, are the most typical, the third, the advisory function, is the best. In the discussion of control policies, these three postures are particularly relevant because the policies generated by the staff group typify the group's posture. When the staff group perceives itself to be merely a service function, it busies itself with administrative details, and puts itself at the beck and call of its masters. In this lackey position, the policies tend to be verbose in an attempt to cover every sort of activity.

Such a basically insecure, I'm Not OK management tends to create a caste system in the company; bestowing privileges and approval according to one's level in the organization. Certain levels may do things that other levels cannot do. Almost every instance must be covered in the control policies, so that never again will a decision have to be reached by the staff function. The authority of the staff group is heavily dependent on the "ins," and the staff makes every effort to please and appease them. Staff people frequently find themselves in the position of having to defend the management against the "antiestablishments." "In establishment we trust" is their motto, because like the vassals long ago, they defend those that provide them with security.

The second posture may be worse because it blocks creative growth at every turn. Limits on behavior, dress, manner, custom, and thinking are dictated through the Holy Policy. The control policy is written with lots of teeth, and the staff group adopts those "dentures" with a vengeance. No one escapes their venom. When management dares to abridge a policy *as written*, memos fly and everything stands still until a pound of flesh has been exacted. If there was ever a time when conformity was promoted, it is through the dictatorial policy. It covers every instance not so much by specific reference as by inference—"You just can't do anything." This staff function is really a control function. If it could regulate trips to the washroom, it would. This staff's motto is "In conformity we trust."

When the staff group adopts the third posture, the advisory function, the policies emanating tend to guide corporate behavior toward uniformity, equity in treatment, and innovative interpretation of intent. The staff function in this instance assumes an I'm OK—You're OK stance. The power is vested in personal authority rather than statutory authority. The staff tries to give decision-making authority to all levels of the organization and has faith in the integrity of the individual. The staff tries to make its control policies realistic, meaningful, and flexible. The motto of this posture is "In the individual we trust."

* November 1974, p. 846.

This last posture is recommended in the writing of policies. With this attitude, the compensation administrator can develop a motivated, free-moving organization that will foster creativity and growth. Effective control policies are those written by the Adult for the Adult. They are policies in which authority is vested in people and based on their professionalism, rather than being vested in statutory dictates emanating from an organizational hierarchy.

The wage and salary program is itself a control system. It establishes the values of jobs, and suggests the expectations of the jobs, if not the duties themselves. It identifies the proper levels for compensation and parameter extremes, the minimums and maximums of the pay structure.

When a system and its structure are implemented, it should be expected that there will be employees who "fall out of the system." The jobs of some employees will be assigned to job grades in which their pay is in some instances higher than the maximum of the range and in some instances lower than the minimum of the range. The terms used to refer to these situations are "red" and "blue" circle rates. Red circle rates are situations in which the employees are paid in excess of the maximum of the range to which they are assigned. Blue circle rates are situations in which the employees are paid less than the minimum of the range to which they are assigned. Both are problems that should be expected at the outset. Both should be resolved. No matter how consistently and logically the grades have been formed, the parameters of those grades, the minimums and maximums, are nonetheless arbitrary lines. They suggest the policy norms or parameters for fair payment for employees in that range. Though red and blue circle rates are to be discouraged, they will exist. Compensation administrators have been known to be so zealous in preventing red and blue circle rates that they have reclassified employees, reevaluated jobs, or simply pulled out "anomalies" so that there would be no red or blue circle rates in *their* system.

Both the maximum and the minimum of any range are arbitrarily assigned, even though they result from arithmetic consistency. While there is a general tendency for administrators to pull up blue circle rated employees to the minimum of the grade range assigned, there is a strong tendency *not* to pull red circle rates down to the maximum of the range assigned. Whether these tendencies are the result of a 1–9 management grid position—the high, people-oriented position that personnel persons are often characterized as having—or the result of past experience in dealing with the ugliness of taking an employee's money away, the common practice is to invoke the "grandfather clause" and let red circle rates remain constant and pull blue circle rates up to the minimum.

There are some guides to help in reconciling this problem. The first, mentioned above, is to hold pay constant. The implementation of a wage and salary system is predicated on the idea that each job is worth just so much to the organization. The reason for putting in a system is to try to eliminate inequities, that is, to stop overpaying or underpaying employees. In an inflationary economy, holding the pay of employees constant is tantamount to reducing their disposable income. While this may seem an incorrect procedure, it must be remembered that the basis of pay in a capitalistic society is the productivity, not the need, of the employee. If the organization wants to increase the pay of the red circle rate, it really has little need for a system of payment in the first place. It is recognized that this is an inflexible position. The structure, with its arbitrary maximums, suggests guidelines for performance. While there may be instances when the organization may want to increase red circle rates, the practice should not be encouraged. The option of decreasing a red circle rate to bring it within the parameters of the range should not be overlooked. Red circle employees who are informed of their "overpayment" status may develop guilt feelings and may feel pressure which will adversely affect their performance. In some instances the reduction of a red circle rate can be a better solution for the employees than might have been thought. It permits them to assume the posture of equity with their peers, removes the burden of guilt or the need to outdo everyone else, and permits them to grow financially when the structure again moves up.

Whatever is done, the employees should be counseled about their situation. The well-informed supervisor is the best one to do this. The compensation administrator must assume responsibility for the best possible outcome of the counseling. How the employees got into this predicament must be explained to them. This suggests that the evaluation system, the job description or questionnaire used, the survey process, the structure development, as well as growth opportunities must be discussed with them. Red circle employees should be encouraged to continue to do good work and to seek higher-paying jobs in which they will be properly rewarded. The ever-rising labor market will also be working in their favor. Each year the labor market rises, as does the pay structure. It can be determined how long the red circle rate will remain a red circle rate. If it is a grossly overpaid situation, the employees should be so informed. If it is just a matter of time before the structure catches up and absorbs their rate, the problem will be short-lived and little action need be taken. The presence of a red circle rate suggests that the evaluation of the job be carefully examined to determine its accuracy, and, further, that the employees' value to the organization be carefully assessed to ensure proper payment.

Blue circle rates are usually considered to be a lesser problem. Positive action can be taken which will be perceived as such. It must be remembered, however, that the installation of the structure created the blue circle rates. They are the result of an arbitrary, but arithmetically correct, placement of minimum pay for a job. If red circle rates are tolerated to remain constant, it follows that blue circle rates may be similarly held constant. The tendency is to move them up to the minimum, however. To hold them constant and hire similarly qualified employees at higher rates is a deplorable action and is perhaps the best reason for increasing blue circle rates to the minimum.

Blue circle rated employees should be counseled. They should be told how they got to be blue circle rates. This means that job evaluation, job description or questionnaire, survey, structure development all need to be disclosed to ensure their understanding and acceptance of their position and the action to be taken.

Their positions and performance should be assessed to make sure that their jobs are properly evaluated and that they are truly performing the work assigned at a satisfactory level of competence.

If it is deemed that these employees should be paid within the range assigned, a program should be designed to rectify the situation. That program must take certain issues, such as the cost of the program, into consideration. The amount of money to bring the total number of blue circle rates up to the minimum is usually the largest cost of the program. From the company standpoint this suggests that rather than push everyone up to the minimum right away, increases should be made over a period of time. Individuals who are found to be far short of the minimum pay may require huge boosts to reach the minimum. Although it may seem hard to imagine, people respond more favorably to frequent smaller increases in pay than they do to one large increase. People actually have difficulty assimilating any significant shock in a sensitive area such as money. A periodic movement toward the minimum is better for the individual and for the company.

To make moves in which increases are granted the employees simply on the basis of policy is merely a giveaway program. To give the increases meaning and to restore confidence in supervision, the supervisors of the blue circle rated employees should be the ones to initiate, monitor, and control the movement of the employees' pay to the minimum. The supervisors should do this based on the individuals' performance.

Policy should dictate the maximum percentage award that can be made in such periodic reviews. Such a maximum percentage ensures equity and regulates the means by which supervisors themselves perform. These periodic increases should be regulated in time as well as percentage. "Periodic" implies a regular interview period such as every six months.

Taking all of these factors into consideration, a policy statement that may be used is: "Upon *implementation* of the program, the *supervisor* has the option, based on the employee's *performance*, to increase the pay of the employee *toward* the minimum of his assigned range at a rate not to exceed 7 *percent*. Thereafter, the employee should be reviewed for performance and like consideration every *six months* until the minimum has been reached."

This policy amortizes or spreads out the cost incurred in the implementation of the program, vests the authority for taking the action in the supervisors, suggests that the criterion for pay increase is performance, regulates the amount of increase for consistency and equity, grants frequent "strokes" to the employees, permits the employees to adjust to new levels of pay gradually, and establishes a uniform method of handling the problem.

A final note: The installation of a wage and salary program will usually produce red and blue circle rates; otherwise there'd be little need for the program. Both red and blue circle rates can be avoided even then if necessary. This is done by increasing the spread of the ranges used. It must be realized that the red and blue circle rates were established primarily because of the depth of the ranges, 50 percent in exempt, 30 percent in the nonexempt. If those depths were increased, they could absorb the blue and red circle rates. It is not a solution that is recommended, but it is one which is taken by companies that want to cover the problem, for cost or other reasons. Having ranges in excess of the typical depth permits gross overpayment and underpayment to exist while producing a semblance of order. For the company that can't handle the problem in another way, this is better than having no program at all, providing that sooner or later the grade depths are restored to the more typical spreads.

The establishment of a salary range once meant that new hires were automatically started at the minimum. This practice is still found. Other control policies in hire rates dictate that no one can be hired at greater than the midpoint of the range. Still other organizations insist that the compensation administrator "sign off" on all hire salaries. All of these policies probably have some basis in logic or did at one time. Compensation administrators must remember at all times what they are trying to control. They are trying to control or direct salaries so that those that contribute to the success of the company will get the higher pay. In addition to paying for contribution, they are trying to control payroll so as to promote internal and external equity.

It is hoped that the evaluation process and the structure will contribute to both of these equity stabilizations. A new hire salary is often perceived as a disturbing influence in this "sea of tranquility" and so is viewed with great suspicion. If the ranges and grades have been created on the basis of external equity, any newcomer will be integrated into the system with little difficulty. To limit newcomers to the minimum of the salary range is folly. It pays no heed to the salary level the newcomers have developed in their career. If the employees have no work experience and the minimum is acceptable to them, then and only then is such a practice feasible.

To restrict hiring up to the midpoint of the range is not without some folly as well. Theoretically the midpoint reflects the average paid in the market for that job. That suggests that if new hire salaries are limited to the midpoint, the only candidates eligible for hire are less than the average performer, or novices. Neither recruiters nor the management requisitioning new employees will stand for that.

When compensation administrators set themselves up as the control device for new hire salary sign-off, they are allowing themselves to be trapped. Recruiters have a goal to hire the best employees possible. They have another goal which is more pressing and less altruistic—they must fill openings. Recruiters "sell" their candidates to management to fill openings. Their zeal is for quantity, and if quality occurs as well, so much the better. The pressure is extreme, however, and their success is measured in quantity, since quality is not so obvious. Pity the poor compensation administrators who stand in the way of this tidal wave. They are simply bowled over by the force, dazzled by the footwork, and "diddled" by recruiter and manager alike. What role do compensation administrators play? First, they have set up salary ranges. Second, they have set up criteria for the jobs in education and experience requirements. Third, they remain the conscience of equity in the managers' minds.

To duel with the recruiter is foolish. The recruiter's job is to recruit, select, and present numbers of applicants to fill openings. If compensation administrators stand in the way of this process, the managers who are hiring can point to the compensation administrators and accuse them of sabotaging their projects for which they need new employees. Recruiters and managers can also alter the "specs," increase the salary range, misclassify, and otherwise completely "snow" compensation administrators. Managers and recruiters can also "go over the head" of compensation administrators as well and force the issue. Needless to say, if this happens too many times, there's something terribly wrong, and compensation administrators place themselves in jeopardy if this occurs.

Compensation administrators are there to promote equity. Will these new hires, no matter what part of the salary range their new salary places them in, disrupt internal equity? Who is in the best position to make such a judgment? The recruiter? The compensation administrator? Neither. Hiring managers must be the ones held responsible for promoting equity in their own organization. New hires must be compared with employees already in the department. Assessments must be made of their value in comparison with their new peers. A ranking should be made for these comparisons. Even though the new hires are an unknown, compared to the managers' current employees, the managers must have made some judgment as to how the new hires compare. Such a ranking, with their salaries charted, will reveal whether a problem is created by the new hires. If a new hire is average in the opinion of the manager, his salary should be the average of his new peers. Notice that the term "average" was used, not "midpoint." The average may be higher or lower than the midpoint. If a new hire is likened to Superman, it follows that his salary should be super as well. Such an assessment on the part of the manager thrusts the responsibility for equity control and maintenance where it should be—on the hiring manager. The compensation administrator's job is to monitor the process and seek its continuity in practice. Their responsibility is thus fulfilled, the manager has a new employee, and the recruiter can mark the requisition "filled."

Upon implementation of the program, the employees were classified by jobs, and assigned grade ranges. Seldom will conditions remain static. Even before implementation, organization changes, market conditions, and economic conditions reveal their indifference to even the most perfectly designed system. The dynamics of industry today dictate that update and audit procedures are a constant process, not a once-a-year exercise. The maintenance of the system is the responsibility of all of its participants, not just the compensation administrator. Job descriptions, job questionnaires, organizational charters all change at unpredictable, irregular rates. First, if the evaluation plan has parameters within which reasonable change can occur without necessitating significant modifications in job evaluation, the problem is abated. Second, changes indicating increased or decreased responsibility are usually first detected by the employee.

In some cases the administrator must be aware of other jobs in the system. Perhaps another job already exists, in which case all that's needed is a reclassification of the employee. The administrator should always be alert to the opportunity to eliminate unused jobs and titles. Remember that even though no one occupies a job, it is possible that someone will in time. The administrator is prudent if he contacts all organizations which use the unpopulated title and sees what the chances are that it will be populated. If it won't be populated, he can eliminate it.

One of the most troublesome changes is the combination and consolidation of jobs. In every business downturn, for example the recession of the mid-seventies, layoffs occur which reduce the number of jobs. Jobs are consolidated, and some remain this way even when times improve. The remaining employees must endure the consolidation of the jobs and carry the load formerly borne by several employees. In such circumstances pressure is brought on the compensation administrator to reevaluate the remaining, consolidated job. In job content evaluation systems, good cases can be made for increases in evaluation and resultant pay. Such a situation occurs when the employee claims that he is doing what five or so had been doing. Therefore, the job is obviously underrated and underpaid. Although the activities may have increased, it is possible that the results are no more contributive than they were before the change. In a contribution-based system, in which the pay is based on the contribution rather than the activities, a more reasonable assessment can be made. If the contribution has increased, then by all means increase the evaluation and the resultant pay. More often than not, however, only the activities will have changed, not the contribution. When explained this way, even the employee can understand why the pay remains the same.

Wage and hour audits are a continuing control on the system as well. Those mentioned earlier, especially the use of a review board, constitute good control measures of the essential bases of exempt/nonexempt status.

The organization structure chart is a useful means not only of communicating relationships but of control. The simple maintenance of the chart goes far in controlling movement throughout the organization. The dynamics of industry usually wreak havoc on attempts to maintain such a chart. There have been various moves away from chart-making, primarily because it was so difficult to maintain the chart itself. A simple means should be employed in sustaining the chart. Readers familiar with Abbott and Costello will see that the primary interest is an organizational version of their routine "Who's on First?" Control of titles, reporting relationships, and channels of communication are at stake in organizational charting and can be vital to the process of exercising control.

The main concern is to identify organizational entities and the leaders of those entities. The assumption of titles and inference of organization can be the most confusing element of all and can contribute to a lack of control. One way to chart the "players" and maintain control of titles is to chart the process by invoking the wage and hour nomenclature. By simply identifying those categorized as executive by wage and hour standards the issue can be clear-cut. Such identified jobs can be charted in the appropriate box. All nonexecutive, that is, professional, administrative, and outside sales, jobs are identified, citing their titles and naming the persons holding the titles. All nonexempt positions can be listed by title and numbers of employees holding the title.

The purpose of this approach is that the chartist can use the legal basis for whose name "gets in a box" and whose doesn't. Nonexempt employees are usually high turnover employees. Their jobs have less impact than exempt jobs. They are frequently transferred from one group to another. These are reasons for not listing their names. The use of solid lines indicating reporting relationships can also be a "fun" game. To reduce the gamesmanship, simply identify who is responsible for the next merit review and increase. Dotted lines are to be avoided. They are usually the result of high-level game playing in which there has developed a lack of candor. This is obviously a hindrance to productivity and should be avoided.

Control can also be exercised through the simple analysis of "compa-ratio." The term simply signifies a means of determining the relationship of salaries paid to the midpoint of the salary range. This comparative relationship indicates several things. It can suggest which departments are underpaying, which are in need of review, and which jobs are the most dynamic in the system.

When the average salary paid equals the midpoint of the range, the compa-ratio is 100. In a 50 percent range spread, when the average salary paid equals the maximum of the range, the compa-ratio is 120. When the average salary equals the minimum of the range, the compa-ratio is 80.

$$\frac{\text{Average salary of incumbents in range} \times 100}{\text{Midpoint of salary range}} = \text{compa-ratio}$$

The compa-ratio for all grades will indicate the general status of each grade with the market. In a 50 percent spread, a compa-ratio of 80 to 90 suggests that the range is highly marketable, that is, tuned to the market. A ratio of 100 suggests that the range is competitive with the market. A ratio of 110 to 120 suggests that the structure is aged and may need to be made more marketable. A comparison of the compa-ratios of several departments can be very revealing about the pay practices in various departments, suggesting appropriate action. For example, a compa-ratio of 10 percent in the sales department and 92 in the production control department indicates that the leaders in sales need to pay high in order to produce and that the leaders in production may be too frugal with pay increases and may need guidance. The compa-ratio is an indicator, not a divining rod.

Control can be exercised through transfers and promotions. It is always amusing to hear how ironclad some compensation administrators think their control is. They are quite proud of the control they have over pay increases for merit. "No one gets a pay increase until I have okayed it," they puff up and say. Yet when asked what control they exercise over promotions, they reply, "None." Those that do have policies controlling promotion increases admit that many promotions coincide with merit increase time. The result is that the employee receives a double increase. Yet, why did the employee get the promotion? It certainly wasn't due to bad performance.

What constitutes a promotion, anyway? I've asked that question many times of hundreds of administrators, and I've always received mixed answers. To some it means merely a change in job functions. To others it means the increase of evaluative points. To others it is an increase in job grade. To others it is the movement to a higher position on the organization chart. Each of these is an incomplete definition of promotions. An increase in evaluation points or a grade could merely mean the progression through a family of jobs—from engineer to senior engineer—which is often a function of time. How many "promotions" to higher positions of the organization chart have really been kicks upstairs and *not* promotions? Even when accompanied by hoopla in the company news media and a token increase to salve the employee's ego? Who actually controls promotions?

Nobody. Not even the CEO. Movement occurs as the result of many things, few of them controllable. When it gets right down to it, a real promotion often is a movement to higher responsibility, as a result of meritorious performance. In other words, the pay increase for promotion should be viewed as is a pay increase for merit. The movement of pay is a single issue, not a dual issue. A policy of control should not differentiate between promotion or merit; it should do one thing, help in the determination of a pay increase based upon frequency, percentage, and level of pay.

· 21 ·

Pay for Performance

The common idea that success spoils people by making them vain, egotistic, and self complacent is erroneous; on the contrary, it makes them, for the most part, humble, tolerant, and kind. Failure makes people cruel and bitter.

SOMERSET MAUGHAM

FEEDBACK is a natural process. It's just that each of us renders feedback in a different manner. Some are flamboyant and generous in offering congratulations, while others with different natures render feedback by saying nothing at all. "If you don't hear from me, you'll know everything's OK" is a common expression among leaders. There is abundant literature which indicates that the animal thrives with feedback and withers without it. If we don't know how to give feedback or feel uncomfortable about it, we refrain from doing it. Stroking is an essential to life, amd leaders must be aware of it and learn how to do it successfully. Once they succeed in doing it, once their own behavior is positively reinforced, they will find it a gratifying experience and will do it again. We do what we find pleasure and satisfaction in doing, all else we avoid. If we enjoy playing tennis, we play it again and give up golf, in which we did not have a good experience.

If supervisors learn the needs and techniques of counseling and feedback, they can do it successfully. Successful experiences in the exercise will encourage them to do it again. Without such training and in the absence of policy, supervisors will fall into a scattering of some giving feedback and others not giving it. Although rendering feedback is a natural process, active feedback is to be encouraged while feedback in the form of lack of informa-

212

tion is to be discouraged. In other words, as a matter of optimizing the feedback process, it is deemed more beneficial to all parties if the feedback is a deliberate exercise of citations of desired behavior and undesired behavior. A policy for performance review is a worthwhile device. Without it, there is not only a lack of order but reduced motivation.

M. S. Myers gives the best illustration of the need for feedback in his bowling example. The bowler enjoys bowling because there is instantaneous feedback and visibility of results. When he bowls the ball down the alley and hits the pins, they scatter, make noise, and are dispatched. His associates view this, applaud, and smile. When he next begins to bowl, he pitches the ball down the alley to knock down the remaining pins. If he has a split, he must either choose between the two pins, or take a chance on getting them both. He at least has the means of planning his attack. Any other combination presents the same challenge, but he clearly sees his objective and takes action to accomplish that objective because of the positive feedback he receives. If a curtain were to be placed between the bowler and the pins, he would have difficulty in formulating his approach to meet his objective. If he were to cast the ball down the alley, it would disappear behind the curtain and he might or might not receive any feedback as the result of his action. His friends would have little to cheer about and they would leave. Depending on the bowler, he would leave, too, and seek another alley in which he received some gratification.

If a person were placed at the curtain who could see both the action behind the curtain and the bowler, he could relate what was happening. Let's call him the supervisor. The supervisor watches the bowler bowl, sees the ball hit the pins, and can advise the bowler as to his achievements. Suppose when the bowler asks how he did, the supervisor says, "You did fine, do it again." No more direction than that. The bowler bowls, the ball disappears, no noise; "How'd I do?" The supervisor replies, "Just fine. . . . Do it again." Sooner or later, with no more feedback than that, the bowler leaves and seeks out another alley or another activity in which there is more feedback.

The example is full of parallels with the feedback process. There is a need for feedback. It is a control policy when we consider "control" as being "directional." If we develop a policy or a system which encourages feedback, we will be encouraging higher performance standards and their accomplishments. But it takes more than just having a policy stating that the supervisors shall report feedback to their subordinates; they must be trained in the techniques of the feedback process so they will find it a good experience. Thus encouraged, they will continue to do it. The policy must state that supervisors will report feedback to their employees. Such feedback should be

given whenever necessary to guide the subordinate to higher levels of performance. If a subordinate is heading on the wrong track, he should be so advised at an early date to ensure good performance.

Although frequent feedback is helpful and should be periodic though not
necessarily scheduled, there should be a session at least once a year in which
the feedback is an in-depth review of performance and goal setting. The
documentation of the review process is a helpful adjunct. The document
serves as a guide for discussion and structures thought. The document also
becomes a matter of record, and when properly done, gives tangible evidence of good and not so good performance tendencies for the employee to
digest. For disciplinary purposes the document is invaluable and becomes a
vital instrument for action. This is a rather negative connotation but a practical realization, a reminder that the company may be Theory Y but the
government is Theory X. "Where there is law, no man receives justice."

The employee's role in the documentation is mixed. He should be
apprised of what the document relates. Some feel it is good to have the
employee see the data. Others feel that it intimidates the supervisor in what
he puts on the document. Some feel the employee should sign the document. If he does, it should be made clear that he is signing his acknowl-
edgment of the data contained in the document, but not necessarily that he
agrees with it. Copies of the form are placed in the employee's file. The employee should have a copy of it also, and he should have it in a visible place
to serve as a reminder. The document should be more than just a performance review form. It should serve the purpose of looking to the future and
identifying mutually desirable and attainable goals that have been approved
by all parties. The attainment of goals is not necessarily tied to a year's duration. Goals should be structured so as to permit visibility of progress through
the year. Alterations and shifting of emphasis are essential to such a program, since it is difficult to anticipate the many events through the year that
will influence the progress toward the goals or the goals themselves.

The system just described is a means by which performance and goal setting are discussed. The problem with most review systems is that they are directly tied to the amount of money awarded in the merit program. Knowing
this, the employee sits restlessly in his chair, waiting to hear the magic
words which dictate the amount of money he can look forward to spending.
Unfortunately the employee hears little of the performance counseling and
does not really attend to the problem of goal setting. This has led many to
try to have separate performance discussions and merit award discussions.

It remains true that money must be awarded as a function of performance and whether separated by one day or six months, the effect is still the
same if the performance discussion and the award are irrevocably con-

nected. The answer, then, is to make them two separate entities not only in time but in concept. Discuss performance and goal setting, and then discuss merit increase with entirely different criteria, but based on performance. Economic criteria are really the basis for salary progression. A part of economic criteria is the productivity factor of the individual, which is, after all, the result of his performance. Payment for results or output is the *only* sensible approach to a successful performance appraisal program.

The timing of the review is of considerable importance. There are two basic approaches, each with multiple variations. One approach is to review all persons at the same time of the year. The other is to review each employee on a date which is peculiar to the employee.

The first approach, reviewing everyone at one time in the year, is quite common in industries both large and small. Its advocates suggest that it enables a more equitable treatment of all employees since they are each looked at under the same conditions, the same time of year, and with the same emphasis. It is also claimed that a smaller staff is needed to maintain such a system because the review is done just once a year. Claims are similarly made that this system deals with the issue of performance appraisal once and for all and therefore makes more efficient use of management's time. Financially, the company can better plan its compensation costs, since the major increase to payroll and the corresponding benefits occur once a year. All of the auxiliary forces, such as the EDP department and the payroll department, can be called upon for the one major effort in a carefully scheduled manner.

The opponents of the once-a-year exercise refer to it as the "herd" approach, the connotation being that the employees are treated like a herd of cattle going through a mechanized process, thereby reducing the motivational element of individual importance. There is a practical problem as well. To be effective, performance appraisal must be personally oriented and cannot wait until a specific time of the year to attend to the several exigencies that occur through the year. Changes in assignments, performance variations, accomplishments, promotions, and new hires are events which continually occur and destroy any once-a-year timing. "Out of cycle" raises, "interim increases," and "off sequence adjustments" are the terms that suggest that the once-a-year timing is simply impractical. Between-cycle pay increases become the rule, and instead of requiring a smaller staff to handle pay increases, the need is for more analysts to handle the "exceptions." The bulk of increases happening once a year is a mammoth job for management to handle while still conducting business. It becomes a chore, an add-on activity which either suffers in execution or hampers normal business operation.

At any rate, performance sessions are time-consuming and exhausting. To do many of them in a short period of time assures that fatigue will reduce their usefulness to the employees. The expression on employees' faces permits much gamesmanship as well. The name of the game is "See what Harry got" by the look on his face. This prompts Harry to play "You'll never guess what I got," a game of high tension. There is also the Christmas syndrome. As the review period approaches, employees have been known to vastly alter their behavior, knowing that "Santa Claus is coming to town." Such a period of high spirits is followed by a period of depression, resignation, and "I told you so."

It's more than a coincidence that many organizations have review time at the end of the fiscal year, when planning the new year. In such a state, changes are anticipated, producing anxieties, and much that is done is accompanied by insecure attitude sets about the future. Frequently the review is done after there have been several "leaks" about how badly the organization did the last year, and the aura of gloom and doom prevail. Hardly the right setting for performance review, but to the controller it sets the "correct" mood for spartanism and frugality.

There are variations on the herd approach. One is to schedule each department at a different time in the year, one department in January, another in February, and so on. This reduces the load, yet has all people in a department reviewed at one time. The problem is that each month is not the same as another. Some months are psychologically happier than others. One can go through the year and identify certain attitude sets with many of the months. January, the blahs; February, cold and miserable; March, never-ending winter month; April, IRS time; May, the promise of spring; June, traditional freedom time, starting with school being out, which can have mixed effects on people whether they relate to summer vacation themselves or anticipate the kids being around the house; July to August, summer doldrums and vacation, with many empty desks; September, end of the summer; October, brace for winter; November to December, finish what was supposed to be finished months earlier, plus holiday preparation. Depending on the month assigned to the department, it can always be good or always be bad.

The other approach is to schedule a review on a date peculiar to the individual. This is often his anniversary date. It sometimes is his birthday. Anniversary dates are altered on occasion by out-of-sequence raises which prompt new review dates. At any rate, the date selected is one with which the individual can relate intimately. It emphasizes the individual and has high motivational appeal. For management, it spreads increases through the year, reducing the time spent during any one month. Costs are similarly spread through the year, which is advantageous to the company. The complaint has been heard that equity is difficult to achieve because it's impossible to recall how others have been treated. This problem can be overcome by doing performance planning with all employees at one time of the year, yet dealing with each individual at the time of his review period. Modifications are acceptable, but, at least, all comparisons come from the same general review of all employees.

In populations of any size, the actual practice is to alert management of subordinates whose review dates are coming due. The changes in pay or status are not necessarily made on the exact anniversary date, but are modified to conform with a date feasible and compatible with payroll processing dates. Consequently, changes occur in some organizations once a month, twice a month, or every week, depending on the payroll system dates. The system remains individualized, conforms to feasible business dates, spreads out the time and the money spent in the system, and is based on a common ground of comparability. This approach seems to have the best of both worlds and has been adopted by many.

Several references have been made to salary planning and budgeting. It has been suggested that this is an annual exercise wherein the increase for every employee is planned in relation to the increases for his peers. It has also been suggested that control is necessary for good salary administration in directing the payroll dollar to those contributing to the success of the enterprise. Payroll will continue to grow; the need is to direct it better. One method of control is the planning and budgetary phase of pay. Reference has already been made to the need for controlling the movement of payroll and individual pay regardless of the reason for pay increases. Pay budgeting should be established for all contingencies—merit, promotions, and new hires. Responsible managers should be judged on how well they utilize the total resources available to them. Payroll is just as good a measure of resource utilization as money spent on machines or in the purchase of more money.

In other words there should be little distinction between budget on merit, promotion, or new hires. A manager becomes stronger by exercising such gross control. Personnel technicians, under the guise of guidelines, usurp management prerogatives and weaken the very management they are allegedly trying to support. They do it by playing games like splitting budgets between merit and promotions; or controlling merit money but not budget; or by forcing managers to get rid of highly paid employees and to hire lower-paid employees, or vice versa. In every instance the company loses, the manager loses, the administrator loses, and the employees lose.

Salaries should be planned for every employee. The manager should be given a percentage of his payroll based on the micro and macro economies the organization finds itself in. The percentage of his budget which makes up his payroll is an important calculation. Let's explore an approach which may be used; it is called the "attrition effect," because what occurs is due in large part to attrition. There are other influences as well. The "whys" of the phenomenon are interesting but not as relevant as the fact that it occurs at all.

Basically, the attrition effect is the increase in payroll prompted by a particular increase to employees the year before. Each organization has its own pattern—its own style, policies, practices, and personalities. When an organization gives an increase to its employees, it shows up one year later in payroll in a somewhat lesser amount. This is due to employees leaving and coming. The variations in companies are due to the number of employees receiving the increase. When one organization gives an average increase of 10 percent to its employees, it may result in a 9 percent increase in payroll a year later. Another company with different practices may have a 5 percent increase in payroll as a result of an average increase of 10 percent given to its employees.

All one needs is to gather statistics peculiar to the organization regarding payroll growth and average percentage given. By tracing such data for a series of typical years, the attrition effect can be learned. It will be found that this amount is fairly consistent for each organization, but it varies from that of another organization. Obviously, the number of employees receiving the increase, the age of the employees, and the normal turnover influence the attrition effect. These phenomena vary from organization to organization, and therefore so does the attrition effect.

More important, this phenomenon is not just a "gee whiz" statistic but has application in the planning and budgeting function as well. When management goes through its planning exercise, it tries to forecast sales and income or services and budget. An integral part of the costs of those calculations is how to plan or predict labor costs. If it is known that a particular average percentage given to the employees will produce a predictable outcome in payroll increase, then by using that predictive tool, labor costs can be planned and the compensation administrator becomes a vital member of the planning team. The attrition effect can be a vital tool to the fiscal-minded compensation administrator, and its use will give him great personal satisfaction and reward.

The planning process naturally brings up the company issue of cost of living or general increase. In recent years there has developed a general awareness of the cost of living. This has prompted many companies to grant pay increases to all employees based on the increase in the cost of living.

This practice was prevalent in the first half of the seventies but has somewhat subsided. This is due in large part to the economy, not to sound logic. In other words if the economy permitted companies to continue their give-away program, many companies would. It can only be concluded that the well-meaning titans of industry wanted to be pictured as benevolent masters so they would be loved by all. This paternalistic attitude prevails in the top ranks and the dues to the club used to be "Give ever'body sothin'."

If the cost of living increase is not already a dead issue in your company, you might want to consider some of these thoughts: We often give cost of living increases to all employees, based on one common percentage. If the cost of living increased by 8 percent, then everyone gets 8 percent. Is there logic to this? Are people at all levels of income impacted by the cost of living at the same rate? The answer is a resounding NO. Although there have been recent attempts to show the contrary, the Samuelson economics principle of disposable income still prevails. Basically, it states that the higher the income, the less of the total income is spent.*

To expand on that concept, let's further identify that the governmental calculation of cost of living increase is based on purchases of staple items. If the average income of the American laborer is $10,000 and cost of living goes up by 8 percent, then statistically his cost of living goes up by 8 percent. A person making twice that amount doesn't have a like increase because he does not spend the same percentage of his income on those items measured for cost of living. His increase is a lesser amount. How much less is not known, though it could be calculated. A person making less than $10,000 probably incurs an even higher cost of living increase since a higher percentage of his income is spent on those staple items measured. To give everyone the same cost of living increase is not a realistic approach. If an organization felt compelled to do so, it could give a cost of living increase equal to the stated national cost of living to those earning the average income. Note that the tie was with national cost of living index. Local costs of living vary from the national. Some exceed the national, some lag behind it. Such data may be obtained and "massaged," but why do it? This leads us to the next consideration.

What obligation, legal or moral, does an organization have to keep an employee's income sound in a rising economy?

Many who are asked this question are stumped by it. There is little doubt that there is no legal obligation, but it's amazing how after talking about the need for paying for contribution, and nothing but contribution, the minds of many will be boggled by this question. They suddenly shift to

---

* Paul A. Samuelson, *Economics*, 9th ed. (New York: McGraw-Hill, 1973).

an attitude of wanting to pay not for contribution but for need of the employee. The moral obligation is, of course, a very personal thing. It suggests altruistic motives, but there are selfish motives as well. If a company maintains a high profile, sells a consumer product, or is a major employer in a community, the organization is more sensitive to the "moral" obligation. More often than not, however, organizations will realize that they have no moral obligation to their employees. Pay should be based on output or contribution or productivity. Pay based on need of the employee has a tendency to reduce the drive of the employee, which has a detrimental effect on output, contribution, or productivity. In a rising economy, when employees contribute to the increase in productivity, they should derive some reward for their labors. That should be the basis of their pay, not the mere fact that their need has increased. Yet, many organizations rush to initiate some kind of blanket increase to their employees when the cost of living goes up; then they wonder why productivity has failed to grow.

Which employee benefits the most from an across-the-board increase, the high-performing employee or the low-performing employee? The answer is the low-performing employee. He recognizes that he gets a raise in pay no matter what he does. The better-performing employee perceives this lack of reward for performance, and he either ceases to perform or he leaves to join an organization which discriminates among levels of performance and rewards accordingly.

Often a company gives an across-the-board increase because another, unionized, company does it. In order to remain nonunion, the company feels compelled to emulate the union company's practice. This action does not prevent unionization, it encourages it! Not only does emulating the union company condone the union's action, it suggests that the union is a good thing. The employees are quick to note this. More important, however, rather than fighting the union movement, this actually sets the company up for an attempt at unionization.

The logic behind this statement is that, as has already been stated, an across-the-board increase benefits the poor employees. The good employees leave for a more discriminating employer. When the good ones resign, only the poor ones are left behind. What kind of employees seek unionization? It's not the better performer who has confidence in himself; it is the poorer employee who lacks confidence and wants a third party to negotiate for him. Therefore, the issuance of a general increase emulating a union action in another company does not discourage unionization, it actually abets it. It also follows that to fight unionization, the organization should discriminate among performers, reward the better ones, and get rid of low performers.

Only by not giving a raise to some, can others, the good performers, gain pay raises to accommodate rising costs and also recognize money given as a result of meritorious performance. The last half of the seventies will continue to see a modest GNP and a high cost of living. Only by withholding pay increases from some can pay increases go to others. The successful organization will be the one that differentiates between good and bad performers.

What percentage of employees should receive an increase each year? There is no absolute answer to that question. Each organization is different. Organizations who disdain the general increase yet have a merit program in which almost all employees get an increase are fooling themselves. They have no merit program; they have a general increase. The general increase may vary from one employee to another, but as long as everyone, or nearly everyone, gets an increase, the company has a general increase program, not a merit program. As a rule of thumb, if more than 85 percent of the employees receive a pay increase during the year for any reason at all, merit, promotion, or some kind of adjustment, the organization has a general increase program, no matter what it is called.

How does an organization control the percentage of employees receiving an increase? One way is to write or state the percentage as a matter of policy. This is not recommended, however. The statement of such a policy is fraught with problems—the writing of it, the justification for it, and especially the inflexibility of it. There may be some years in which it will be desirable to give a higher percentage, and others when a lower percentage may be optimal. The way to control the percentage subtly yet effectively is through the distribution of the budget dollar itself. By giving each department less than the desired pay increase percentage, the manager is forced to make certain discriminations. The manager, good or bad, will want to see to it that the employees who make him look good, add to his survival, and are the contributors will receive the higher rewards.

For example, in a year in which the cost of living rises at 6 percent, the manager wants to make sure that the good performers get at least the cost of living plus some merit increase. If he were given a 6 percent budget, he could give every employee 6 percent, a general increase, with no merit, no discrimination. By giving him less than 6 percent, he is forced to give some employees nothing so he can give the better employees at least the cost of living and some perceived merit money. Such a percentage can be altered each year. The variables are the success of the organization and the money available, the desired percentage for each recipient, and the cost of living. By arithmetically determining these factors, each manager can be given a percentage of his payroll to spend. He will then control it, and no policy need be stated.

Control as used here means direction. An added directional control is to see that no one receives too small a raise. The old-timer might feel that no raise is too small, but this is not so. A raise perceived to be too small can be terribly damaging to the organization. First, when dealing with pay raises, it is necessary to talk in percentages and not in dollars. It is the *relative* change in pay rate which is significant to both the giver and the recipient. A $50 raise is good or bad depending on the base. To a person making $1,000 a month, it's a small raise.

There is a need to establish control guidelines for pay-raise percentages. During the late fifties and early sixties the minimum was usually 3 percent, with a high of 10 percent. During the late sixties and early seventies, the low was 5 percent, with a high between 12 and 15 percent. During the rest of the seventies, due to the GNP, labor supply, and the reduced rate of increase in the cost of living, it is likely that the parameters of good pay practice will be a low of 3 percent and a high of 10 percent. This suggests that no pay raise for any reason should be less than 3 percent, and further, that any pay raise over 10 percent should be reviewed as an exception. A stated policy in this particular is useful. The policy should be simply worded and make no distinction about the reason for the increase, that is, whether it be for merit, promotion, or adjustment.

The compilation of statistics in pay raises, particularly high, low, average, and median percentages of awards, prepares compensation administrators very admirably for guiding management in pay distribution. Thus prepared, their guidance can be very subtle and can exert great influence over pay actions merely by casting a shadow of knowledge on the transaction. Their counsel will be sought before a pay raise is given, since they have the norm information. They will find that they don't have to sign pay actions because their influence will be felt before the act and not afterward. Their authority is vested in their professional ability, not in statutory dictates. The satisfaction of the job will be high, and they will be very productive.

While it is essential to control the percentage of award, control of the frequency is equally significant. The time for formal review should be based on a date peculiar to the individual. Turnover statistics can assist in choosing the frequency of review, especially among new employees during their first year. A common practice is to review nonexempt jobs after a month, three months, or six months on the job. A particular frequency should not be adopted merely because other companies use it. The decision should be based on objective data. By compiling turnover statistics, when people leave the company can be determined. High leave-rates usually occur during the first year of employment. This can be costly. By analyzing the data, the best time to perform reviews can be determined. If new employees tend to leave after four months of service, perhaps a review at the end of three months will have a positive effect on their attitude, and they will not leave. If people leave after 90 days, maybe the first review period should be at the end of 60 or 80 days.

There is no set rule. Each organization should make its own decision for the first review period, based on its own data. New employees do need orientation, and a performance review is really part of that orientation. This is true not only with nonexempt employees but with anyone who is entering the labor force for the first time, such as a college graduate. The review period should be established, based on the organization's own needs as shown by its statistics, turnover being a notable indicator. After the first year, the pay increases should be controlled so that a particular period is considered to be the norm by policy. The norm for nonexempt jobs is usually six months; for exempt jobs it is 12. In other words, a normal review period is every 12 months, but seldom more frequent than every six months.

The technology and sophistication of the organization's business are usually the determinants of the length of time between reviews. The more sophisticated, the wider apart the reviews, since it takes more time for a sophisticated company to measure the results of its actions. Note that performance review and counseling should occur whenever they are needed, whether this be hourly, monthly, or yearly. Pay increases should be controlled so that employees are eligible for them every year. This should be the case with all levels. The "stretch-out" practice that some organizations have is deplorable. According to it, executives who have reached a certain level of pay are eligible for an increase only after 18 months. The increase in 18-month periods is usually the same percentage other employees get in a 12-month period. This practice is actually a penalty for having been successful in reaching higher income levels.

It is argued that persons at the higher income levels don't *need* the same increase treatment as others. Pay should not be based on need, it should be based on contribution. To motivate executives, it is imperative that they have the same eligibility for pay increases as other employees. It is conceivable that programs and projects for which the high executive is held accountable may not be finished in a 12-month period. In that event the total award for which he is eligible should be calculated on an annual basis, such as 150 percent of the normal annual award if the award is given after 18 months. Another approach would be to assess the progress toward the objective on an annual basis. If the project is 80 percent complete at the end of

12 months, the executive should receive 80 percent of the eventual award. Frequency is important to employees at all levels regardless of income. It is a form of positive stroke, and even executives need positive stroking.

Another significant control of pay is the level to which the increase brings the salary. CEOs like to influence this control area. With salary levels constantly rising, the CEO often fails to recognize that what once constituted a high salary no longer does. When the CEO of a very large computer-making firm was a junior executive, $10,000 was a hefty salary. In the early seventies, it was merely the average pay in the company. Nevertheless, as CEO, he insisted on seeing all increases that brought salaries to $10,000 or more. How much review the increases received is mere conjecture. The company did have significant problems due in large part to the attention the CEO was giving to pay increases instead of other elements of the business. He finally realized this, and now sees only the higher pay-level increases, which is as it should be.

This review shouldn't be based on dollar levels, per se, however. The CEO should see the top 10 percent earner levels. The next level of the executive management should have approval authority up to all other salary levels. Each level of management can thus be structured to have approval for a certain percentage of the total earners. In this way, the number of signatures on pay increases will be kept to a minumum, instead of the "laundry lists" that seem to be required in some companies. The percentage assignments would be divided among the several layers in the particular organization's hierarchy. The salary level approval authority would be stated in dollars and would probably have to be adjusted every year for streamline operation as the salary levels increase. Such a system permits management to exercise control, to maintain visibility of salary levels, and to expedite pay actions.

When compensation administrators realize that they are responsible for pay actions rather than others who sign the pay action, they seek information on the issue of "how much is enough." The data necessary includes diagrams showing:

◇ percentages of increases, averages, medians, highs and lows by department classification, location, etc.

◇ salary levels by department classification, location, etc.

◇ turnover by department, classification, location, etc.

Such charts can be drawn by hand or by computer. Current relevant data is essential, and compensation administrators should equip themselves accordingly.

Computerization is the best means of controlling the data. In order to do this, compensation administrators must organize the data they need to retrieve. This includes readouts that enumerate such data as:

⬧ Name, employee number, date of hire
⬧ Classification, grade, range
⬧ Salary, compa-ratio, ranking
⬧ Department, location, site
⬧ Date, amount of last three increases by dollar and percentage

Control is the result of knowledge. Knowledge is augmented by statistical compilations and audits. Compensation administrators will discover that they can exert more control and direction by equipping themselves with statistical data and using judgment in its interpretation than in trying to place themselves between employees and their bosses, which is the typical situation. It has already been stated that compensation administrators do not have to sign pay actions to control them. In fact, asserting their will at that time may cause them to lose control and merely be caught up in the politics of the situation. Statistical data will serve them far better as a source of authority for their actions than will any statutory dictate.

·22·

Another Look
at Performance Appraisal

Quality is like buying oats. If you want nice, clean, fresh oats, you must pay a fair price. However, if you'll be satisfied with oats that have already been through the horse, that comes a little cheaper.

THE most challenging personnel problem confronting the organization is the performance appraisal of employees. Getting them in the door is not all that hard. The recruitment and selection process is like the courtship and romance. The actual employment is like the marriage itself, after the honeymoon period, with the ups and downs of successes and failures, problems and joys. The analogy ends with the performance appraisal. That's where corporate life is "one up" on marriage. Corporate life dictates that a formal performance appraisal shall take place in which past successes and failures are reviewed and goals are established for the future. It is a difficult exercise—generally too difficult for the marriage scene. If it is too difficult for the intimacy of marriage, imagine how difficult it is in the business scene. Yet it must be done. Employees must know how they're doing, what they are to do, and how they feel about their job. If it is done correctly, performance appraisal is an essential adjunct to productivity.

However, it is seldom done well. Not too long ago we were an agrarian nation. Few organizations existed and the differences between manager and subordinate were very great. Now all that has changed. We live in an organized society, most of us work in organized environments, and the differences between manager and managed are greatly reduced. The manager

226

must have the means to motivate employees and to measure the success of his ability to do so. That measurement is the performance appraisal. It is likened to an audience listening to a singer. When the performer sings a song recognized by the audience, the audience applauds. The audience is applauding itself for having recognized the selection. So, too, the manager must review the results of his ability to lead through the performance appraisal of his subordinates. Now it becomes apparent why many managers neglect to conduct the performance appraisal. They don't like facing up to their own failures. It was this absence of performance appraisals that prompted personnel technicians to action. They knew that employees need feedback.

Personnel technicians answered this need by designing guidelines, forms, and standards that would "help" the manager in the onerous exercise. The personnel technicians went even further and introduced systems that organized the thought for the manager. The manager reacted to the "Simon says" conditions by going through the motions of the appraisal exercise. This watered-down attempt to categorize performance often dealt with input characteristics, such as attitude, getting along with others, and organizing the work.

To further "help" the manager, personnel experts developed the all-encompassing, fail-safe, idiot-proof matrix in which all behavior was boiled down to a particular square in the grid. All the supervisor had to do was to categorize the employee in relation to a norm. He had five "flavors" of performance from which to choose: distinguished, commendable, acceptable, fair, and marginal. The placement of employees had to conform to a normal, bell-shaped curve. In fact, every department is often required to have a specific percentage of each type of performance, 60 percent of the employees have to be acceptable, 15 percent fair, and 15 percent commendable, leaving 5 percent to be distinguished and 5 percent to be marginal. The matrix dictated the percentage reward for each level of performance, depending on the employee's placement in the range (usually, if the employee was low in the range, the percentage was higher and the frequency of getting a raise was greater, apparently to encourage the poorer employee, but with the effect of penalizing success). In addition, certain levels of performance could go just so far into the range.

While this method is theoretically and statistically defensible, human behavior and its measurement don't lend themselves to such neat configurations. The smarter managers soon began backing into the system. Knowing what percentage increase they wanted to give their employee, they'd fudge the system up or down so the employee would be in the right place to get that percentage. For instance, an employee who was commendable but already paid too high in relation to his peers, would be classified as acceptable or lower so that the employee could get the percentage raise that the manager wanted to give him. If, however, an employee was doing only marginal work but other forces dictated that he be given a high increase, the manager would rate him as acceptable or higher in order to give him a lower percentage increase. Thus the matrix was compromised, and the system failed to be a good method of rewarding performance. In instances such as the above, the supervisor compromises himself and company policy fails, but the big loser is the employee. He gets neither information about nor the true expression of his performance. Because most managers tend to overrate their employees, every year the percentages skew a little more toward the right; in other words, there are more commendable and distinguished employees and fewer marginal and fair ones. This could be the result of a weeding-out exercise or the improvement of the performance level of all employees, but chances are it is just the result of gamesmanship in the organization.

This type of performance appraisal system, which is in widespread use today, fails to take into account the human element that doesn't lend itself to easy categorization. This is not a "performance" system, it is a *conformance* system in which the subjective thoughts of the manager about his subordinates' performance are forced to fit corporate standards of behavior, organized into specific categories of performance, and assigned a rank under a bell-shaped curve.

It is precisely this type of system which has prompted the moot issue of the mixing of performance appraisal with the merit award process. The argument against doing both at the same time has been that the employee is unable to take in the counseling because he is so concerned about the amount of money he will receive as a result of being pronounced "acceptable, marginal, fair, commendable, or distinguished." The "separatists" argue that the performance appraisal session should be separate from the dollar award discussion. Yet the dollar award must be based on performance. No matter what separates the performance appraisal session from the dollar award session, there remains a problem. If the systems are interrelated, the employee hears nothing except how much more he will get in his pocket.

The issues must be separate, yet they are inseparable. How can that be? Let's look at the problem closely. What are the objectives of the whole review process? They are to review accomplishments, discuss shortcomings, establish goals, develop strategy, reward performance, and advance salary. The first four deal with the philosophical issues of performance. This is a learning and growing exercise. The last two deal with the economic issues, how much and when. Both groups have dimensions in the past and future. The philosophical issues discuss the past and what can be done in the future. The economic issues deal with the existing salary history and the salary that should be expected. Like the church and the state, the two concepts of performance appraisal—philosophy and economics—must be dealt with separately.

We have already discussed the need for performance appraisal counseling. There are countless books on the subject of how to discuss performance with the employee. Let's leave this philosophical part to those qualified to handle it—and turn our attention, in this volume on compensation, to the role of economics. Is there an economic approach that is related to both performance and the labor market? Can this approach be oriented both to the person and to sound business concepts? Can such an approach be taken for large as well as small organizations? The remainder of this chapter presents a multivariant approach to compensation progression. This approach reviews a change of salary from different angles, using multiple techniques. These multiple techniques include:

◆ *individual salary curve*—line of regression showing the employee's personal growth measured in salary increases during his work experience. (This also bears on past performance since it reveals how past supervisors have regarded the employee's performance.)

◆ *peer ranking*—"totem pole" ranking of peer group done by the supervisor. This reveals the supervisor's current regard for the individual and highlights inequities if they exist.

◆ *survey data*—internal and external data showing the distribution of like employees and the salaries paid.

◆ *marketability*—a formula for estimating the individual's worth on the market as seen by other employers competing for his services.

The objectives of the multivariant approach are:

◇ to motivate the employee through recognition of personal contribution, reward, and growth.

◇ to ensure equitable treatment with employee's peers, local and distant, in-house and in-market.

◇ to retain the company's competitive position in both the labor market and the product market.

◇ to provide guides to supervision in the determination of just and proper compensation progression problems.

The task of the supervisor in supporting a salary advance for a subordinate is one of justification. While he is aware of subjective data that warrants the proposed action (e.g., a recent accomplishment or achievement, a promotion, an inequity, a new level of contribution, higher performance), it is not always easy to show in quantifiable terms *why* the proposed action is just.

The multivariant approach to compensation progression is an attempt to *help* the supervisor show just cause for advancing the salary of the employee. As the name implies, it is a technique for approaching the problem from many different angles to objectively justify the salary increase.

It uses as a basis for study the employee's performance posture and individual growth as developed in his tenure. This attention to individuality is the key to obtaining the most motivational value from the dollar. Studies have shown that individual attention and recognition are high if not on top of a list of things which motivate the employee. When an employee knows that his individual posture is the basis for a salary program, he is encouraged and motivation results.

Next the analysis moves to the employee's peer group and reviews the equity of salaries paid to the individuals as ranked by their supervisor. In spite of the many efforts to keep individual salaries confidential, employees often learn of the salaries received by their peers. There is probably no greater inhibitor to motivation, no greater negative motivator, than having salary inequity in a group. No other influence can be as damaging to a merit program than paying salaries disproportionately to the ranked members of a peer group.

The visibility of the analysis then broadens in the company. Internal grade and salary integrity must be maintained throughout. This analysis adds to that integrity.

The market is the next comparison. Applicable surveys from management counseling firms, associations, and surveying companies may be used as a measure of the market.

The last technique used is a marketability formula. This formula is an attempt to consider the value of an employee in the market as determined by his proven performance.

Finally, the results from these techniques are collated and reviewed. When these techniques have been used for a period, the disparity between the results will be minimal, and the salary deemed reasonable for the employee becomes evident. The significance is that this is a positive approach. No harangues, no emotional outbreaks, no hostility result. The salary change is either justified or not justified. Objectivity pervades, and the analyst need not stumble through the forest with indecision haunting him. The supervisor can be satisfied with his "day in court" and now has gained the assurance that his employees are being fairly compensated. He can go to his subordinates with positive statements regarding their compensation standing instead of having nothing to say or, worse, making up a story as to why "they" (usually meaning management) took the action they did.

Now let us review the four techniques.

1. The *individual salary curve* is a line connecting the successive salary increases granted by the supervisors to the employee through his performance during his work experience. It is generally understood that a person progresses at a speed peculiar to his drive and motivation. This usually follows a pattern as shown in Figure 7. The person progresses rapidly at first and receives ever-diminishing increases, producing a plateau effect after a period of time.

A first-degree least-squares line (L) applied to this growth rate reveals the employee's long-term growth tendency. When this least-squares line and a

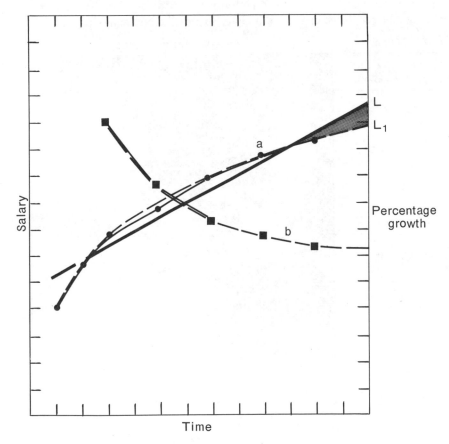

Figure 7. Individual salary curve.

second least-squares line (L$_1$), which traces the latest data, are extrapolated, the parameters within which the employee's next salary point is *likely* to be are revealed. A person is *not* committed to the past, however, and current conditions may compel consideration of other salary points. When the first-degree least-squares line is measured from year to year, the percentage growth of the employee emerges, yielding average increases gained and, when plotted, they dramatically confirm the plateau effect mentioned above.

2. *Peer ranking* is perhaps the key to gaining the most out of the company's motivational dollar in the paying of salaries. The supervisor's ranking of a homogeneous group of peers and their being remunerated on the basis of their placement in that ranking assures the employee that compensation progression is truly the result of performance. Moreover, the supervisor, in recognizing and heeding this principle, spends the company's payroll dollar

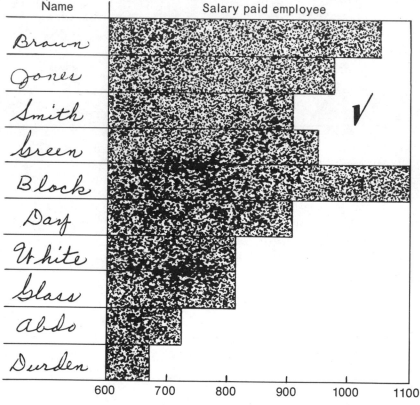

Figure 8. Peer ranking.

wisely. A peer ranking such as the one in Figure 8 should be thought of as a picture of a situation as it exists at that moment. When the next picture is taken, the arrangement of the subjects may have changed. Constant juggling of ranking, however, reveals serious problems. The suggested criterion for ranking persons is "value to the company." This concept is purposely left undefined. A supervisor is responsible for the product of his group. The methods by which he leads his employees differ from the methods used by other supervisors. Supervisors' evaluations of employees' work differ also. There are several considerations for evaluations that are common to all groups, however:

Initiative	Quality of work
Loyalty	Quantity of work
Tact	Timeliness of work
Attitude	Absenteeism
Enthusiasm	Tardiness
Dependability	Individual job objectives

Note that these characteristics must be applied to the dimension of time in order for their full value to be realized. As shown, an employee's worth may be a measured characteristic to be realized in time, but not necessarily now. The mix used and the value given to each characteristic as a function of time are peculiar to the supervisor.

3. *Survey data,* perhaps the most well known and most misused technique, may yield insight into what the total market deems it advisable to pay certain occupations. By choosing to vary its pay for these occupations, the company may further refine this data. Using the familiar statistical sampling approach, one can extract from the peer ranking placement of the employee and determine what the placement "would pay" in the internal and external distributions. For example, a person ranking in the seventy-fifth percentile of his peer group should compare favorably with like occupational groups displayed in internal and external surveys.

Figure 9 represents the data from an internal salary survey of employees in like classifications. The normal (bell-shaped) curve indicates that Q_1 equals about $800 per month, Q_2 about $900, and Q_3 about $940. If the manager has ranked an employee in the third quartile of his group, then he should compare the salary of that seventy-fifth percentile performer with the salaries being paid in the company at Q_3. Similarly, the manager should also refer to an expanded universe in evaluating the employee's salary—that is, the salary should also relate to the Q_3 found in the national labor market, represented as a maturity curve in Figure 10.

4. *Marketability* involves a formula which attempts to answer the ques-

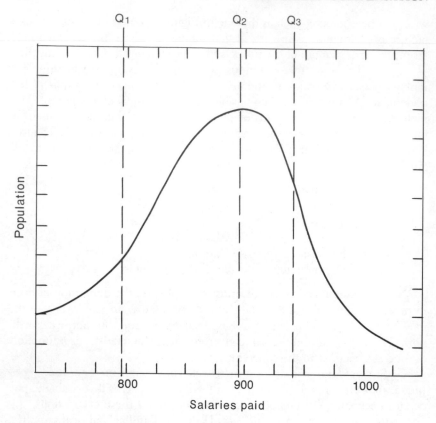

Figure 9. Internal classification distribution.

tion posed by the employee concerned about the salaries earned by similar graduates from the same discipline but with no experience. By projecting on the base of salaries offered similar graduates, the average annual percentage increase multiplied by the number of years of experience of that employee shows his market worth as viewed by competitors bidding for his services.

$$\text{Marketability} = S + SEG$$

where S = current beginning salary earned by graduates from the same discipline but with no experience
E = number of years of experience
G = average annual growth of individual (percent)

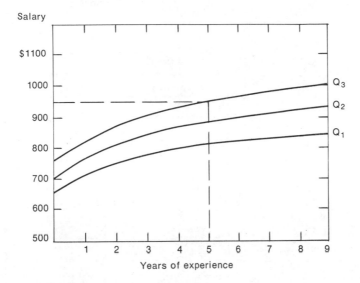

Figure 10. National survey (years of experience versus salary).

For example:

$$\text{Marketability} = \$710 + (\$710)(5 \text{ yrs})(7\%)$$
$$= 710 + (710)(35\%)$$
$$= 710 + 248.50$$
$$= \$958.50$$

The marketability analysis of compensation progression usually results in a higher figure than the other techniques of the multivariant approach, since it uses broad market data rather than individual or organization data. Nevertheless, it is important to take the marketability analysis into consideration since these factors, broad as they may be, are used by personnel recruiters.

In this section, we have used several economic indicators to determine the quantifiable reasons for a salary increase. The focus has been on the individual, recognizing his unique development and performance as measured by salary increases. He is compared to his peer group, which reduces inequity problems and encourages motivation by paying the employee for his value to the company. Once this internal integrity has been established, national surveys confirm his place in the labor market. As a check on this, the marketability formula is used to place the employee in today's market, with a growth rate unique to his own development.

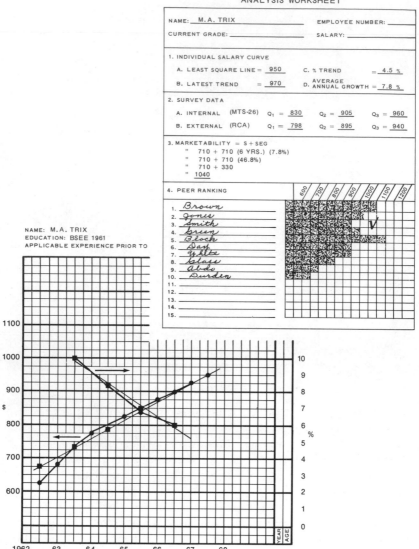

Figure 11. Implementation.

When these four techniques are continuously applied to a population, the results will be very close together. When they differ, the prime motivating factor suggesting the raise, as measured by this approach, should be used.

The implementation for this approach is accomplished as shown in Figure 11.

·23·

Dealing
with the Consultant

A prominent clergyman was asked to give his opinion of consulting in the United States. He hesitated to make any comment on consulting, but he did offer to pray for those who had to make a living at it.

THE development of the compensation program is an arduous task. It is fraught with political problems and dire threats and consequences. It is difficult to please everyone all of the time, and sometimes it seems that some of the people can't be pleased even some of the time. The compensation administrator sometimes seems like the man who lost a divorce case on the grounds of impotency and, on the same day, also lost a paternity case—he just can't win.

The possibility of using a consultant in the development of the compensation program should not be overlooked. Consultants are being used in every phase of business. In some parts of the country they are actually status symbols: "I've got two consultant firms working for me, how many do you have?" The retention of the consultant was once viewed as an admission of failure or lack of expertise. These attitudes are disappearing in the more cosmopolitan areas. Compensation administrators are often reticent about using consultants because of the inadequacy they frequently feel about their jobs in the first place. Many times they adopt the posture of I'm Not OK and feel that their function isn't important enough to retain counsel. Yet, the controller retains a squad of CPAs, EDP retains computer consultants, every organization retains legal counsel, and recruitment managers pay fees to search firms.

As mentioned earlier, if nothing else, consultants should be able to bring expertise and objectivity to compensation administrators. The plan designed with the help of a consultant can be far less expensive than the plan designed internally. The design and development of a compensation program need continuity and attention to detail. Compensation administrators have countless tasks to accomplish that prevent them from devoting sufficient attention to the developing plan, thus jeopardizing the plan's consistency.

The consultant can usually contribute fresh ideas and experience gained from past encounters. The reinvention of the wheel may bring pride to the inventor but it is a timely and costly process. The consultant should be able to save the company much time and expense in the development process. Compensation administrators would do well to not let their egos prevent them from hiring a consultant. Very frugal compensation administrators will often refuse to be the ones to retain the consultant. However, where possible, compensation administrators should make sure that they do the retaining. If a consultant is hired over the head of the compensation administrator, that compensation administrator really has a problem—he is condemned to the position of spectator. The consultant will usually be unflagging in his devotion to the party that brought him into the organization. Be that party. This is the best way to control the situation. Many feel that to even talk to a consultant will cost money. While some consultants charge for even the smallest inquiry, most will share ideas with the client or potential client at no cost or obligation.

There are many consulting firms in the country that are qualified to assist in the development of part or all of the compensation plan. Some are large, well-known, established firms, while others are small, independent, even one-person shops. Both the large and small firms have advantages as well as disadvantages.

The large, well-known firm has a reputation to uphold. Such a firm will take extensive and expensive measures to safeguard its name. This is both an advantage and a disadvantage to the client. The client can be assured that the results of the engagement will be thoroughly analyzed and reviewed by several members of the consulting firm before they leave under their letterhead. Such reviews do have a moderating effect. But there may also be an attempt to keep the client happy, which often means to not give him anything of a disturbing or changing nature. The process of review means that many high-priced consultants will add their names (and charges) to the engagements. Incidentally, most firms insist that all people at all levels remain "chargeable," that is, they charge some if not all of their time to a client account. These costs mount up dramatically. The client pays not only for the hourly wage of the consultant but for the consulting firm's overhead and profit. A recent article in *Nation's Business* indicated that the larger the consulting firm, the larger the fee.*

Often the large firm will have experts on hand who are nationally known and can render great service. Frequently, however, these "front men" sell the program and, in the interest of both firm and client, they assign a junior consultant to perform the engagement, with guidance from the "ace." More than once the "ace" has arrived at the client's office with the report of the engagement, and both client and "ace" have read it for the first time. This can be very embarrassing and costly, if revealing.

One of the reasons used most frequently for retaining a "name" consultant is "the hedge." The thought behind this is: "Hiring a consultant is a little risky and expensive. If the engagement accomplishes nothing, I'll really be in hot water. I want to protect myself by hiring a well-known consultant. Then if the job goes sour, I can at least say, 'I hired the best, what more could I do?' " This rationale is used more often than anyone would like to acknowledge.

The large firm has backup. If for some reason the consultant becomes unavailable, the large firm has someone who can pick up where the other one left off. This can be done with minimal loss in continuity. The one-person operation has no backup.

The large firm may have greater experience from which to draw to complete an engagement. It must be remembered that conformity to a standard and homage to the firm name are critical to the large firm. Standards abound as do manuals on a variety of subjects. Firms that hold themselves out as experts in all fields are suspect. The engagement is as good as the consultant working on it. Many times the consultant is relatively new in the field and thus has little experience, yet the cost of the engagement is based on the firm's name and reputation. Allegiance to firm name and conformance to standards by consultants at all levels of the organization are probably the greatest failings of the large firm. They make creativity and pioneering almost impossible.

Independent consultants are likely to run very hard for their clients. They are always trying to establish and maintain their reputation and can do so only by dutifully serving the needs of their clients. Independent consultants may have served only a few clients over the past years. Such client lists are the independent consultants' badge of honor, and they will have them available at a moment's notice.

Obviously the lack of staff overhead and formal procedures will reduce the cost of the engagement, and this is a great benefit in retaining the in-

* September 1975, p. 9.

dependent consultant. Moreover, if he's good, he will hold himself out as a specialist in a field, not a master of all fields.

Independent consultants can be expected to execute the engagement themselves rather than to have a junior or backroom person do the work. A close client-consultant relationship is of utmost importance, and independents can assure this; they have no political bureaucracy with which to contend.

Fresh approaches should be expected from independent consultants since they are not committed to any "standard" ways of solving problems. They probably are independent consultants because they simply are not conformists. Also, they will want to distinguish themselves from the large firms. So long as their ideas are tempered with sound judgment and based on empirical evidence, they should be feasible.

Whether a large firm or an independent consultant is contacted, there are some hints for securing the maximum service for the least money. Contact at least three consulting firms and let them compete for your business. Competition is healthy. One company selected four consulting firms and invited all of them to discuss the company's compensation needs together in a one-day *paid* session. One firm declined to be included in that form of competition and was thus eliminated from consideration. The other three received their normal daily fee and as a group discussed the needs of the company and suggested the means by which each would satisfy the identified needs. That one day's session cost the company three days' fees, but it reaped a harvest of advice and counsel and it provided an excellent means by which to select the best consultant for the company.

Make sure all consulting firms have the same specifications of the problem, the company's needs, and the scope of the engagement. Otherwise, their ideas and advice will not be comparable, and it will be difficult to choose the best firm.

Identify how much it would cost if the company developed the program without outside help. These costs include time away from the job, research of the plans, travel to other companies, survey costs, and additional full- or part-time help. The feasibility of hiring a consultant can then be determined.

Establish the internal capability of designing the program. This involves not only the expertise, but the time available to attend to the program and the ultimate acceptability of the program designed internally versus the acceptability of the one designed externally.

Determine if the bulk of the work should be done internally with assistance from the consultant, or externally with assistance from the company staff. This will allow the consultant to indicate if he can serve you by the hour, the day, or the proposal. If the company designs the program, assistance can be rendered by the consultant, and the fee could be hourly or daily, but the responsibility for the development rests with the internal staff. When a consultant submits a proposal, the responsibility for developing the program rests with the consultant, with assistance rendered by the internal staff.

The proposal method is by far the best for both parties. It clarifies for both parties what is expected of each and how they are to relate to one another. The proposal should have four parts to it. The first part details the needs of the company and the scope of the engagement as perceived by the consultant. This ensures that both are clear regarding the task to be accomplished. The second part details the approach to be taken—how the consultant will fill the needs identified. It should enumerate the steps to be taken and the expected tangible results of those steps. The third part indicates the consultant's rationale for taking the chosen approach. As a test of logic and reasonability, the benefits derived from taking that approach can be compared with the rationale offered by competing consultants. The fourth part covers the time and cost parameters of the proposed engagement. The consultant should be able to estimate how long it will take to complete the engagement. The cost of the engagement should be a range indicating a minimum and a maximum. The maximum should be no more than 35 to 40 percent higher than the minimum. The costs proposed should include not only the consultant's fee but the expenses to be incurred in the execution of the engagement. An open-ended "and other out-of-pocket expenses incurred" clause should not be tolerated. The consultant should be held accountable for his expenses.

With such a proposal, compensation administrators are in a good position to determine if they should retain a consultant or do the job themselves. If they feel they should have help, the proposal gives them all they need to make a wise decision. Once the decision is made, the proposal also serves as a means to monitor and control the program's development. During the execution of the engagement, compensation administrators need only check the progress of the steps that are detailed in the approach portion of the proposal against the monthly billing to see if both are moving at the right speed. The compensation administrators remain in charge of the engagement.

The consultant selected should be professional, personable, have integrity, and inspire trust and confidence. The outside consultant can be a perfect complement to the internal consultant. The use of the outside consultant permits the company to "run lean" and to hire and fire consultants as needed, rather than to swell the payroll with additional permanent in-house consultants.

Postscript

God grant me the serenity to accept the things I can't change . . .

the courage to change the things I can, and . . .

the wisdom to know the difference.

THE design and development of the wage and salary program can be the finest achievement in a person's career. Such an opportunity does not present itself often. One should seize the opportunity to design a program, if for no other reason than that it looks great on a resume. Obviously the motivation ought to be sounder and higher than that. Compensation administrators must remember that they have a heady responsibility in assisting executive management in a very critical area—the reinvestment of the payroll dollar. They must execute this responsibility wisely. They must design programs that pay for contribution and identify responsibility. The programs must not be so cumbersome or inflexible that they or the companies collapse under their weight. The programs must satisfy internal equity so that employees perceive that their organization is treating them fairly. The programs must be credible, so credible that every element—the compensable factors, the job description, the survey summary data, the structure, the classifications, the conversion charts, and the pay practices—can stand the light of day. No motivation programs, no matter how well designed or administered, can have the desired effect if the employees do not perceive equity in the pay. Acceptance of the pay programs is therefore essential.

Compensation administrators should remain cognizant of both the macro and micro economies in which their organizations move. They should anticipate shifts in the classic demand-supply movements and seize opportunities for their organizations and employees to benefit from them.

By relating the evaluation program and the performance appraisal program to contribution or output or results, compensation administrators are fulfilling an important responsibility. Productivity has not been encouraged in this country, *activity* has. The programs oriented to job content or input or activity that have been designed in the last 30 years have promoted bureaucracy and not productivity. These systems are still in wide use, and because they are so entrenched in the workings of the organizations, they will probably continue to be used until compensation administrators with more than the normal amount of intestinal fortitude stand up and yell "Enough!" If they don't, the managements will rid their organizations of these "pay distributors" and take back the reins of pay control. A final warning: The pay systems installed in the booming years when labor was scarce and needed to be enticed into our organizations are inappropriate when labor is in abundant supply and economic growth is moderate. New approaches must and will be taken! By whom? By compensation administrators who recognize these facts of life or by CEOs who refuse to let traditional compensation administrators bungle up the pay practices.

To be able to innovate is a success in itself. There is satisfaction in knowing that one has succeeded in doing something worthwhile. Maslow called this gratification of the need for self-actualizing or self-fulfillment. I encourage the compensation administrator to aspire to satisfying that need. The achievement of something different, something new, is in itself gratifying. There is a distinction between achievement and success. Achievement is the knowledge that you have studied and worked hard and done the best that is in you. Success is being praised by others. It may be important, it satisfies one's ego need, but it is not so important or satisfying as achievement. Aim for achievement and forget about success.

Learn from the past, sift through the Parent tapes, heed the Child in you by reacting spontaneously to a new situation. To do what you feel is correct without compromising your ideals is very satisfying and is quite possible in the compensation administrator's job.

It is hoped that the preceding chapters have given you some insight into what's been done in the field that's good and not so good. You must select from and build upon the past and create something appropriate for your needs and the needs of the organization you serve. No book on compensation administration can tell you exactly what you should do; it can, however, give you a basis on which to develop.

Kahlil Gibran said of the teacher: "If he is indeed wise he does not bid you enter the house of *his* wisdom, but rather leads you to the threshold of your own mind." *

* *The Prophet* (New York: Alfred A. Knopf, 1923), p. 56.

INDEX

245